µC/OS

The Real-Time Kernel

Jean J. Labrosse

R & D Publications

Lawrence, Kansas 66046

R & D Publications, Inc.
1601 West 23rd Street, Suite 200
Lawrence, Kansas 66046-0127

The programs in this book are presented for instructional value. The programs have been carefully tested, but are not guaranteed for any particular purpose. The publisher does not offer any warranties and does not guarantee the accuracy, adequacy, or completeness of any information and is not responsible for any errors or omissions or the results obtained from use of such information.

Trademarks:
Borland Turbo C++, Borland International
IBM-PC, International Business Machines Corp.
Intel 8080 etc., Intel Corporation
Hitachi H8/xxx, etc., Hitachi Corporation
Motorola 68xxx, etc., Motorola, Inc.
MS-DOS, Microsoft Corporation.

Distributed by **Prentice Hall**

ISBN 0-13-031352-1

To my lovely wife Manon, our son James

and to our parents

Table of Contents

Appendix D
LISTC & HPLISTC

Appendix E
TO

Appendix F
Real-Time Kernel Manufacturers

Preface

Many books have been written about operating systems. This is, however, the first book ever written describing the internals of a portable, ROMable, preemptive, real-time multitasking kernel for microprocessors. µC/OS manages up to 63 user tasks, with performance comparable to many commercially available kernels.

This book is intended for the programmer, software engineer, or electrical engineer designing real-time control systems using microprocessors. This book is also ideal for students learning about real-time software.

To benefit from this book, you should be familiar with the C Programming Language (ANSI X3J11), and have minimum understanding of assembly language for the Intel 80x86 family of microprocessors.

Writing the kernel in C allows µC/OS to be easily ported to other microprocessors. For instance, µC/OS can be ported to the following microprocessors (to name a few):

Motorola:
6800/01/02/03
6809
68HC11
68HC16
680xx
683xx

Intel:
8080/85
80x86/88

Hitachi:
H8/3xx
H8/5xx
64180

Zilog:
Z-80
Z-8
Z-180
Z-280
Z-8000

Etc.

Integrating µC/OS in your application can be done in less than one day. µC/OS can be ported to a different microprocessor within a few days, because assembly language has been kept to a minimum,. Full source code for μC/OS is provided in this book. I have adopted rigorous coding conventions to ensure that the source code is as clean and as neat as possible. Having the source code along with a description of the code allows you to add features to μC/OS. μC/OS can thus be used as a stepping-stone to your own implementation of a real-time kernel.

Acknowledgements

I would like to thank my wife for her support, patience and understanding while I was writing this book. I would also like to thank the people at R&D Publications for giving me the opportunity to write this book, with special thanks to Dr. Bernard Williams. His advice, knowledge and criticism have made this project possible. I would also like to thank Mr. Tyler Sperry, editor of *Embedded Systems Programming* magazine, for allowing me to publish an earlier version of μC/OS in his magazine and for allowing me to use the kernel manufacturer survey presented in appendix F. Finally, I would like to thank my fellow workers at Dynalco Controls for their moral support.

List of Figures

Table of Code Listings

Introduction

This book describes the design implementation of μC/OS, a portable, ROMable, preemptive, real time, multitasking kernel for microprocessors. Most of μC/OS is written in C with target microprocessor specific code written in assembly language. Assembly language is, however, kept to a minimum. An earlier version of μC/OS was originally published in the May and June 1992 issues of *Embedded Systems Programming* magazine.

μC/OS (pronounced "Micro–C O S") stands for **Micro-Controller Operating System**. The initial goals for μC/OS were to create a small but powerful kernel for the Motorola MC68HC11 microcontroller. As the design evolved, the target specific limitations of μC/OS were removed to make μC/OS portable for use with other microprocessors.

μC/OS was tested on an IBM-PC compatible system using Borland International's Turbo C++ V3.00. For this reason, the implementation of μC/OS shown in this chapter is for an Intel 80186/80188 microprocessor (SMALL memory model). μC/OS will also work on 80286, 80386 and the 80486 based computers because these processors are all upward compatible with the 80186/80188. Although developed on an IBM-PC compatible, μC/OS is targeted for embedded systems. The Intel 80186/80188 was chosen because the 8086/8088 is a poor choice for embedded control applications since it requires additional support circuitry. A minimum 80188 system can be built with only four chips (80188, RAM, EPROM and 8255 PPI).

μC/OS can be ported to just about any microprocessor as long as the microprocessor provides a stack pointer and the CPU registers can be pushed onto and popped from the stack. The C compiler must be ANSI compatible and provide in line assembly or language extensions that allow you to enable and disable interrupts. Keeping the code written in assembly language to a strict minimum allows μC/OS to be ported to other target environments with minimal efforts. If μC/OS is to be ported to a non Intel 80x86 processor, the keywords 'near' and 'far' will need to be #defined to:

```
#define near
#define far
```

Chapter 1 introduces operating system concepts such as critical sections, multitasking, scheduling, reentrancy, mutual exclusion, semaphores, intertask communication, task synchronization, task coordination and interrupts.

Chapter 2 introduces µC/OS and its internal structure. The explanations detail how a task is implemented in µC/OS, how a task moves between its six states, what a task control block is and how it's implemented, how to create and delete a task, how µC/OS decides which task will get control of the CPU, how to change the priority of a task and how to delay execution of a task for a user specified number of clock ticks.

Chapter 3 discusses interrupt processing and how it relates to µC/OS, how µC/OS affects interrupt latency, response and recovery. Finally, this chapter explains what a clock tick is and how it is handled.

Chapter 4 describes intertask communication, synchronization and coordination using µC/OS, and details how µC/OS implements semaphores, message mailboxes and message queues.

Chapter 5 explains how to configure an application to use µC/OS. This chapter also describes how to initialize µC/OS and how to start the multitasking process.

Chapter 6 provides a reference manual to all of the services provided by µC/OS. Timing information for the Intel 80186/80188 microprocessor (SMALL memory model) is also provided, indicating how long functions will take to execute under certain circumstances.

Chapter 7 presents two examples which run on an IBM-PC/AT or compatible. The examples demonstrate how easy it is to integrate µC/OS in your application.

Appendix A provides the complete source code for the microprocessor independent portion of µC/OS.

Appendix B contains the 80186/80188 microprocessor specific code (SMALL memory model).

Appendix C explains the conventions I used to write µC/OS. Not only did these conventions help me for the design of µC/OS but also serve in all my programming projects.

Appendix D presents a utility that I use to print C source code. The utility prints C source code in compressed mode (i.e. 17 CPI) and allows you to specify page breaks. Two versions are available, one for a Hewlett Packard (HP) Laserjet II type printer and one for an Epson FX-80 type printer.

Appendix E contains a utility that I use to move between MS-DOS directories without having to use the CHDIR command.

Appendix F examines some pros and cons for choosing between purchasing a kernel and writing your own. The appendix also provides a list of real-time kernel manufacturers, in case you opt to purchase a kernel.

Appendix G provides a bibliography of reference material I used to write this book.

Appendix H provides you with information on how to obtain the companion diskette to this book. The diskette contains all the source code presented in this book on either a 5 1/4 inch (360K) or 3 1/2 inch (720K) DOS format.

Chapter 1

Real-Time Kernel Concepts

Real-time systems are characterized by the fact that severe consequences will result if logical as well as timing correctness properties of the system are not met. There are two types of real- time systems: SOFT and HARD. In a SOFT real-time systems, tasks are performed by the system as fast as possible but don't have to finish by specific times. In HARD real-time systems, tasks have to be performed not only correctly but also in a timely fashion. This book assumes SOFT real-time systems.

Real-time applications cover a wide range. Most applications for real-time systems are *embedded*. This means that the computer being used is built into a system and is not seen by the user as being a computer. Examples of embedded systems are:

- Process control
    - Food processing
    - Chemical plants
- Automotive
    - Engine controls
    - Anti-lock braking systems
- Office automation
    - FAX machines
    - Copiers
- Computer peripherals
    - Printers
    - Terminals
    - Modems

- Robots
- Aerospace
    - Flight management systems
    - Weapons systems
    - Jet engine controls
- Domestic
    - Microwave ovens
    - Dishwashers
    - Washing machines

Real-time software applications are typically more difficult to design than non real-time applications. The use of a real-time kernel will simplify the design process by allowing the application to be divided into multiple tasks managed by the kernel. This chapter describes real-time kernel concepts.

μC/OS

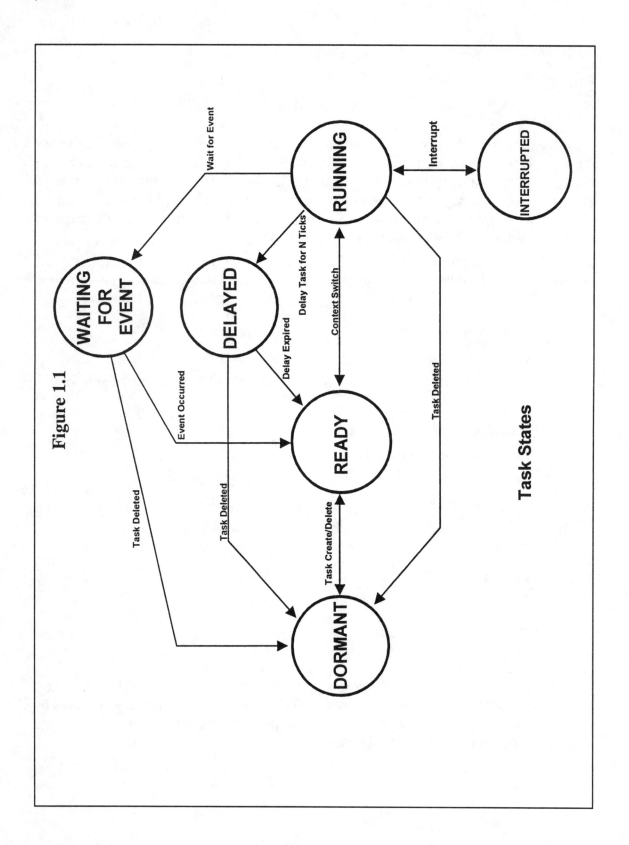

Figure 1.1

Task States

6

1

Critical Section of Code

A critical section of code, also called a *critical region*, is code that needs to be treated indivisibly. Once the section of code starts executing, it must not be interrupted. To ensure this, interrupts are typically disabled prior to executing the critical code and enabled when done. (See the following discussion of interrupt handling.)

Resource

A resource is any entity used by a task. A resource can thus be an I/O device such as a printer, a keyboard, a display etc. or a variable, a structure, an array etc.

Shared Resource

A shared resource is a resource which can be used by more than one task. Each task should gain exclusive access to the shared resource to prevent data corruption.

Multitasking

Multitasking is the process of scheduling and switching the CPU between several tasks; a single CPU switches its attention between several sequential tasks. Multitasking maximizes the utilization of the CPU and also provides for modular construction of applications. One of the most important aspects of multitasking is that it allows the application programmer to manage complexity inherent in real-time applications. Application programs are typically easier to design and maintain if multitasking is used.

Task

A task, also called a thread, is a simple program that thinks it has the CPU all to itself. The design process for a real-time application involves splitting the work to be done into tasks which are responsible for a portion of the problem. Each task is assigned a priority, its own set of CPU registers and its own stack area (as shown in Figure 1.2). Each task is typically an infinite loop that can be in any one of six states: **DORMANT, READY, RUNNING, DELAYED, WAITING FOR AN EVENT** or **INTERRUPTED** (see Figure 1.1). The **DORMANT** state corresponds to a task which resides in memory but has not been made available to the multitasking kernel. A task is **READY** when it can execute but its priority is less than the current running task. A task is **RUNNING** when it has control of the CPU. A task is **DELAYED** when the task suspended itself until a certain amount of time has elapsed. A task is **WAITING FOR AN EVENT** when it requires the occurrence of an event: waiting for an I/O operation to complete, a shared resource to be available, a timing pulse to occur, etc. Finally, a task is **INTER-RUPTED** when an interrupt occurred and the CPU is in the process of servicing the interrupt.

Context Switch or Task Switch

When the multitasking kernel decides to run a different task, it simply saves the current task's context (CPU registers) in the current task's context storage area (see Figure 1.2). Once this operation is performed, the new task's context is restored from its storage area and then resumes execution of the new task's code. This process is called a *context switch* or a *task switch*. Context switching adds overhead to the application. The more registers a CPU has, the higher the overhead. The time required to perform a context switch is determined by how many registers have to be saved and restored by the CPU. Performance of a real-time kernel should not be judged on how many context switches the kernel is capable of doing per second.

Kernel

The kernel is the part of a multitasking system responsible for the management of tasks (that is, managing the CPU's time) and communication between tasks. The fundamental service provided by the kernel is context switching.

Scheduler

The scheduler, also called the dispatcher, is the part of the kernel responsible for determining which task will run next. Most real-time kernels are priority based. Each task is assigned a priority based on its importance. Establishing the priority for each task is application specific. In a priority based kernel, control of the CPU will always be given to the highest priority task ready to run. *When* the highest priority task gets the CPU, however, is determined by the type of kernel used. There are two types of priority based kernels: non-preemptive and preemptive.

Non-Preemptive Kernel

Non-preemptive kernels require that each task does something to explicitly give up control of the CPU. To maintain the illusion of concurrency, this process must be done frequently. Non-preemptive scheduling is also called *cooperative multitasking*; tasks cooperate with each other to relinquish control of the CPU. Non-preemptive kernels are much simpler to design than preemptive kernels. One of the advantages of a non-preemptive kernel is that interrupt latency is typically low. (See the later discussion of interrupts.) Non-preemptive kernels can also make use of non- reentrant functions (at the task level). Non-reentrant functions can be used by each task without fear of corruption by another task. This is because each task can run to completion before it relinquishes the CPU. Non-reentrant functions, however, should not be allowed to give up control of the CPU.

Another advantage of non-preemptive kernels is the smaller need to guard shared data through the use of semaphores protecting shared variables, because each task owns the CPU without the fear of being preempted. This is not an absolute rule and

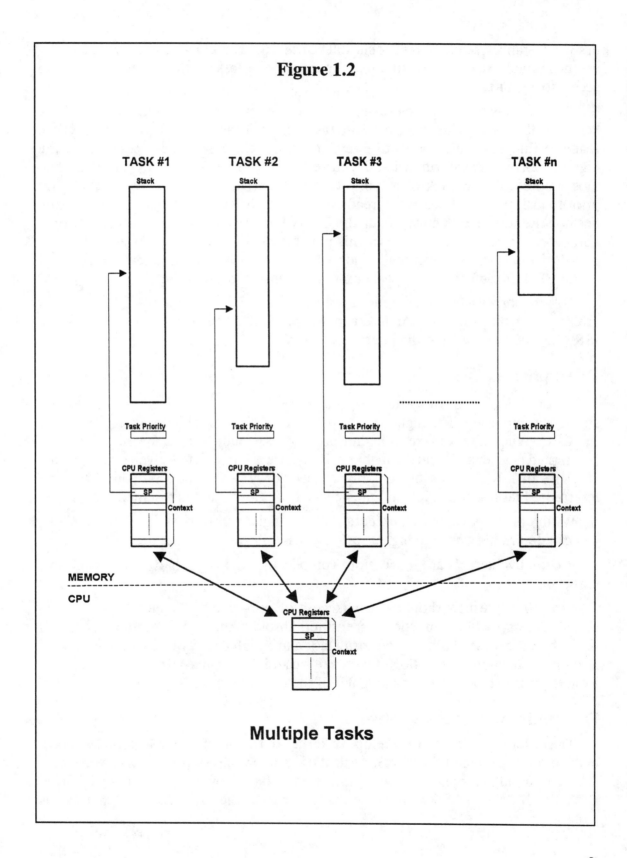

Figure 1.2

Multiple Tasks

in some instances, semaphores should still be used. Shared I/O devices may require the use of mutual exclusion semaphores; for example, a task might still need exclusive access to a printer.

The only way a task can be preempted is from an interrupt; an *Interrupt Service Routine* (ISR) always has priority over a task. The ISR can make a higher priority task ready to run. The ISR, however, always returns to the interrupted task. Again, the higher priority task will run when the current task gives up control of the CPU. The most important drawback of a non-preemptive kernel is responsiveness. A higher priority task that has been made ready to run may have to wait a long time to run, because the current task must give up the CPU when it is ready to do so. Most real-time kernels are preemptive because of this possible delay. Non-preemptive kernels are non-deterministic; you never really know when the highest priority task will get control of the CPU. It is up to your application to relinquish control of the CPU.

To summarize, a non-preemptive kernel allows each task to run until it voluntarily gives up control of the CPU. An interrupt will preempt a task. Upon completion of the ISR, the ISR will return to the interrupted task.

Preemptive Kernel

µC/OS is a preemptive kernel. A preemptive kernel is used when system responsiveness is important. The highest priority task ready to run is always given control of the CPU. When a task makes a higher priority task ready to run, the current task is preempted (suspended) and the higher priority task is immediately given control of the CPU. If an ISR makes a higher priority task ready, when the ISR completes, the interrupted task is suspended and the new higher priority task is resumed.

With a preemptive kernel, execution of the highest priority task is deterministic; you can determine *when* the highest priority task will get control of the CPU.

Preemptive kernels are much more complicated to design than non- preemptive kernels.

Preemptive kernels should not make use of non-reentrant functions unless exclusive access to these functions is ensured through the use of mutual exclusion semaphores, because both a low priority task and a high priority task can make use of a common function. Corruption of data may occur if the higher priority task preempts a lower priority task which is making use of the function.

Preemptive vs Non-Preemptive

The differences between a preemptive kernel and a non-preemptive kernel is shown in the timing diagram of Figure 1.3. As the flow diagram shows, three tasks are created. TASK 1 has a higher priority than TASK 2 which has a higher priority than TASK 3. Both TASK 2 and TASK 3 are made ready to run by the *TICK ISR*. Another ISR is used to send a message to TASK 1. When the ISR sends a message to TASK 1, TASK 1 is made ready to run.

For the non-preemptive kernel, the *TICK ISR* occurs at time (A) and makes TASK 2 and TASK 3 ready to run. When the *TICK ISR* returns, TASK 2 is given control of the CPU (B). When the other interrupt occurs (C), TASK 2 is temporarily suspended to service the interrupt. When the ISR completes, TASK 2 is resumed (D). When TASK 2 gives up control of the CPU, TASK 1 is executed (E) because it has a higher priority than TASK 3. At the completion of TASK 1, the CPU is relinquished and TASK 3 is given control of the CPU (F).

For the preemptive kernel, the *TICK ISR* is serviced in the same way as for the non-preemptive kernel (A). TASK 2 is given control of the CPU at the completion of the *TICK ISR* (B). When the other interrupt occurs (C), TASK 2 is suspended. At the completion of the ISR, the preemptive kernel will execute TASK 1 since it has a higher priority than the interrupt task (i.e. TASK 2). TASK 1 is thus given control of the CPU (D). TASK 2 is resumed when TASK 1 completes (E). Finally, TASK 3 will be processed at the completion of TASK 2.

Reentrancy

A reentrant function is a function that can be used by more than one task without fear of data corruption. A reentrant function can be interrupted at any time and resumed at a later time without loss of data. Reentrant functions either use local variables (i.e. CPU registers or variables on the stack) or protect data when global variables are used. An example of a reentrant function is shown below:

```
void strcpy(char *dest, char *src)
{
        while (*dest++ = *src++){
                ;
        }
        *dest = NUL;
}
```

An example of a non-reentrant function is shown below (Var1 is declared global). Since the function accesses a global variable, it is non-reentrant.

```
void foo(void)
{
    .
    .
    .
    Var1 += 23;
    .
    .
    .
}
```

The function can be made reentrant, however, by protecting the critical section of code.

```
void foo(void)
{
    .
    .
    Disable interrupts;
    Var1 += 23;
    Enable interrupts;
    .
    .
    .
}
```

Compilers specifically designed for embedded software will typically provide reentrant libraries. Floating point math is performed through library functions when a microprocessor does not have hardware floating point math capability. This does not mean, however, that the library functions are reentrant. For instance, both the Borland C++ V3.x and Microsoft C/C++ V7.0 do not support reentrant libraries (math and standard run time library), because these compilers are intended for a single tasking operating system, MS-DOS. Fortunately, alternate sources exist for such libraries.

Round Robin Scheduling

When two or more tasks have the same priority, the kernel will allow one task to run for a predetermined amount of time and then select the next one in turn. This is also called *time slicing*. The kernel gives control to the next task in line if: a) the task doesn't have any work to do during its time slice or b) the task completes before the end of its time slice. µC/OS does not allow round robin scheduling.

Task Priority

A priority is assigned to each task. The more important the task, the higher the priority given to it.

Static Priorities

Task priorities are said to be *static* when the priority of each task does not change during the application's execution. Each task is thus given a fixed priority at compile time.

Dynamic Priorities

Task priorities are said to be *dynamic* if the priority of tasks can be changed during the application's execution; each task can change its priority at run time. µC/OS allows task priorities to be changed dynamically.

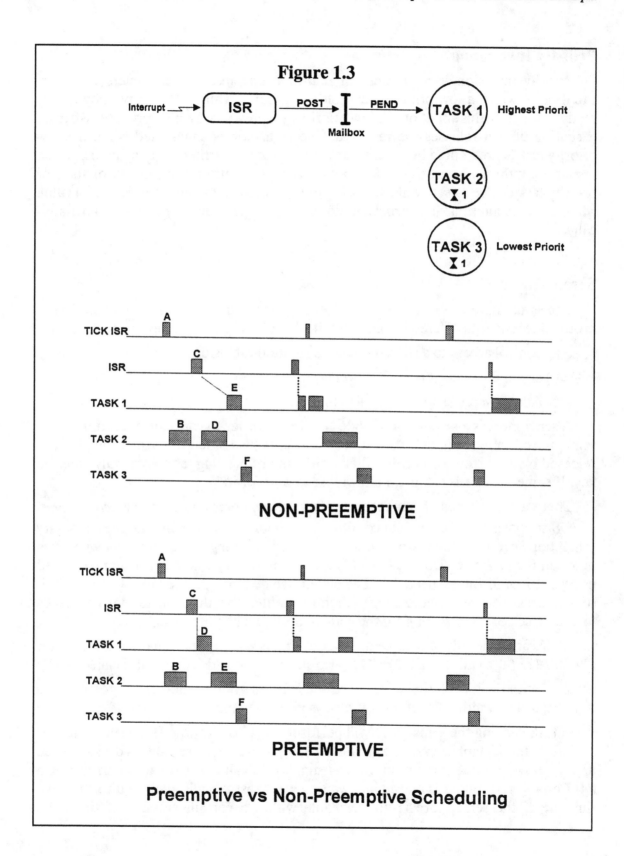

Figure 1.3

NON-PREEMPTIVE

PREEMPTIVE

Preemptive vs Non-Preemptive Scheduling

Priority Inversions

Priority inversion is a problem in real-time systems. Priority inversion is any situation in which a low priority task holds a resource while a higher priority task is ready to use it. In this situation the low priority task prevents the high priority task from executing until it releases the resource. The condition is aggravated when the low priority task is preempted by other tasks (or interrupts), further delaying access to the resource by the high priority task. To correct this situation, the priority of the low priority task can be raised while accessing the resource and restored to its initial value when done. A multitasking kernel should thus allow priorities to be changed dynamically.

Semaphores

The semaphore was invented by Edsger Dijkstra in the mid 60s. A semaphore is a protocol mechanism offered by most multitasking kernels. Semaphores are used to:

a) control access to a shared resource (mutual exclusion)

b) signal the occurrence of an event

c) Allow two tasks to synchronize their activities

A semaphore is a key that your code acquires in order to continue execution. If the semaphore is already in use, the requesting task is suspended until the semaphore is released by its current owner. In other words, the requesting task says: "Give me the key. If someone else is using it, I am willing to wait for it!"

There are two types of semaphores: *binary semaphores* and *counting semaphores*. µC/OS supports both binary and counting semaphores. As its name implies, a binary semaphore can only take two values: 0 or 1. A counting semaphore allows values between 0 and 255, 65535 or 4294967295, depending on whether it is implemented using 8, 16 or 32 bit, respectively. The actual size depends on the kernel used; 32 bit semaphores are rarely used. Along with the semaphore's value, the kernel also needs to keep track of tasks waiting for the semaphore's availability.

There are generally only three operations that can be performed on a semaphore: *INITIALIZE* (also called *CREATE*), *WAIT* (also called *PEND*) and *SIGNAL* (also called *POST*).

The initial value of the semaphore must be provided when the semaphore is initialized. The waiting list of tasks is always initially empty.

A task desiring the semaphore will perform a *WAIT* operation. If the semaphore is available (the semaphore value is greater than *0*), the semaphore value is decremented and the task continues execution. If the semaphore's value is *0*, the task performing a *WAIT* on the semaphore is placed in a waiting list. Most kernels allow you to specify a timeout; if the semaphore is not available within a certain amount of time, the requesting task is made ready to run and an error code (indicating a timeout occurred) is returned to it.

A task releases a semaphore by performing a *SIGNAL* operation. If no task is waiting for the semaphore, the semaphore value is simply incremented. If any task is waiting for the semaphore, however, one of the tasks is made ready to run and the semaphore value is not incremented; the key is given to a waiting task. Depending on the kernel used, the task which will receive the semaphore is either:

a) the highest priority task waiting for the semaphore or

b) the first task that requested the semaphore (First In First Out)

Some kernels allow you to choose either method through an option when the semaphore is initialized. If the readied task has a higher priority that the current task (the task releasing the semaphore), a context switch will occur and the higher priority task will resume execution; the current task will be suspended until it again becomes the highest priority task ready to run. µC/OS will make the highest priority task waiting for the semaphore ready to run and does not support First In First Out order (FIFO).

Mutual Exclusion

Imagine what would happen if two tasks were allowed to send characters to a printer at the same time. The printer would contain interleaved data from each task. For instance, if task #1 tried to print "I am task #1!" and task #2 tried to print "I am task #2!" the printout could look like this:

"I Ia amm t tasask k#1 #!2!"

To prevent this situation, exclusive access to the printer by each task is necessary until each task completes its print job. A binary semaphore is used in this case to provide mutual exclusion; the semaphore is initialized to 1. The rule is simple, to access the resource you must first obtain the resource's semaphore. Figure 1.4 shows the tasks competing for a semaphore to gain exclusive access to the printer. Note that the semaphore is represented symbolically by a key indicating that each task must obtain this key to use the printer.

The above example implies that each task must know about the existence of the semaphore in order to access the resource. There are situations when it is better to encapsulate the semaphore. Each task would thus not know that it is actually acquiring a semaphore when accessing the resource. For example, an RS-232C port is used by multiple tasks to send commands and receive responses from a device connected at the other end of the RS-232C port. A flow diagram is shown in Figure 1.5. The function *CommSendCmd()* is called with three arguments: the ASCII string containing the command, a pointer to the response string from the device and finally, a timeout in case the device doesn't respond within a certain amount of time. The pseudo code for this function is shown below:

Figure 1.4

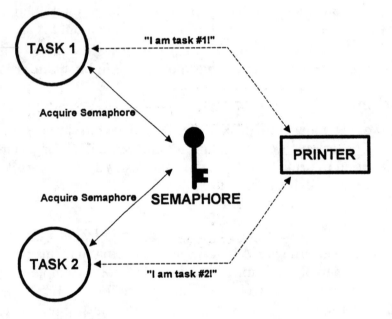

Two tasks competing for a printer

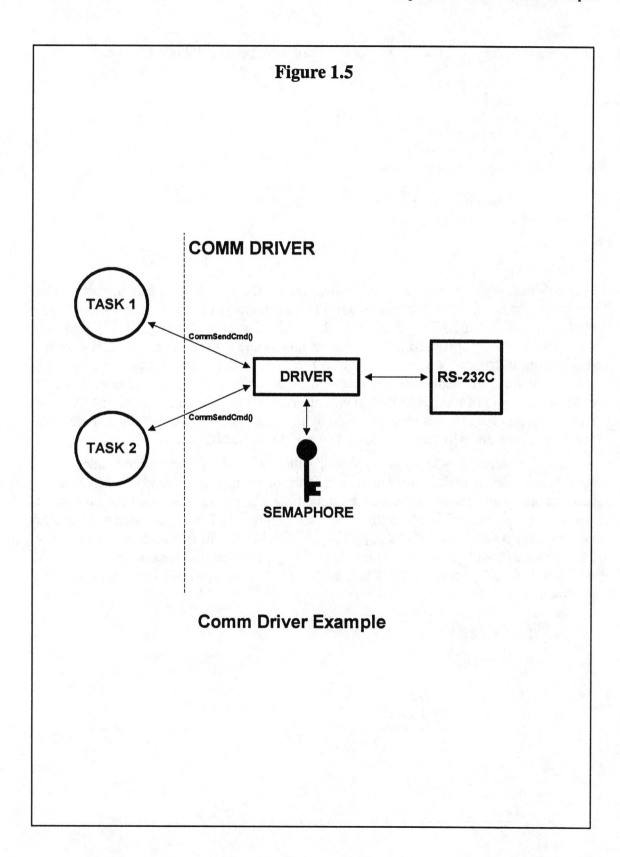

Figure 1.5

Comm Driver Example

```
UBYTE CommSendCmd(char *cmd, char *response, UWORD timeout)
{
    Acquire port's semaphore;
    Send command to device;
    Wait for response (with timeout);
    if (timed out) {
        Release semaphore;
        return (error code);
    } else {
        Release semaphore;
        return (no error);
    }
}
```

Each task which needs to send a command to the device calls this function. The semaphore is assumed to be initialized to 1 (i.e. available) by the communication driver initialization routine. The first task that calls *CommSendCmd()* will acquire the semaphore and thus proceed to send the command and wait for a response. If another task attempts to send a command while the port is busy, this second task will be suspended until the semaphore is released. Where the second task is concerned, it made a call to a normal function that will not return until the function has performed its duty. When the semaphore is released by the first task, the second task will acquire the semaphore and will thus be allowed to use the RS-232C port.

A more general type of semaphore, called a *counting semaphore*, allows the semaphore value to take positive values. A counting semaphore is used when a resource can be used by more than one task at the same time. For example, a counting semaphore is used in the management of a buffer pool (see Figure 1.6). Let's assume that the buffer pool initially contains 10 buffers. A task would obtain a buffer from the buffer manager by calling *BufReq()*. When the buffer is no longer needed, the task would return the buffer to the buffer manager by calling *BufRel()*. The pseudo code for these functions is shown below:

```
BUF *BufReq(void)
{
    BUF *ptr;

    Acquire a semaphore;
    Disable interrupts;
    ptr           = BufFreeList;
    BufFreeList = ptr-BufNext;
    Enable interrupts;
    return (ptr);
}
```

```
void BufRel(BUF *ptr)
{
    Disable interrupts;
    ptr-BufNext = BufFreeList;
    BufFreeList = ptr;
    Enable interrupts;
    Release semaphore;
}
```

The buffer manager will satisfy the first ten buffer requests (since there are ten keys). When all semaphores are used, a task requesting a buffer would be suspended until one becomes available. Interrupts are disabled to gain exclusive access to the linked list (this operation is very quick). When a task is finished with the buffer it acquired, it calls *BufRel()* to return the buffer to the buffer manager; the buffer is inserted into the linked list before releasing the semaphore. By encapsulating the interface to the buffer manager, the caller doesn't need to be concerned with the actual implementation details.

Semaphores are often overused. The use of a semaphore to access a simple shared variable is overkill in some situations. The overhead involved in acquiring and releasing the semaphore can consume valuable time. Disabling and enabling interrupts could do the job more efficiently. All real-time kernels will disable interrupts during critical sections of code. You are thus basically allowed to disable interrupts for as much time as the kernel does without affecting interrupt latency. Obviously, you need to know how long the kernel will disable interrupts. (See the following discussion of Interrupt Latency, Response and Recovery.)

For example, let's suppose that two tasks are sharing a 16 bit integer variable. The first task increments the variable while the other task clears it. If you consider how long a processor takes to perform either operation, you do not need a semaphore to gain exclusive access to the variable. Each task simply needs to disable interrupts before performing its operation on the variable and enable interrupts when done. A semaphore should be used, however, if the variable to manipulate is a floating point and the microprocessor doesn't support floating point in hardware. In this case the processing time involved in processing the floating point variable could affect interrupt latency.

Deadlock (or Deadly Embrace)

A deadlock, also called a *deadly embrace*, is a situation in which two tasks are unknowingly waiting for resources that are held by each other. For instance, if task T1 has exclusive access to resource R1 and task T2 has exclusive access to resource R2. Now if T1 needs exclusive access to R2 and T2 also needs exclusive access to R1, neither

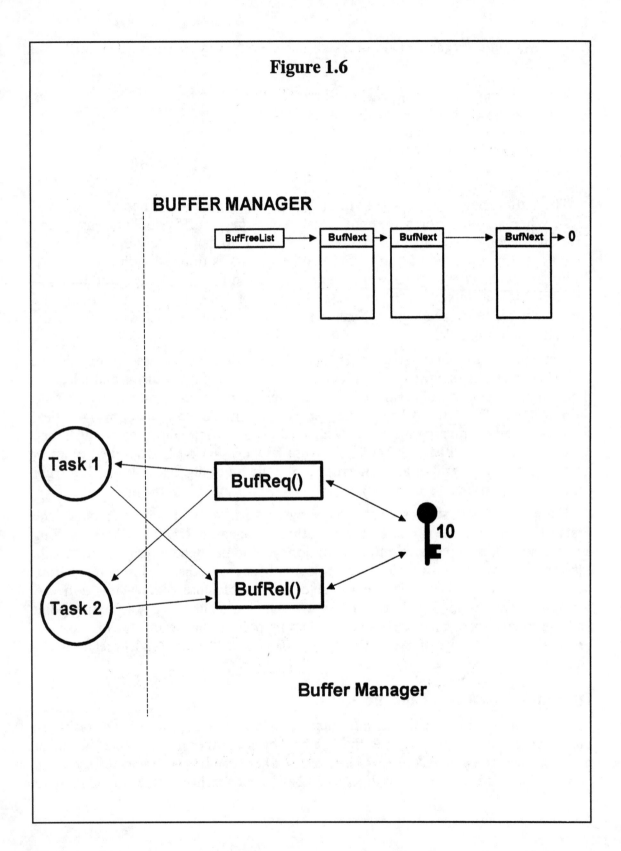

Figure 1.6

task can continue — they are deadlocked. The simplest way to avoid a deadlock is for both tasks to:

    a) acquire all resources before proceeding and

    b) acquire the resources in the same order.

Synchronization

A task can be synchronized with an ISR or another task when no data is being exchanged, by using a semaphore as shown in Figure 1.7. Note that, in this case, the semaphore is drawn as a flag, to indicate that it is used to signal the occurrence of an event rather than being used for mutual exclusion, which would be drawn as a key. When used as a synchronization mechanism, the semaphore is initialized to *0*. Using a semaphore for this type of synchronization is also called a *unilateral rendezvous*. For example, a task initiates an I/O operation and then waits for the semaphore. When the I/O operation is complete, an ISR (or another task) signals the semaphore and the task is resumed.

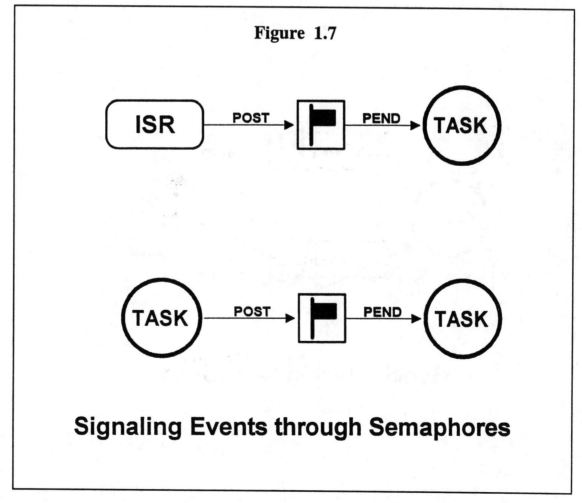

Figure 1.7

Signaling Events through Semaphores

If the kernel supports counting semaphores, the semaphore would accumulate events that have not yet been processed.

Note that more than one task can be waiting for the event to occur. In this case, the kernel could signal the occurrence of the event either to:

a) the highest priority task waiting for the event to occur

b) the first task waiting for the event

Depending on the application, more than one ISR or task could signal the occurrence of the event.

Two tasks can synchronize their activities by using two semaphores as shown in Figure 1.8. This is called a *bilateral rendezvous*. A bilateral rendezvous is similar to a unilateral rendezvous except that both tasks must synchronize with one another before proceeding. For example, two tasks are executing as shown below. When the first task reaches a certain point, it signals the second task and then waits for a signal from the second task. Similarly, when the second task reaches a certain point, it signals the first

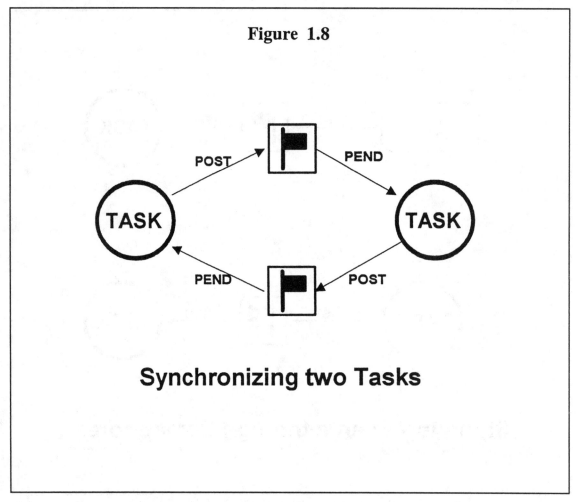

Figure 1.8

Synchronizing two Tasks

task and then waits for a signal from the first task. At this point, both tasks are synchronized with each other. A bilateral rendezvous cannot be performed between a task and an ISR.

```
Task1()
{
    while (1) {
        Perform operation;
        Signal task #2;
        Wait for signal from task #2;
        Continue operation;
    }
}

Task2()
{
    while (1) {
        Perform operation;
        Signal task #1;
        Wait for signal from task #1;
        Continue operation;
    }
}
```

Event Flags

Event flags are used when a task needs to synchronize with the occurrence of multiple events. The task can be synchronized when any of the events have occurred. This is called *disjunctive synchronization* (Logical *OR*). A task can also be synchronized when all events have occurred. This is called *conjunctive synchronization* (Logical *AND*). Disjunctive and conjunctive synchronization are shown in Figure 1.9.

Common events can be used to signal multiple tasks as shown in Figure 1.10. Events are typically grouped. A group consists of 8, 16 or 32 events. Tasks and ISRs can set or clear any event in a group. A task is resumed when all the events it requires are satisfied. The evaluation of which task will be resumed is performed when a new set of events occurs.

Intertask Communication

It is sometimes necessary for a task or an ISR to communicate information to another task. This information transfer is called intertask communication. Information may be communicated between tasks in two ways: through global data and by sending messages.

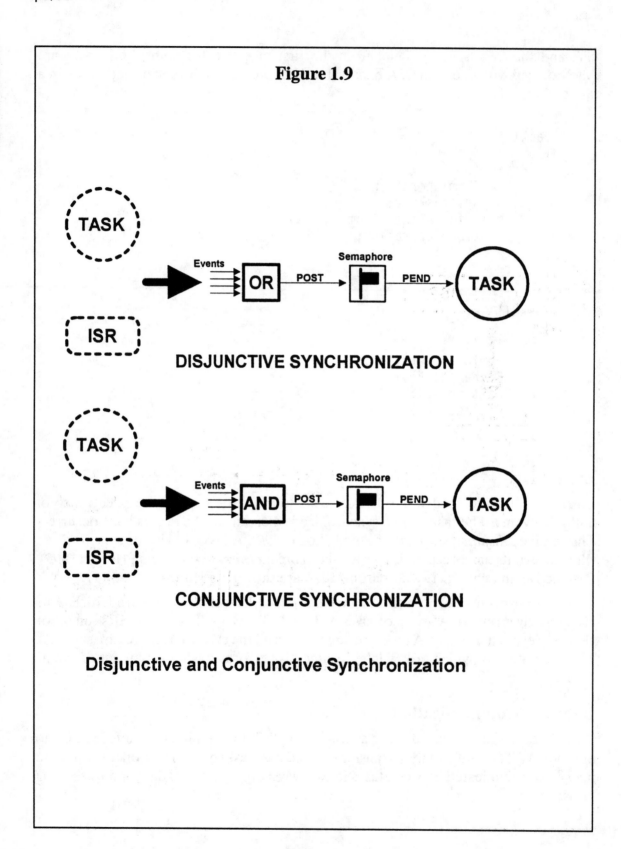

Figure 1.9

DISJUNCTIVE SYNCHRONIZATION

CONJUNCTIVE SYNCHRONIZATION

Disjunctive and Conjunctive Synchronization

Figure 1.10

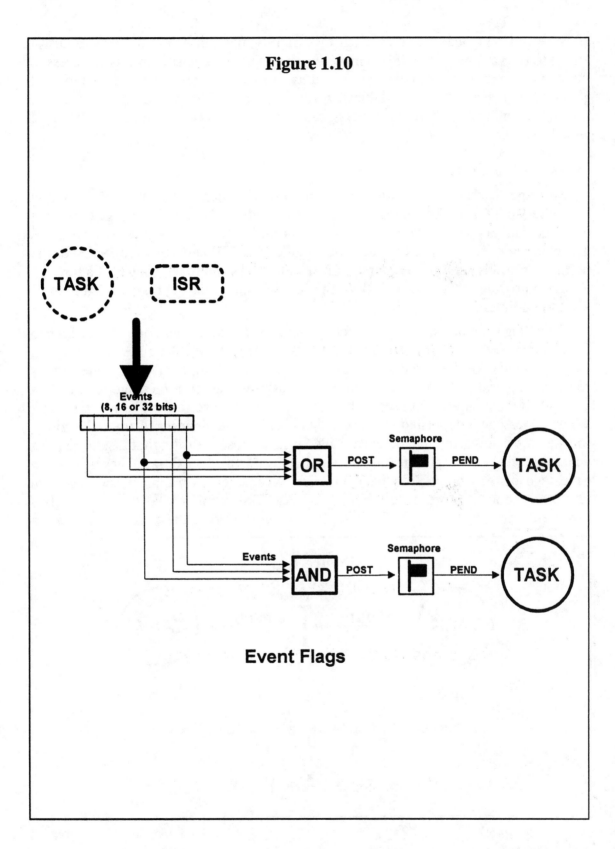

Event Flags

When using global variables, each task or ISR must ensure that it has exclusive access to the variables. If an ISR is involved, the only way to ensure exclusive access to the common variables is to disable interrupts. If two tasks are sharing data each can gain exclusive access to the variables by using either disabling/enabling interrupts or through a semaphore. Note that a task can only communicate with an ISR by using global variables.

Message Mailboxes

Messages can be sent to a task through kernel services. The two most common kernel services for sending messages are the Message Mailbox and Message Queue. A Message Mailbox, also called a *message exchange*, is typically a pointer size variable. Through a service provided by the kernel, a task or an ISR can deposit a message (the pointer) into this mailbox. Similarly, one or more tasks can receive messages through a service provided by the kernel. Both the sending and receiving task will agree as to what the pointer is pointing to.

A waiting list is associated with each mailbox in case more than one task desires to receive messages through the mailbox. A task desiring to receive a message from an empty mailbox will be suspended and placed on the waiting list until a message is received. Typically, the kernel will allow the task waiting for a message to specify a timeout. If a message is not received before the timeout expires, the task is resumed. When a message is deposited into the mailbox, either the highest priority task waiting for the message is given the message (called priority based) or the first task to request a message will be given the message (called FIFO). Figure 1.11 shows a task depositing a message into a mailbox. Note that the mailbox is represented graphically by an I-beam and the timeout is represented by an hourglass. The number next to the hourglass represents the number of clock ticks (described later) that the task will wait for a

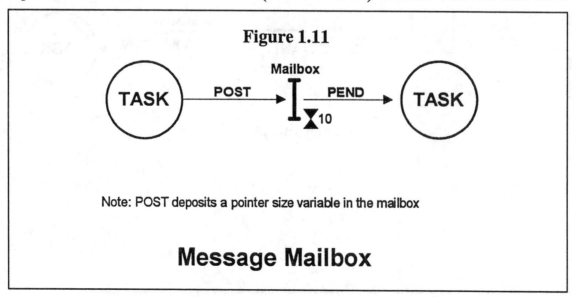

Figure 1.11

Note: POST deposits a pointer size variable in the mailbox

Message Mailbox

message to arrive. µC/OS supports message mailboxes with timeouts. When a message is deposited into a mailbox, µC/OS will give the message to the highest priority task waiting for a message (if any task is waiting). µC/OS does not support FIFO order.

Message Queues

A message queue is used to send one or more messages to a task. A message queue is basically an array of mailboxes. Through a service provided by the kernel, a task or an ISR can deposit a message (the pointer) into a message queue. Similarly, one or more tasks can receive messages through a service provided by the kernel. Both the sending and receiving task will agree as to what the pointer is actually pointing to. Generally, the first message inserted in the queue will be the first message extracted from the queue (FIFO).

As with the mailbox, a waiting list is associated with each message queue in case more than one task is to receive messages through the queue. A task desiring to receive a message from an empty queue will be suspended and placed on the waiting list until a message is received. Typically, the kernel will allow the task waiting for a message to specify a timeout. If a message is not received before the timeout expires, the task is resumed. When a message is deposited into the queue, either the highest priority task or the first task to wait for the message will be given the message. Figure 1.12 shows an ISR depositing a message into a queue. Note that the queue is represented graphically by a double I-beam. The 10 indicates the number of messages that can be accumulated in the queue. A 0 next to the hourglass indicates that the task will wait forever for a message to arrive. µC/OS supports message queues with timeouts. When a message is deposited into a queue, µC/OS will give the message to the highest priority task waiting for a message (if any task is waiting). µC/OS does not support FIFO order.

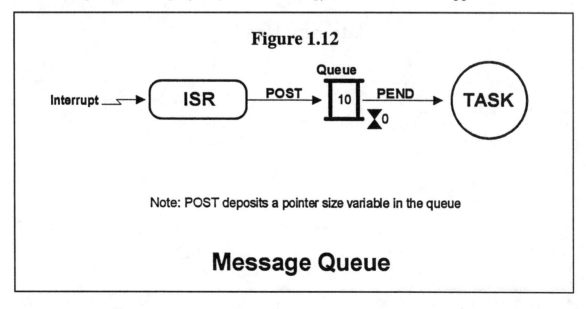

Figure 1.12

Note: POST deposits a pointer size variable in the queue

Message Queue

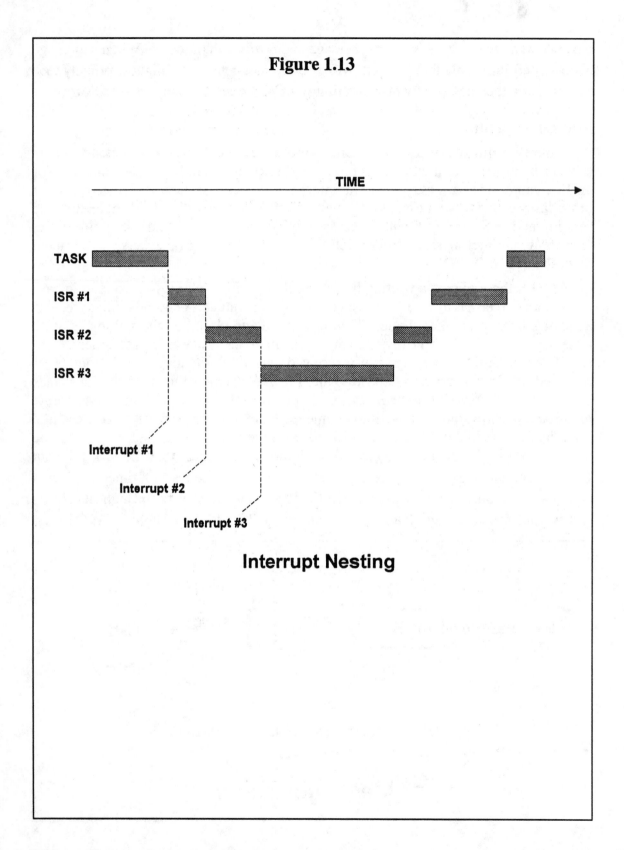

Figure 1.13

Interrupt Nesting

Interrupts

An interrupt is a hardware mechanism used to signal the CPU that an asynchronous event has occurred. When an interrupt is recognized, the CPU saves part (or all) of its context and jumps to a subroutine called an Interrupt Service Routine or ISR. The ISR processes the event and upon completion of the ISR, the program returns to:

a) The interrupted task for a non-preemptive kernel

b) The highest priority task ready to run for a preemptive kernel

Interrupts allow a microprocessor to process events when they occur. This prevents the microprocessor from continuously polling an event to see it this event has occurred. Microprocessors allow interrupts to be ignored and recognized through the use of special instructions: disable interrupts and enable interrupts. Processors generally allow interrupts to be nested. This means that while servicing an interrupt the processor will recognize and service other interrupts as shown in Figure 1.13.

Interrupt Latency, Response and Recovery

An important issue in real-time systems is the time required to respond to an interrupt and to actually start executing user code to handle the interrupt (see Figure 1.14).

All real-time kernels disable interrupts when manipulating critical sections of code. Interrupt latency is given by:

Maximum amount of time interrupts are disabled +

Time to start executing the ISR

The longer a kernel disables interrupts, the higher the interrupt latency. Before executing user code, the processor's context must be saved. If a non-preemptive kernel is used, the user ISR code is executed next. If a preemptive kernel is used, a special function provided by the kernel is called. This function is used to notify the kernel that an ISR is in progress and allows the kernel to keep track of interrupt nesting. The response time to an interrupt is given by:

Non-preemptive:

Interrupt latency +

Time to save the CPU's context

Preemptive:

Interrupt latency +

Time to save the CPU's context +

Execution time of the kernel ISR entry function

Interrupt recovery time is the time required for the processor to return to the interrupted code. In a non-preemptive kernel, interrupt recovery simply involves restoring the processor's context and returning to the interrupted task. For a preemptive kernel, interrupt recovery is typically performed by a function provided by the kernel. When all interrupts have nested, the kernel will determine if a higher priority task has been made ready to run as a result of the ISR. If a higher priority task is ready to run as a result of the ISR, this task is resumed. Note that the interrupted task will be resumed when it becomes the highest priority task ready to run. Interrupt recovery is thus given by:

Non-preemptive:

Time to restore the CPU's context +

Time to execute the return from interrupt instruction

Preemptive:

Time to restore the CPU's context +

Time to determine if a higher priority task is ready +

Time to execute the return from interrupt instruction

ISR Processing Time

While ISRs should be as short as possible, there are no absolute limits on the amount of time for an ISR. One cannot say that an ISR must always be less than 100 µS, 500 µS, 1 mS etc. If the ISR's code is the most important code that needs to run at any given time, then it could be as long as it needs to be. In most cases, however, the ISR should recognize the interrupt and signal a task that will perform the actual processing. You should consider whether the overhead involved in signaling a task is more than the processing of the interrupt. Signaling a task from an ISR (i.e. through a semaphore, a mailbox or a queue) requires some processing time. If processing of your interrupt requires less than the time required to signal a task, you should consider processing the interrupt in the ISR itself.

Non-Maskable Interrupts (NMIs)

Sometimes, an interrupt must be serviced as quickly as possible and cannot afford to have the latency imposed by the kernel. In these situations, you may be able to use the Non-Maskable Interrupt (NMI) provided on most microprocessors. Since the NMI cannot be disabled, interrupt latency, response and recovery are minimal. The NMI is generally reserved for drastic measures such as saving important information during a power down. If, however, you application doesn't have this requirement, you could use the NMI to service your most time critical ISR.

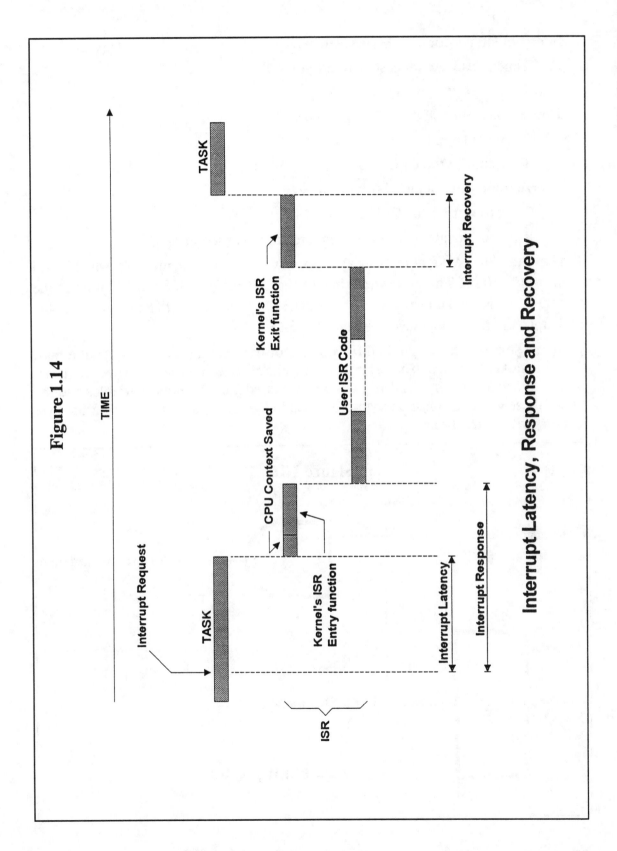

Figure 1.14

Interrupt Latency, Response and Recovery

Interrupt latency for an NMI is given by:

Time to execute longest instruction +

Time to start executing the ISR

The response time of an NMI is given by:

Interrupt latency +

Time to save the CPU's context +

Interrupt recovery of an NMI is given by:

Time to restore the CPU's context +

Time to execute the return from interrupt instruction

I have used te NMI feature in an application to respond to an interrupt which could occur every 150 µS. The processing time of the ISR took from 80 to 130 µS and the kernel I used disabled interrupts for about 45 µS. As you can see, if I had used maskable interrupts, the ISR could have been late by 25 µS.

When you are servicing an NMI, you cannot use kernel services to signal a task. NMIs cannot be disabled to access critical sections of code. You can, however, still pass parameters to and from the NMI. Parameters passed must be global variables and the size of these variables must be read or written indivisibly, that is, not as separate byte read or write instructions.

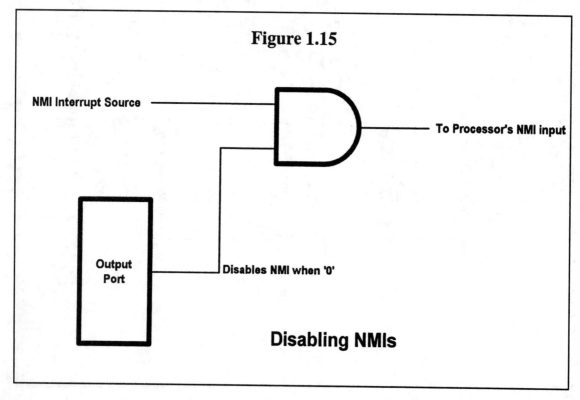

Figure 1.15

NMI Interrupt Source ——————

To Processor's NMI input

Output Port

Disables NMI when '0'

Disabling NMIs

NMIs can be disabled by adding external circuitry as shown in Figure 1.15. Assuming that both the interrupt and the NMI are positive going signals, a simple AND gate is inserted between the interrupt source and the processor's NMI input. Interrupts are disabled by writing a *0* to an output port. You wouldn't disable interrupts to use kernel services, but you could use this feature to pass 8, 16, or 32 bit parameters to and from a task.

Now, suppose that the NMI service routine needs to signal a task every 40 times it executes. If the NMI occurs every 150 µS, a signal would be required every 6 mS. You cannot use the kernel to signal the task, but you could use the scheme shown in Figure 1.16. In this case, the NMI service routine would generate a hardware interrupt through an output port. Since the NMI service routine typically has the highest priority, the interrupt would not be recognized until the end of the NMI service routine. At the completion of the NMI service routine, the processor would be interrupted to service this hardware interrupt. This ISR would clear the interrupt and post to a semaphore that would wake up the task. As long as the task services the semaphore well within 6 mS, your deadline would be met.

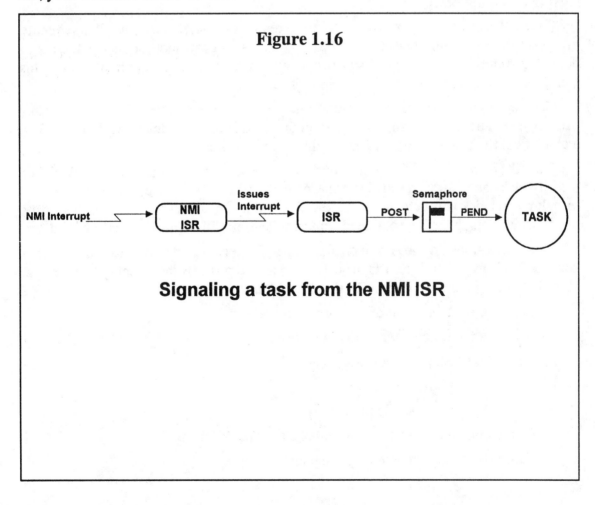

Figure 1.16

Signaling a task from the NMI ISR

Clock Tick

A *clock tick* is a special interrupt that occurs periodically. This interrupt can be viewed as the system's heartbeat. The time between interrupts is application specific and is generally between 10 and 200 mS. The faster the tick rate, the higher the overhead imposed on the system. The clock tick interrupt allows tasks to be delayed for an integral number of clock ticks and to provide timeouts when tasks are waiting for events to occur.

All kernels allow tasks to be delayed for a certain number of clock ticks. The resolution of delayed tasks is 1 clock tick, however, this does not mean that its accuracy is 1 clock tick.

Figures 1.17 through 1.19 are timing diagrams showing a task delaying itself for 1 clock tick. The shaded areas indicate the execution time for each operation being performed. Note that the time for each operation varies to reflect typical processing which would include loops and conditional statements (i.e. if/else, switch and ?:). The processing time of the Tick ISR has been exaggerated to show that it too is subject to varying execution times.

Case 1 (Figure 1.17) shows a situation where higher priority tasks and ISRs execute prior to the task which needs to delay for 1 tick. As you can see, the task attempts to delay for 20 mS but because of its priority, actually executes at varying intervals. This will thus cause the execution of the task to jitter.

Case 2 (Figure 1.18) shows a situation where the execution times of all higher priority tasks and ISRs are slightly less than one tick. If the task delays itself just before a clock tick, the task will execute again almost immediately!

Case 3 (Figure 1.19) shows a situation where the execution times of all higher priority tasks and ISRs extends beyond one clock tick. In this case, the task that tries to delay for 1 tick will actually execute 2 ticks later! In this case, the task missed its deadline. This might be acceptable in some applications but in most cases, it would not.

These situations are not unique to one specific kernel and exist with all real-time kernels. They are related to CPU processing load and possibly incorrect system design. Here are some possible solutions to these problems:

- Increase the clock rate of your microprocessor

- Increase the time between tick interrupts.

- Rearrange task priorities

- Avoid using floating point math

   (if you must, use single precision)

- Get a compiler that performs better code optimization

- Write some code in assembly language

1

- Upgrade to a faster microprocessor in the same family, e.g.

8086 to 80186

68000 to 68020

etc.

Regardless of what you do, jitter will always occur.

Performance

A number of factors affect a real-time kernel's performance:

a) Context Switching Time: Context switching time is really determined by the microprocessor and generally doesn't change from one kernel to another. Saving and restoring a processor's context depends on how many registers a processor has. Context switching time is not a meaningful benchmark.

b) Interrupt Response: An important criterion for a real-time kernel is how quickly it responds to an interrupt.

c) Determinism: An important performance issue in a real-time kernel is determinism. Kernel services should be deterministic by specifying how long each service call will take to execute. Having this information allows you to better plan your application software. All services provided by µC/OS are deterministic and µC/OS's performance does not depend on the number of tasks in your application (except when processing a clock tick).

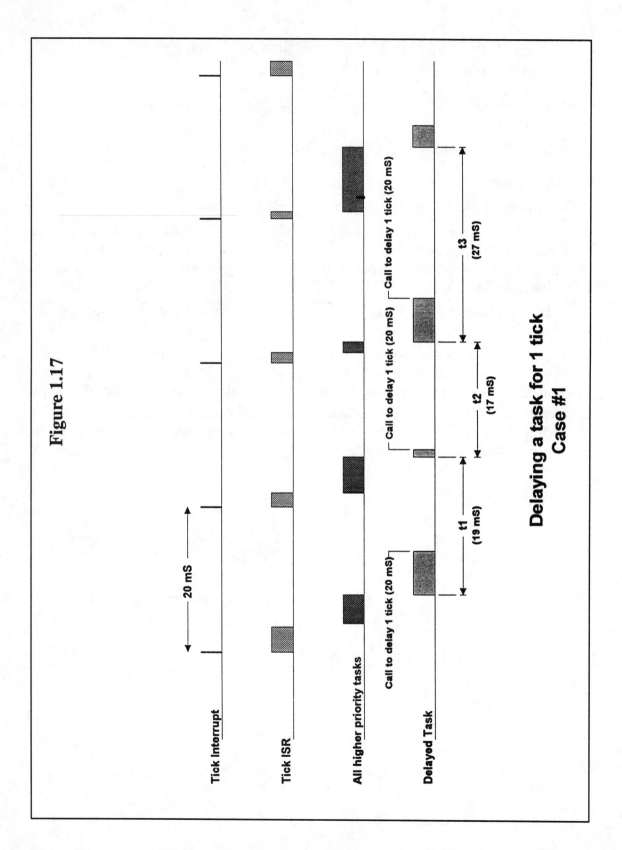

Figure 1.17

**Delaying a task for 1 tick
Case #1**

Figure 1.18

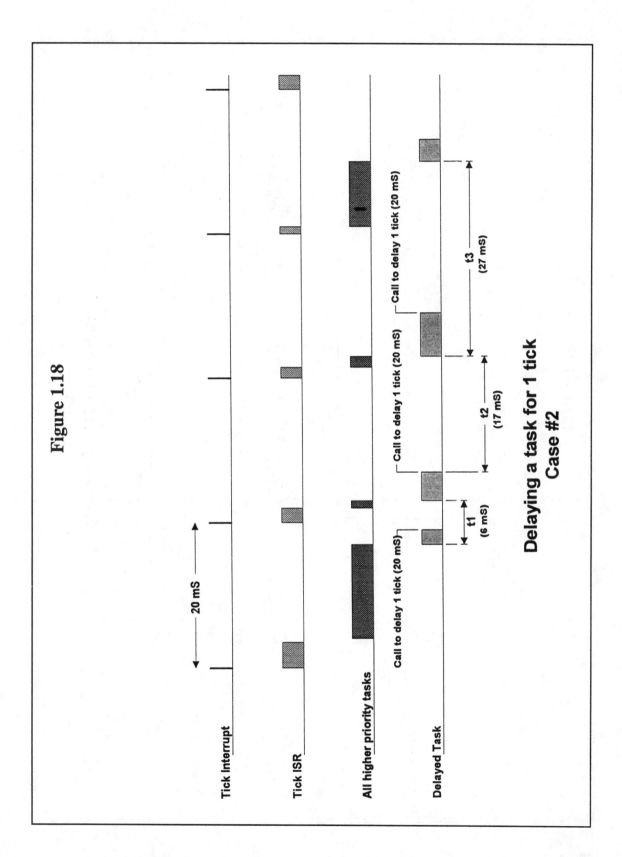

Delaying a task for 1 tick
Case #2

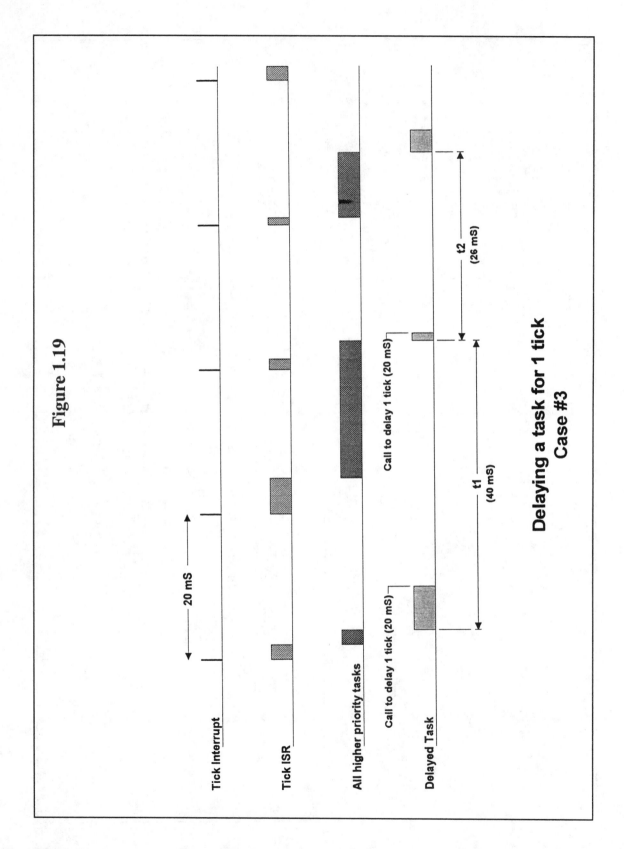

Figure 1.19

Tick Interrupt

Tick ISR

All higher priority tasks

Call to delay 1 tick (20 mS)

Delayed Task

20 mS

Call to delay 1 tick (20 mS)

t1
(40 mS)

t2
(26 mS)

Delaying a task for 1 tick
Case #3

Chapter 2

Kernel Structure

μC/OS can manage up to 63 tasks and its performance is comparable to many commercially available kernels. μC/OS was originally targeted for an 8 bit microcontroller. Including only required kernel services in an application keeps the amount of EPROM and RAM to a minimum. The stack size for each task can be independently specified, reducing the amount of RAM required. μC/OS provides a number of system services such as mailboxes, queues, semaphores, time related functions, etc., explained in succeeding chapters. μC/OS is priority driven and always runs the highest priority task ready to run. μC/OS is also fully preemptive. Interrupts can suspend the execution of a task and if a higher priority task is awakened as a result of the interrupt; the highest priority task will run as soon as the interrupt completes. Interrupts can be nested up to 255 levels deep.

Critical Sections

When μC/OS is in the process of updating critical data it must ensure that it is not interrupted to avoid corrupted data. To guaranty that μC/OS has exclusive access to a critical section of code, μC/OS disables interrupts prior to executing this code and enables interrupts when it is done. The macros *OS_ENTER_CRITICAL()* and *OS_EXIT_CRITICAL()*, which are target microprocessor specific, are used to disable and enable interrupts, respectively. Macros are used for portability. Disabling and enabling interrupts can be done through language extensions or by inline assembly language (if the compiler permits this). (See chapter 3 for the discussion of interrupt handling.)

Interrupts are never disabled for more than 500 CPU clock cycles (80186/80188). An additional 200 CPU clock cycles is required to save the processor's context and notify μC/OS that an interrupt is being processed. Interrupt response is thus about 700 CPU clock cycles. The execution times of all μC/OS kernel services are deterministic.

μC/OS has certain limitations. Tasks that execute under μC/OS must have a unique priority number and thus, no two tasks can have the same priority. Because of this limitation, μC/OS cannot do round robin scheduling. μC/OS system calls cannot be made from the non-maskable interrupts (NMI) service routine because μC/OS must disable interrupts to execute critical sections of code. Most if not all commercially available kernels have this limitation. Finally, the execution time of the function used to process a clock tick depends on the number of tasks in an application (but is still deterministic).

TASKS

A task is an infinite loop function or a function which deletes itself when it is done executing. The infinite loop can eventually be preempted by an interrupt that can cause a higher priority task to run. The task can also make a call to one of the following µC/OS services: *OSTaskDel()*, *OSTimeDly()*, *OSSemPend()*, *OSMboxPend()* or *OSQPend()*. A task can thus be declared as follows:

```
void far Task(void *data)
{
   User code;
   OSTaskDel(task's priority);
}
```

or

```
void far Task(void *data)
{
   while (1) {
      Optional user code;
      Call uCOS service to DELAY or PEND;
      Optional user code;
   }
}
```

Your application can have up to 63 such functions. Each task is assigned a unique priority level from 0 to 62. The lower the priority level the higher the task priority, i.e. the more important the task is. The task priority number also serves as the task identifier. The priority number is used by the *OSTaskChangePrio()* and *OSTaskDel()* kernel services. µC/OS always executes the highest priority task ready to run.

Task States

Figure 2.1 shows the state transition diagram for tasks under µC/OS. At any given time, a task can be in any one of six states.

The *DORMANT* state corresponds to a task which resides in EPROM but has not been made available to µC/OS. A task is made available to µC/OS by calling *OSTask-Create()*. When a task is created, it is made *READY* to run. Tasks may be created before multitasking starts or dynamically by a running task. When created by a task, if the created task has a higher priority than its creator, the created task is immediately given

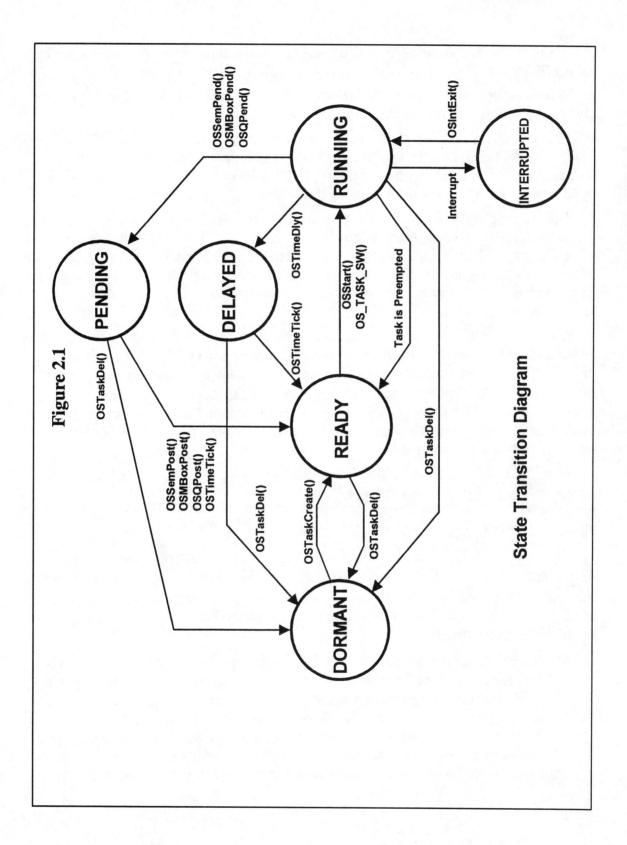

Figure 2.1

State Transition Diagram

control of the CPU. A task can return itself or another task to the dormant state by calling *OSTaskDel()*.

Multitasking is started by calling *OSStart()*. *OSStart()* runs the highest priority task created. This task is thus placed in the *RUNNING* state.

The running task may delay itself for a certain amount of time by calling *OSTimeDly()*. This task is thus placed in the *DELAYED* state and the next highest priority task is immediately given control of the CPU. The delayed task is made ready to run by *OSTimeTick()* when the desired delay time expires (described later).

The running task may also need to wait until an event occurs, by calling either *OSSemPend()*, *OSMboxPend()* or *OSQPend()*. The task is thus *PENDING* for the occurrence of the event. When a task pends on an event, the next highest priority task is immediately given control of the CPU. The task is made ready when the event occurs. The occurrence of an event may be signaled by either another task or an interrupt service routine, ISR.

A running task can always be *INTERRUPTED*, unless the task disables interrupts. When an interrupt occurs, execution of the task is suspended and the ISR takes control of the CPU. The ISR may make one or more tasks ready to run by signaling one or more events. In this case, before returning from the ISR, µC/OS determines if the interrupted task is still the highest priority task ready to run. If a higher priority task is made ready to run by the ISR then the new highest priority task is resumed. Otherwise, the interrupted task is resumed.

When all tasks are either waiting for events or delayed for a number of clock ticks, µC/OS executes the idle task, *OSTaskIdle()*.

Task Control Blocks

When a task is created, it is assigned a Task Control Block, *OS_TCB* (see Listing 2.1). An *OS_TCB* is used by µC/OS to maintain the state of a task when it is preempted. When the task regains control of the CPU the *OS_TCB* allows the task to resume execution exactly where it left off. All *OS_TCB*s reside in RAM. Below is a description of each field in the *OS_TCB* data structure.

> *OSTCBStkPtr* contains a pointer to the current top of stack for the task. µC/OS allows each task to have its own stack but just as importantly, each stack can be of any size. Some commercially available kernels assume that all stacks are the same size unless you write complex hooks. This limitation wastes RAM when all tasks have different stack requirements, because the largest anticipated stack size has to be allocated for all tasks. *OSTCBStkPtr* is the only field in the *OS_TB* data structure accessed from assembly language code (from the context switching

---

Listing 2.1

```
/*
********************************************************************************
*                           uCOS TASK CONTROL BLOCK
********************************************************************************
*/

typedef struct os_tcb {
    void          *OSTCBStkPtr;      /* Pointer to current top of stack                          */
    UBYTE         OSTCBStat;         /* Task status                                              */
    UBYTE         OSTCBPrio;         /* Task priority (0 == highest, 63 == lowest)               */
    UWORD         OSTCBDly;          /* Nbr ticks to delay task or, timeout waiting for event    */
    UBYTE         OSTCBX;            /* Bit position in group  corresponding to task priority (0..7) */
    UBYTE         OSTCBY;            /* Index into ready table corresponding to task priority     */
    UBYTE         OSTCBBitX;         /* Bit mask to access bit position in ready table            */
    UBYTE         OSTCBBitY;         /* Bit mask to access bit position in ready group            */
    struct os_tcb *OSTCBNext;        /* Pointer to next      TCB in the TCB list                  */
    struct os_tcb *OSTCBPrev;        /* Pointer to previous TCB in the TCB list                   */
    OS_EVENT      *OSTCBEventPtr;    /* Pointer to event control block                           */
} OS_TCB;
```

---

code). Placing *OSTCBStkPtr* at the first entry in the structure makes accessing this field easier from the assembly language code.

OSTCBStat contains the state of the task. When *OSTCBStat* is *0*, the task is ready to run. Other values can be assigned to *OSTCBStat* and these values are described in *UCOS.C* (see Appendix A).

OSTCBPrio contains the task priority. A high priority task has a low *OSTCBPrio* value (that is, the lower the number, the higher the actual priority).

OSTCBDly is used when a task needs to be delayed for a certain number of clock ticks or a task needs to pend for an event to occur with a timeout. In this case, this field contains the number of clock ticks that the task is allowed to wait for the event to occur. When this value is zero the task is not delayed or has no timeout.

OSTCBX, *OSTCBY*, *OSTCBBitX* and *OSTCBBitY* are used to accelerate the process of making a task ready to run, or to make a task wait for an event (to avoid computing these values at runtime). The values for these fields are computed when the task is created or when the task's priority is changed as follows:

```
OSTCBX      = priority & 0x07;
OSTCBBitX   = OSMapTbl[priority & 0x07];
OSTCBY      = priority >> 3;
OSTCBBitY   = OSMapTbl[priority >> 3];
```

OSTCBNext and *OSTCBPrev* are used to doubly link *OS_TCB*s. This chain of *OS_TCB*s is used by *OSTimeTick()* to update the *OSTCBDly* field for each task (described later). The *OS_TCB* for each task is linked when the task is created and the *OS_TCB* is removed from the list when the task is deleted. A doubly linked list is used to permit an element in the chain to be quickly removed. (See *OSTaskDel()* in Listing 2.4 and *OSTaskChangePrio()* in Listing 2.9).

OSTCBEventPtr is a pointer to an event control block (described later).

The maximum number of tasks and thus the maximum number of *OS_TCB*s is declared in the user's code. All *OS_TCB*s are placed in *OSTCBTbl[]*, and the number of entries in this table defines how many tasks are available for µC/OS to manage. An extra *OS_TCB* is allocated for the idle task and thus, if storage is allocated for 20 tasks, *OSTCBTbl[]* will have 21 entries. When µC/OS is initialized, all *OS_TCB*s in this table are linked in a singly linked List of free *OS_TCB*s as shown in Figure 2.2. When a task is created, the *OS_TCB* pointed to by *OSTCBFreeList* is assigned to the task and *OSTCBFreeList* is adjusted to point to the next *OS_TCB* in the chain. When a task is deleted, its *OS_TCB* is returned to the list of free *OS_TCB*s.

Creating a Task

Tasks are created by calling *OSTaskCreate()*. This function is target microprocessor specific. The code for the 80186/80188 microprocessor is shown in Listing 2.2. Tasks can either be created prior to the start of multitasking or by a task at run time. A task cannot be created by an ISR. *OSTaskCreate()* is passed four arguments:

task is a pointer to the task's code.

data is a pointer to a user definable data area that is used to pass arguments to the task. This feature is very useful when multiple tasks are needed which use the same body of code. The task's code must know what *data* will be pointing to. For example, a task could be written to handle multiple communication channels. When the task is created, it is passed a pointer to a structure that defines the channel's specifics.

pstk is a pointer to the task's stack area that is used to store local variables and CPU registers during an interrupt. The size of this stack is defined by the task requirements and the anticipated interrupt nesting. Determining the size of the stack involves knowing how many bytes are required for storage of local variables for the task itself, all nested functions, as well as requirements for interrupts (accounting for nesting). *pstk* must point to the highest memory location of the allocated stack area, because the 80186/80188's stack pointer is decremented when elements are pushed onto the stack.

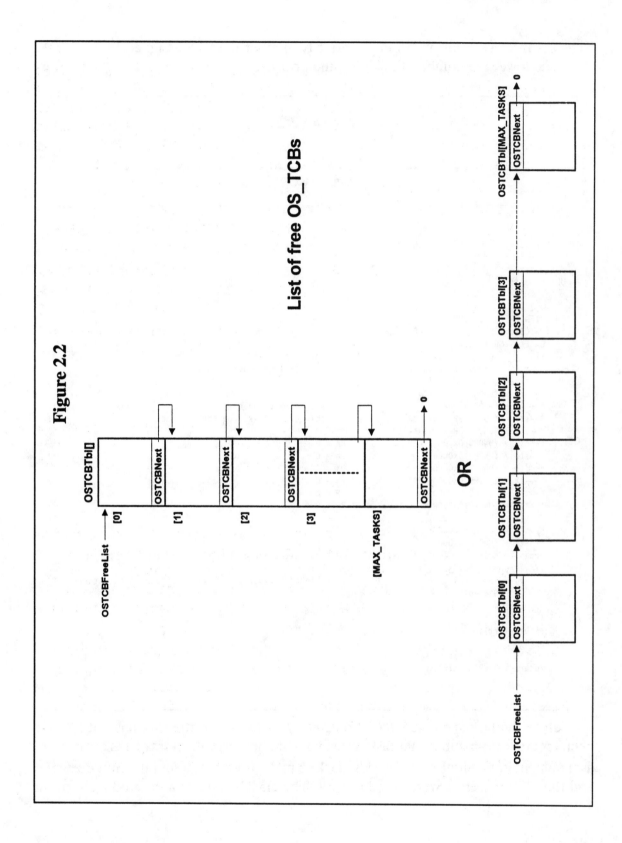

Figure 2.2

List of free OS_TCBs

2

p is the task priority. A unique priority number must be assigned to each task. The lower the number, the higher the priority.

Listing 2.2

```
/*
*********************************************************************************************
*                                    CREATE A TASK
*                                  (80186/80188 Small)
*********************************************************************************************
*/

UBYTE OSTaskCreate(void (far *task)(void *pd), void *pdata, void *pstk, UBYTE p)
{
    UWORD *stk;
    UBYTE  err;


    OS_ENTER_CRITICAL();
    if (OSTCBPrioTbl[p] == (OS_TCB *)0) {   /* Make sure task doesn't already exist at this priority   */
        OS_EXIT_CRITICAL();
        stk    = (UWORD *)pstk;              /* Load stack pointer                                     */
        *--stk = (UWORD)FP_OFF(pdata);       /* Simulate call to function with argument                */
        *--stk = (UWORD)FP_SEG(task);
        *--stk = (UWORD)FP_OFF(task);
        *--stk = (UWORD)0x0200;              /* PSW = Interrupts enabled                               */
        *--stk = (UWORD)FP_SEG(task);        /* Put pointer to task   on top of stack                  */
        *--stk = (UWORD)FP_OFF(task);
        *--stk = (UWORD)0x0000;              /* AX = 0                                                 */
        *--stk = (UWORD)0x0000;              /* CX = 0                                                 */
        *--stk = (UWORD)0x0000;              /* DX = 0                                                 */
        *--stk = (UWORD)0x0000;              /* BX = 0                                                 */
        *--stk = (UWORD)0x0000;              /* SP = 0                                                 */
        *--stk = (UWORD)0x0000;              /* BP = 0                                                 */
        *--stk = (UWORD)0x0000;              /* SI = 0                                                 */
        *--stk = (UWORD)0x0000;              /* DI = 0                                                 */
        *--stk = (UWORD)0x0000;              /* ES = 0                                                 */
        err = OSTCBInit(p, (void *)stk);     /* Get and initialize a TCB                               */
        if (err == OS_NO_ERR) {
            if (OSRunning) {                 /* Find highest priority task if multitasking has started */
                OSSched();
            }
        }
        return (err);
    } else {
        OS_EXIT_CRITICAL();
        return (OS_PRIO_EXIST);
    }
}
```

Before the task is created, *OSTaskCreate()* ensures that the task has not already been created. Remember that tasks must have unique priorities. If the task priority is available, µC/OS initializes the task's stack to make it look as if an interrupt occurred and the CPU registers were saved onto it. The stack frame of a created task for an

80186/80188 is shown in Figure 2.3. When the task executes for the first time, it will have interrupts enabled.

OSTaskCreate() then calls *OSTCBInit()* (Listing 2.3) which obtains an *OS_TCB* from the list of free *OS_TCBs*. If all *OS_TCBs* have been used, the function returns an error code. If an *OS_TCB* is available, it is initialized. A pointer to the task's *OS_TCB* is placed in the *OSTCBPrioTbl[]* using the task priority as the index. The task's *OS_TCB* is then inserted in a doubly linked list with *OSTCBList* pointing to the most recently created task's *OS_TCB*. The task is then inserted in the list of tasks that are ready to run, i.e. the ready list.

2

Listing 2.3

```
/*
*********************************************************************************************
*                                    INITIALIZE TCB
*********************************************************************************************
*/

UBYTE OSTCBInit(UBYTE p, void *stk)
{
    OS_TCB *ptcb;


    OS_ENTER_CRITICAL();
    ptcb = OSTCBFreeList;                                    /* Get a free TCB from the free TCB list  */
    if (ptcb != (OS_TCB *)0) {
        OSTCBFreeList          = ptcb->OSTCBNext;            /* Update pointer to free TCB list        */
        OSTCBPrioTbl[p]        = ptcb;
        ptcb->OSTCBStkPtr      = stk;                        /* Load Stack pointer in TCB              */
        ptcb->OSTCBPrio        = (UBYTE)p;                   /* Load task priority into TCB            */
        ptcb->OSTCBStat        = OS_STAT_RDY;                /* Task is ready to run                   */
        ptcb->OSTCBDly         = 0;
        ptcb->OSTCBX           = p & 0x07;
        ptcb->OSTCBBitX        = OSMapTbl[p & 0x07];
        ptcb->OSTCBY           = p >> 3;
        ptcb->OSTCBBitY        = OSMapTbl[p >> 3];
        ptcb->OSTCBEventPtr    = (OS_EVENT *)0;              /* Task is not pending on an event        */
        ptcb->OSTCBNext        = OSTCBList;                  /* Link into TCB chain                    */
        ptcb->OSTCBPrev        = (OS_TCB *)0;
        if (OSTCBList != (OS_TCB *)0) {
            OSTCBList->OSTCBPrev = ptcb;
        }
        OSTCBList          = ptcb;
        OSRdyGrp          |= OSMapTbl[p >> 3];               /* Make task ready to run                 */
        OSRdyTbl[p >> 3]  |= OSMapTbl[p & 0x07];
        OS_EXIT_CRITICAL();
        return (OS_NO_ERR);
    } else {
        OS_EXIT_CRITICAL();
        return (OS_NO_MORE_TCB);
    }
}
```

If a task is created after multitasking has started (that is, created by a task) the scheduler is called to determine if the created task has a higher priority than its creator. If the new task has a higher priority, the new task is executed immediately, otherwise *OSTaskCreate()* returns to its caller.

Listing 2.4

```
/*
*******************************************************************************************
*                                       DELETE A TASK
*******************************************************************************************
*/

UBYTE OSTaskDel(UBYTE p)
{
    register OS_TCB   *ptcb;
    register OS_EVENT *pevent;


    if (p == OS_LO_PRIO) {                                       /* Not allowed to delete idle task*/
        return (OS_TASK_DEL_IDLE);
    }
    OS_ENTER_CRITICAL();
    if ((ptcb = OSTCBPrioTbl[p]) != (OS_TCB *)0) {              /* Task to delete must exist      */
        OSTCBPrioTbl[p] = (OS_TCB *)0;                          /* Clear old priority entry       */
        if ((OSRdyTbl[ptcb->OSTCBY] &= ~ptcb->OSTCBBitX) == 0) { /* Make task not ready          */
            OSRdyGrp &= ~ptcb->OSTCBBitY;
        }
        if (ptcb->OSTCBPrev == (OS_TCB *)0) {                   /* Remove from TCB chain          */
            ptcb->OSTCBNext->OSTCBPrev = (OS_TCB *)0;
            OSTCBList                  = ptcb->OSTCBNext;
        } else {
            ptcb->OSTCBPrev->OSTCBNext = ptcb->OSTCBNext;
            ptcb->OSTCBNext->OSTCBPrev = ptcb->OSTCBPrev;
        }
        if ((pevent = ptcb->OSTCBEventPtr) != (OS_EVENT *)0) {  /* If task is waiting on event    */
            if ((pevent->OSEventTbl[ptcb->OSTCBY] &= ~ptcb->OSTCBBitX) == 0) { /* ... remove task from */
                pevent->OSEventGrp &= ~ptcb->OSTCBBitY;                        /* ... event ctrl block */
            }
        }
        ptcb->OSTCBNext = OSTCBFreeList;                        /* Return TCB to free TCB list    */
        OSTCBFreeList   = ptcb;
        OS_EXIT_CRITICAL();
        OSSched();                                              /* Find new highest priority task */
        return (OS_NO_ERR);
    } else {
        OS_EXIT_CRITICAL();
        return (OS_TASK_DEL_ERR);
    }
}
```

Deleting a Task

A task may return itself or another task to the *DORMANT* state by calling *OSTaskDel()*. The code for *OSTaskDel()* is shown in Listing 2.4. The priority of the task to delete is

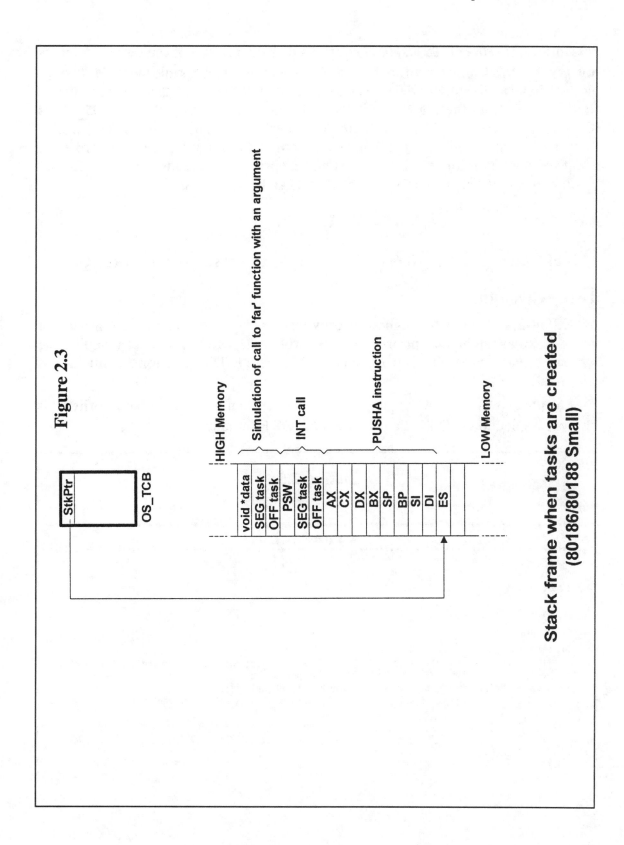

Figure 2.3

Stack frame when tasks are created (80186/80188 Small)

passed to *OSTaskDel()*. *OSTaskDel()* verifies that the priority of the task to delete is not *OS_LO_PRIO*, to prevent an application from deleting µC/OS's idle task. *OSTCBDel()* also verifies that the task to delete has been created. If the task has been created, it is first removed from the ready list (if the task was ready to run), then the *OS_TCB* is unlinked from the *OS_TCB* chain. If the *OSTCBEventPtr* field in the task's *OS_TCB* is nonzero, the task to delete is pending on an event and thus must be removed from the event waiting list. Before finding the next highest priority task ready to run, the *OS_TCB* is returned to the list of free *OS_TCB*s so that it can be used by another task.

WARNING

OSTaskDel() MUST NOT be called by an interrupt service routine (ISR).

Task Scheduling

µC/OS always executes the highest priority task ready to run. The determination of which task has the highest priority and thus will be next to run is determined by the scheduler. Task scheduling is performed by *OSSched()*. The code for this function is shown in Listing 2.5.

Each task is assigned a unique priority level between *0* and *63*. Task priority 63 is always assigned to µC/OS's idle task when µC/OS is initialized.

Listing 2.5

```
/*
*********************************************************************************************************
*                                            uCOS SCHEDULER
*********************************************************************************************************
*/

void OSSched(void)
{
    register UBYTE y;


    OS_ENTER_CRITICAL();
    if ((OSLockNesting | OSIntNesting) == 0) {   /* Task scheduling must be enabled and not ISR level */
        y            = OSUnMapTbl[OSRdyGrp];      /* Get pointer to highest priority task ready to run  */
        OSTCBHighRdy = OSTCBPrioTbl[(y << 3) + OSUnMapTbl[OSRdyTbl[y]]];
        if (OSTCBHighRdy != OSTCBCur) {           /* Make sure this is not the current task running     */
            OSCtxSwCtr++;
            OS_TASK_SW();                         /* Perform a context switch                           */
        }
    }
    OS_EXIT_CRITICAL();
}
```

2

μC/OS's task scheduling time is constant irrespective of the number of tasks created in an application. Each task that is ready to run is placed in a ready list consisting of two variables, *OSRdyGrp* and *OSRdyTbl [8]*. Task priorities are grouped (8 tasks per group) in *OSRdyGrp*. Each bit in *OSRdyGrp* is used to indicate whenever any task in a group is ready to run. When a task is ready to run it also sets its corresponding bit in the ready table, *OSRdyTbl [8]*. To determine which priority (and thus which task) will run next, the scheduler determines the lowest priority number that has its bit set in *OSRdyTbl [8]*. The relationship between *OSRdyGrp* and *OSRdyTbl [8]* is shown in Figure 2.4 and is given by the following rules:

```
Bit 0 in OSRdyGrp is 1 when any bit in OSRdyTbl[0] is 1.
Bit 1 in OSRdyGrp is 1 when any bit in OSRdyTbl[1] is 1.
Bit 2 in OSRdyGrp is 1 when any bit in OSRdyTbl[2] is 1.
Bit 3 in OSRdyGrp is 1 when any bit in OSRdyTbl[3] is 1.
Bit 4 in OSRdyGrp is 1 when any bit in OSRdyTbl[4] is 1.
Bit 5 in OSRdyGrp is 1 when any bit in OSRdyTbl[5] is 1.
Bit 6 in OSRdyGrp is 1 when any bit in OSRdyTbl[6] is 1.
Bit 7 in OSRdyGrp is 1 when any bit in OSRdyTbl[7] is 1.
```

The following code is used to place a task in the ready list:

```
OSRdyGrp          |= OSMapTbl[p >> 3];
OSRdyTbl[p >> 3]  |= OSMapTbl[p & 0x07];
```

where *p* is the task's priority.

As you can see in Figure 2.4, the lower 3 bits of the task's priority are used to determine the bit position in *OSRdyTbl [8]*, while the next three most significant bits are used to determine the index into *OSRdyTbl [8]*. Note that *OSMapTbl [8]* (see Listing 2.6) is a table in ROM, used to equate an index from *0* to *7* to a bit mask as shown in the table below:

Index	Bit mask (Binary)
0	00000001
1	00000010
2	00000100
3	00001000
4	00010000
5	00100000
6	01000000
7	10000000

A task is removed from the ready list by reversing the process. The following code is executed in this case:

```
if ((OSRdyTbl[p >> 3]    &= ~OSMapTbl[p & 0x07]) == 0)
        OSRdyGrp        &= ~OSMapTbl[p >> 3];
```

This code clears the ready bit of the task in *OSRdyTbl[8]* and clears the bit in *OSRdyGrp* only if all tasks in a group are not ready to run, i.e. all bits in *OSRdyTbl[p >> 3]* are *0*. Another table lookup is performed, rather than scanning through the table starting with *OSRdyTbl[0]* to find the highest priority task ready to run. *OSUnMapTbl[256]* is a priority resolution table (shown in Listing 2.6). Eight bits are used to represent when

---

Listing 2.6

```
/*
****************************************************************************************
*                       MAPPING TABLE TO MAP BIT POSITION TO BIT MASK
*
* Note: Index into table is desired bit position, 0..7
*       Indexed value corresponds to bit mask
****************************************************************************************
*/

UBYTE const OSMapTbl[]    = {0x01, 0x02, 0x04, 0x08, 0x10, 0x20, 0x40, 0x80};

/*
****************************************************************************************
*                              PRIORITY RESOLUTION TABLE
*
* Note: Index into table is bit pattern to resolve highest priority
*       Indexed value corresponds to highest priority bit position (i.e. 0..7)
****************************************************************************************
*/

UBYTE const OSUnMapTbl[] = {
    0, 0, 1, 0, 2, 0, 1, 0, 3, 0, 1, 0, 2, 0, 1, 0,
    4, 0, 1, 0, 2, 0, 1, 0, 3, 0, 1, 0, 2, 0, 1, 0,
    5, 0, 1, 0, 2, 0, 1, 0, 3, 0, 1, 0, 2, 0, 1, 0,
    4, 0, 1, 0, 2, 0, 1, 0, 3, 0, 1, 0, 2, 0, 1, 0,
    6, 0, 1, 0, 2, 0, 1, 0, 3, 0, 1, 0, 2, 0, 1, 0,
    4, 0, 1, 0, 2, 0, 1, 0, 3, 0, 1, 0, 2, 0, 1, 0,
    5, 0, 1, 0, 2, 0, 1, 0, 3, 0, 1, 0, 2, 0, 1, 0,
    4, 0, 1, 0, 2, 0, 1, 0, 3, 0, 1, 0, 2, 0, 1, 0,
    7, 0, 1, 0, 2, 0, 1, 0, 3, 0, 1, 0, 2, 0, 1, 0,
    4, 0, 1, 0, 2, 0, 1, 0, 3, 0, 1, 0, 2, 0, 1, 0,
    5, 0, 1, 0, 2, 0, 1, 0, 3, 0, 1, 0, 2, 0, 1, 0,
    4, 0, 1, 0, 2, 0, 1, 0, 3, 0, 1, 0, 2, 0, 1, 0,
    6, 0, 1, 0, 2, 0, 1, 0, 3, 0, 1, 0, 2, 0, 1, 0,
    4, 0, 1, 0, 2, 0, 1, 0, 3, 0, 1, 0, 2, 0, 1, 0,
    5, 0, 1, 0, 2, 0, 1, 0, 3, 0, 1, 0, 2, 0, 1, 0,
    4, 0, 1, 0, 2, 0, 1, 0, 3, 0, 1, 0, 2, 0, 1, 0
};
```

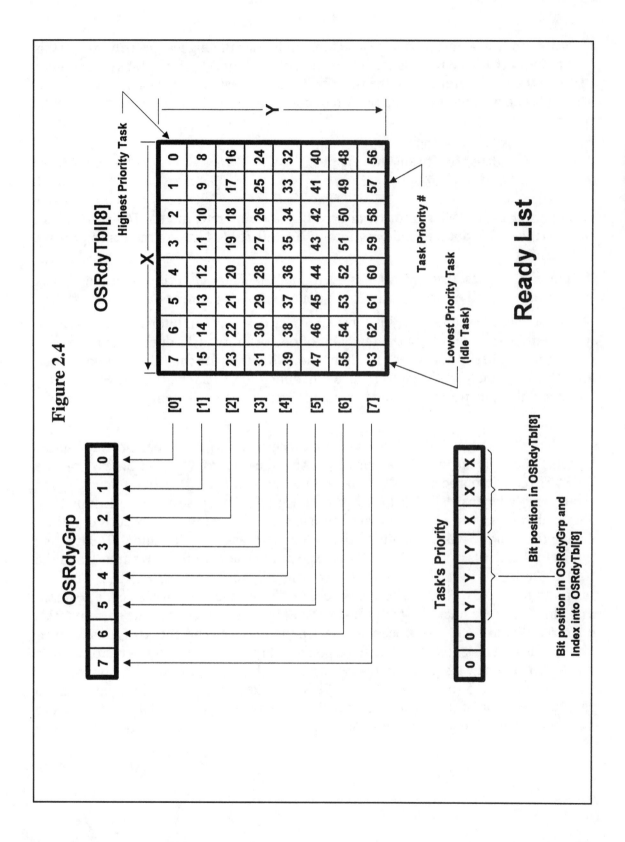

Figure 2.4

Ready List

tasks are ready in a group. The least significant bit has the highest priority. Using this byte to index the table returns the bit position of the highest priority bit set, a number between 0 and 7. Determining the priority of the highest priority task ready to run is accomplished with the following section of code:

```
y = OSUnMapTbl[OSRdyGrp];
x = OSUnMapTbl[OSRdyTbl[y]];
p = (y << 3) + x;
```

Again, p is the task's priority, and getting a pointer to the *OS_TCB* of this task (*OSTCBHighRdy*) is done by indexing into *OSTCBPrioTbl[64]* using the task's priority. (See Listing 2.5)

Once the highest priority task has been found, *OSSched()* verifies that the highest priority task is not the current task. This is done to avoid an unnecessary context switch.

All of the code in *OSSched()* is considered a critical section. Interrupts are disabled to prevent ISRs from setting the ready bit of one or more tasks during the process of finding the highest priority task ready to run. Note that *OSSched()* could be written entirely in assembly language to reduce scheduling time. *OSSched()* was written in C for readability and portability and also to minimize assembly language.

When *OSSched()* finds a higher priority task ready to run it performs a context switch. The context switch is performed by the macro *OS_TASK_SW()*. For the 80186/80188 microprocessor, *OS_TASK_SW()* defines an *INT* instruction that vectors to the assembly language ISR *OSCtxSw* to perform the context switch (see Listing 2.7). Remember that a task stack is initially setup to look as if an interrupt occurred. Before calling *OSCtxSw*, *OSTCBCur* points to the preempted task's *OS_TCB* and *OSTCBHighRdy* points to the new task's *OS_TCB*. *OSCtxSw* expects the stacks of the current task and the new highest priority task to look as shown in Figure 2.5 (at BEFORE). The *INT* instruction *OS_TASK_SW()* pushed the processor's *PSW*, the current task code segment and offset onto the stack. *OSCtxSw* thus starts off by saving the rest of the current task's context onto the stack. The processor's stack pointer for the current task is finally saved into the current task's *OS_TCB*. The stack pointer of the new task to run is restored from its *OS_TCB* (the new task's context is restored). At this point, the stack frame looks as shown in Figure 2.5 (at AFTER). *OSCtxSw* finally executes a return from interrupt to resume execution of the highest priority task. The preempted task has made a call to a function that will not return until the task becomes the highest priority task ready to run.

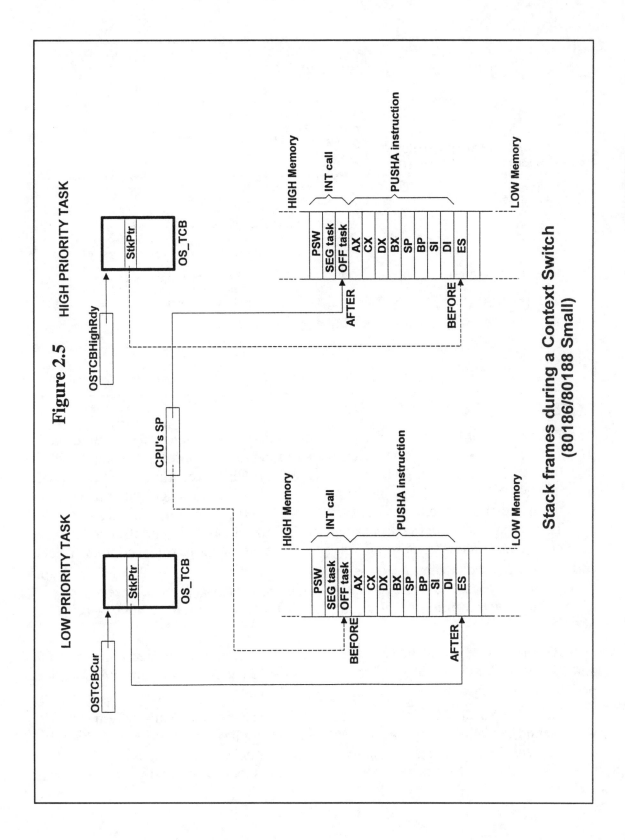

Figure 2.5   HIGH PRIORITY TASK

Stack frames during a Context Switch
(80186/80188 Small)

```
                                Listing 2.7

;******************************************************************************
;                    PERFORM A CONTEXT SWITCH (From task level)
;                              void OSCtxSw(void)
;                             (80186/80188  Small)
;
; Total execution time : 182 bus cycles
;******************************************************************************

_OSCtxSw    PROC    FAR

            PUSHA                               ; 36~, Save current task's context
            PUSH    ES                          ;  8~
            MOV     BX,[_OSTCBCur]              ;  9~, Save stack pointer in preempted task's TCB
            MOV     [BX],SP                     ; 12~
            MOV     BX,[_OSTCBHighRdy]         ;  9~, Point to TCB of highest priority task
            MOV     [_OSTCBCur],BX             ; 12~, This is now current TCB
            MOV     SP,[BX]                    ;  9~, Get new task's stack pointer
            POP     ES                         ;  8~
            POPA                               ; 51~
            IRET                               ; 28~, Return to new task

_OSCtxSw    ENDP
```

LOCK/UNLOCK

The *OSSchedLock()* function is used to prevent task rescheduling until its counterpart, *OSSchedUnlock()*, is called. The code for these functions is shown in Listing 2.8. The task that calls *OSSchedLock()* keeps control of the CPU even though other higher priority tasks are ready to run. Interrupts, however, are still recognized and serviced (assuming interrupts are enabled). *OSSchedLock()* and *OSSchedUnlock()* must be used in pairs. The variable *OSLockNesting* keeps track of the number of times *OSSchedLock()* has been called to allow for nesting. This allows nested functions which contain critical code that other tasks cannot access. µC/OS allows nesting up to 255 levels deep. Scheduling is re-enabled when *OSLockNesting* is *0*. *OSSchedLock()* and *OSSchedUnlock()* must be used with caution because they affect the normal management of tasks by µC/OS.

OSSchedUnlock() calls the scheduler when *OSLockNesting* has decremented to *0* and *OSSchedUnlock()* is called from a task, because events could have made higher priority tasks ready to run while scheduling was locked.

After calling *OSSchedLock()*, your application must not make any system call that will suspend execution of the current task, i.e., your application cannot call *OSTimeDly*, *OSSemPend()*, *OSMboxPend()* or *OSQPend()* until *OSLockNesting* returns to *0*. No other task will be allowed to run, because the scheduler is locked out and your system will lock up.

Listing 2.8

```
/*
*********************************************************************************************
*                                    PREVENT SCHEDULING
*********************************************************************************************
*/

void OSSchedLock(void)
{
    OS_ENTER_CRITICAL();
    OSLockNesting++;                            /* Increment lock nesting level             */
    OS_EXIT_CRITICAL();
}


/*
*********************************************************************************************
*                                    ENABLE SCHEDULING
*********************************************************************************************
*/

void OSSchedUnlock(void)
{
    OS_ENTER_CRITICAL();
    if (OSLockNesting != 0) {
        OSLockNesting--;                        /* Decrement lock nesting level             */
        if ((OSLockNesting | OSIntNesting) == 0) { /* See if scheduling re-enabled and not an ISR */
            OS_EXIT_CRITICAL();
            OSSched();                          /* See if a higher priority task is ready   */
        } else {
            OS_EXIT_CRITICAL();
        }
    } else {
        OS_EXIT_CRITICAL();
    }
}
```

Locking the scheduler gives a task the highest priority after interrupts as shown below:

Highest Priority: Interrupts

Task that locked the scheduler

Lowest Priority: Highest priority task ready to run

Changing Priority

µC/OS allows you to change the priority of a task by calling *OSTaskChangePrio()*. Note that the desired priority must not have already been assigned, otherwise, an error code is returned. (See Listing 2.9.) *OSTaskChangePrio()* verifies that the task to change exists. The priority of the task is changed by performing the following operations:

1) If the task is ready to run, it is removed from the ready list. When the task is given its new priority, it will be placed in the ready list. If the task was not ready to run, the task will not be made ready to run at the new priority level.

2) If the task was waiting for an event to occur (that is, *OSTCBEventPtr* is not *NULL*), the task is removed from the event waiting list and will be inserted in the waiting list at the task's new priority.

3) The task is removed from the *OS_TCB* chain to prevent *OSTimeTick()* from making the task ready to run while it is being given its new priority. At this point, the task is unavailable to µC/OS and thus interrupts can be re-enabled.

With interrupts enabled, the *OS_TCB* fields *OSTCBX*, *OSTCBBitX*, *OSTCBY* and *OSTCBBitY* are recomputed because they are dependent on the new priority level. Interrupts are then again disabled, to put the task under µC/OS's control with its new priority. Note that the *OS_TCB* is now placed at the beginning of the *OS_TCB* chain.

Rescheduling is forced because the *OSTaskChangePrio()* function could make a higher priority task ready to run. If, however, the calling task is still the highest priority task ready to run, no context switch will occur. Changing the priority of a task looks almost as if the task was deleted and then created with the new priority, except for the fact that *OSTCBDly* and *OSTCBEventPtr* are maintained, and the task will still wait at its new priority if it was waiting for an event to occur.

The *OSTaskChangePrio()* function has the longest execution time of any µC/OS function, but more importantly, it disables interrupts for the longest amount of time. Changing a task's priority is an expensive proposition and should be used sparingly.

Delaying a task

A task can delay itself for a number of clock ticks by calling *OSTimeDly()*. (See Listing 2.10). *OSTimeDly()* removes the calling task from the ready list and loads *OSTCBDly* with the desired number of ticks. When *OSTimeTick()* executes, it will decrement *OSTCBDly* down to 0. When *OSTCBDly* reaches 0, the task will be made ready to run again. Valid delays range from 1 to 65535 clock ticks. Note that calling this function with a delay of zero results in no delay and thus the function returns to the caller. When the delay is greater than zero, *OSTimeDly()* always results in a context switch and the current task is suspended until the delayed time runs out.

With a 10 mS tick rate, delays of close to 11 hours can be achieved. You could produce longer delays by placing *OSTimeDly()* in a loop as shown below. This example would result in a delay of close to 7 days!.

```
for (i = 0; i 100; i++)
    OSTimeDly(10000);
```

Listing 2.9

```
/*
*********************************************************************************************
*                              CHANGE PRIORITY OF A TASK
*********************************************************************************************
*/

UBYTE OSTaskChangePrio(UBYTE oldp, UBYTE newp)
{
    register OS_TCB   *ptcb;
    register OS_EVENT *pevent;
            BOOLEAN    rdy;


    OS_ENTER_CRITICAL();
    if (OSTCBPrioTbl[newp] != (OS_TCB *)0) {                     /* New priority must not already exist */
        OS_EXIT_CRITICAL();
        return (OS_PRIO_EXIST);
    } else {
        if ((ptcb = OSTCBPrioTbl[oldp]) != (OS_TCB *)0) {       /* Task to change must exist         */
            OSTCBPrioTbl[oldp] = (OS_TCB *)0;                   /* Remove TCB from old priority      */
            pevent             = ptcb->OSTCBEventPtr;           /* Get pointer to event control block */
            if (OSRdyTbl[ptcb->OSTCBY] & ptcb->OSTCBBitX) {     /* If task is ready make it not ready */
                if ((OSRdyTbl[ptcb->OSTCBY] &= ~ptcb->OSTCBBitX) == 0) {
                    OSRdyGrp &= ~ptcb->OSTCBBitY;
                }
                rdy = TRUE;
            } else {
                rdy = FALSE;
                if (pevent != (OS_EVENT *)0) {                  /* Remove from event wait list       */
                    if ((pevent->OSEventTbl[ptcb->OSTCBY] &= ~ptcb->OSTCBBitX) == 0) {
                        pevent->OSEventGrp &= ~ptcb->OSTCBBitY;
                    }
                }
            }
            if (ptcb->OSTCBPrev == (OS_TCB *)0) {               /* Remove from TCB chain             */
                ptcb->OSTCBNext->OSTCBPrev = (OS_TCB *)0;
                OSTCBList                  = ptcb->OSTCBNext;
            } else {
                ptcb->OSTCBPrev->OSTCBNext = ptcb->OSTCBNext;
                ptcb->OSTCBNext->OSTCBPrev = ptcb->OSTCBPrev;
            }
            OS_EXIT_CRITICAL();
            ptcb->OSTCBPrio = newp;                             /* Setup task control block          */
            ptcb->OSTCBY    = newp >> 3;                        /* ... other fields are unchanged    */
            ptcb->OSTCBBitY = OSMapTbl[newp >> 3];
            ptcb->OSTCBX    = newp & 0x07;
            ptcb->OSTCBBitX = OSMapTbl[newp & 0x07];
```

Listing 2.9 *continued*

```
        OS_ENTER_CRITICAL();
        if (rdy) {                                          /* If task was ready ...              */
            OSRdyGrp                    |= ptcb->OSTCBBitY; /* ... make new priority ready to run */
            OSRdyTbl[ptcb->OSTCBY] |= ptcb->OSTCBBitX;
        } else {
            if (pevent != (OS_EVENT *)0) {                  /* Wait for event if was waiting      */
                pevent->OSEventTbl[ptcb->OSTCBY] |= ptcb->OSTCBBitX;
                pevent->OSEventGrp              |= ptcb->OSTCBBitY;
            }
        }
        OSTCBPrioTbl[newp]    = ptcb;                       /* Place pointer to TCB @ new priority */
        OSTCBList->OSTCBPrev = ptcb;                        /* Link OS_TCB to OS_TCB chain ...     */
        OSTCBList            = ptcb;                        /* ... we assume idle task is present  */
        OS_EXIT_CRITICAL();
        OSSched();                                          /* Run highest priority task ready     */
        return (OS_NO_ERR);
    } else {
        OS_EXIT_CRITICAL();
        return (OS_PRIO_ERR);                               /* Task to change didn't exist         */
    }
  }
}
```

Listing 2.10

```
/*
*********************************************************************************************************
*                          DELAY TASK 'n' TICKS    (n from 1 to 65535)
*********************************************************************************************************
*/

void OSTimeDly(UWORD ticks)
{
    if (ticks > 0) {
        OS_ENTER_CRITICAL();
        if ((OSRdyTbl[OSTCBCur->OSTCBY] &= ~OSTCBCur->OSTCBBitX) == 0) {  /* Delay current task */
            OSRdyGrp &= ~OSTCBCur->OSTCBBitY;
        }
        OSTCBCur->OSTCBDly = ticks;                          /* Load ticks in TCB          */
        OS_EXIT_CRITICAL();
        OSSched();
    }
}
```

Chapter 3

Interrupt Processing

This chapter explains interrupt handling, the importance of interrupt response times, and clock tick interrupts.

µC/OS requires an Interrupt Service Routine (ISR) written in assembly language. For the 80186/80188, an ISR must be written as follows:

```
ISRx    PROC FAR
        STI                 ; Enable interrupts
        PUSHA               ; Save CPU's context
        PUSH  ES
        CALL _OSIntEnter    ; Notify uCOS of ISR
        CALL _UserISRCode   ; Execute user code
        CALL _OSIntExit     ; Notify uCOS of end of ISR
        POP   ES            ; Restore CPU's context
        POPA
        IRET                ; Return from interrupt
ISRx    ENDP
```

Interrupts are enabled early in this ISR, in case other interrupts have higher priority. Your ISR, however, doesn't have to enable interrupts this early. You could execute some code with interrupts disabled as shown below, but you should save the rest of the CPU's context before you execute any code.

```
ISRx    PROC FAR
        PUSHA               ; Save CPU's context
        PUSH  ES
        CALL _UserCode      ; User code with interrupts disabled
        STI                 ; Enable interrupts
        CALL _OSIntEnter    ; Notify uCOS of ISR
        CALL _UserISRCode   ; Execute user code
        CALL _OSIntExit     ; Notify uCOS of end of ISR
        POP   ES            ; Restore CPU's context
        POPA
        IRET                ; Return from interrupt
ISRx    ENDP
```

Remember that by executing code before you enable interrupts, you are increasing the interrupt latency of other interrupts (discussed later in this chapter).

µC/OS requires that the function *OSIntEnter()* (see Listing 3.1) is called prior to making any kernel system calls. *OSIntEnter()* keeps track of the interrupt nesting level. µC/OS allows interrupts to be nested up to 255 levels deep. When *OSIntEnter()* returns, the user's ISR code is invoked. Note that the user code is responsible for clearing the interrupt. *OSIntEnter()* also enables interrupts.

Listing 3.1

```
/*
*******************************************************************************************
*                                        ENTER ISR
*******************************************************************************************
*/

void OSIntEnter(void)
{
    OS_ENTER_CRITICAL();
    OSIntNesting++;                              /* Increment ISR nesting level              */
    OS_EXIT_CRITICAL();
}


/*
*******************************************************************************************
*                                        EXIT ISR
*******************************************************************************************
*/

void OSIntExit(void)
{
    OS_ENTER_CRITICAL();
    if ((--OSIntNesting | OSLockNesting) == 0) { /* Reschedule only if all ISRs completed & not locked */
        OSIntExitY   = OSUnMapTbl[OSRdyGrp];
        OSTCBHighRdy = OSTCBPrioTbl[(OSIntExitY << 3) + OSUnMapTbl[OSRdyTbl[OSIntExitY]]];
        if (OSTCBHighRdy != OSTCBCur) {          /* No context switch if current task is highest ready */
            OSCtxSwCtr++;
            OSIntCtxSw();                        /* Perform interrupt level context switch    */
        }
    }
    OS_EXIT_CRITICAL();
}
```

The conclusion of the ISR is marked by calling *OSIntExit()* which decrements the interrupt nesting level. When the nesting level is *0*, that is all interrupts have completed, µC/OS determines if a higher priority task has been awakened by the ISR (or any other event that might have interrupted this ISR). If a higher priority task is ready to run, the ISR will return to the higher priority task rather than the interrupted task. Note that μC/OS will return to the interrupted task if scheduling has been disabled (*OSLockNesting! = 0*).

OSIntExit() calls the assembly language function *OSIntCtxSw* (see Listing 3.2) instead of *OSCtxSw*. There are two reasons to do this. First, half the work is already done because the interrupt has already saved the PSW, the CS and IP of the interrupted task and all other registers were saved at the beginning of the ISR. The second reason is that *OSIntExit()* allocates local variables (the SI register for the 80186/80188) on the interrupted task's stack and makes a call to *OSIntCtxSw*.

Listing 3.2

```
;******************************************************************************************
;                       PERFORM A CONTEXT SWITCH (From an ISR)
;                              void OSIntCtxSw(void)
;
; Total execution time : 142 bus cycles
;******************************************************************************************

_OSIntCtxSw PROC    NEAR

            ADD     SP,6                    ;  4~, Ignore calls to OSIntExit and OSIntCtxSw
            MOV     BX,[_OSTCBCur]          ;  9~, Save stack pointer in old TCB
            MOV     [BX],SP                 ; 12~
            MOV     BX,[_OSTCBHighRdy]      ;  9~, Point to TCB of highest prio. task ready to run
            MOV     [_OSTCBCur],BX          ; 12~, This is now current the TCB
            MOV     SP,[BX]                 ;  9~, Get new task's stack pointer
            POP     ES                      ;  8~
            POPA                            ; 51~
            IRET                            ; 28~, Return to new task

_OSIntCtxSw ENDP
```

To make the stack frame look as if a simple context switch is in progress, the processor's stack pointer needs to be adjusted as shown in Figure 3.1. Note that the number to add to the SP register depends on the compiler used and the choice of compile time options. The number to add is four (4) plus the number of registers saved at the beginning of the *OSIntExit()* function. The best way to find out how many registers were saved is to have the compiler produce an assembly language file (most good compilers have this option) and to examine the assembly code generated at the beginning of this function.

If your ISR does not make any calls to the kernel, *OSIntEnter()* and *OSIntExit()* are not required and your ISR would look like this:

```
ISRx    PROC FAR
            STI                 ; Enable interrupts
            PUSHA               ; Save CPU's context
            PUSH  ES
            CALL _UserISRCode   ; Execute user code
            POP   ES            ; Restore CPU's context
            POPA
            IRET                ; Return from interrupt
    ISRx    ENDP
```

Interrupt latency, Response and Recovery

An important issue in real-time systems is the time required to respond to an interrupt and to actually start executing user code to handle the interrupt (see Figure 3.2).

All real time kernels disable interrupts when manipulating critical sections of code. µC/OS disables interrupts for a maximum of 500 CPU clock cycles (80186/80188). Interrupt latency is given by:

Maximum interrupt disable time (500) +

Time to vector to the ISR (50)

µC/OS's worst case interrupt latency is thus 550 CPU clock cycles. Before executing user code, the processor's context must be saved and if µC/OS services are required, *OSIntEnter()* must be called. The response time is given by:

Interrupt latency (550) +

Time to save all registers (60) +

Execution time for OSIntEnter() (75)

µC/OS's worst case interrupt response time is thus 685 CPU clock cycles.

Since µC/OS disables interrupts for up to 500 CPU clock cycles (80186/80188), an application can do the same without affecting the worst case interrupt latency. For example, your application could disable interrupts up to 500 CPU clock cycles to access critical sections of code or to access shared data.

The interrupt recovery time is the time required for the processor to restore its context and return from interrupt. Interrupt recovery is performed by *OSIntExit()*. If a higher priority task has been made ready to run as a result of the ISR, the worst case interrupt recovery time is 450 CPU clock cycles (See Figure 3.2).

Clock Tick

µC/OS allows tasks to either suspend execution for a number of "clock ticks" or wait until an event occurs with a timeout. A clock tick is typically provided by a periodic interrupt and can be viewed as the system's heartbeat. The time between interrupts is application specific and is typically between 10 mS and 200 mS. The faster the tick rate, the higher the overhead imposed on the system. The worst case overhead for an 80186/80188 microprocessor is about 2% when the tick rate is 20 Hz (50 mS) and all 63 tasks are delayed or are waiting for events with a timeout. This 2% figure might seem high, but if all tasks are delayed, the processor is only servicing the tick interrupt! The code to process a tick interrupt can be implemented as follows (80186/80188):

```
TickISR     PROC FAR
            STI                     ; Enable interrupts
            PUSHA                   ; Save CPU's context
            PUSH  ES
            CALL  _OSIntEnter       ; Notify µC/OS of ISR
            CALL  _OSTimeTick       ; Execute tick handler
;
;           User code to clear the tick interrupt
;
            CALL  _OSIntExit        ; Notify µC/OS of end of ISR
            POP   ES                ; Restore CPU's context
            POPA
            IRET                    ; Return from interrupt

TickISR     ENDP
```

The tick ISR calls *OSTimeTick()* (See Listing 3.3) which decrements the *OSTCBDly* field for each *OS_TCB* if it is nonzero. *OSTimeTick()* follows the chain of *OS_TCB* starting at *OSTCBList* until it reaches the idle task. When the *OSTCBDly* field of a task's *OS_TCB* is decremented to zero, the task is made ready to run. The execution time of *OSTime-Tick()* is directly proportional to the number of tasks created in an application.

If you don't like to make ISRs any longer than they must be, *OSTimeTick()* can be called at the task level. To do this, you would allocate task priority *5* to service a tick as follows (priority *0* through *4* are reserved for future use):

```
TimeTask()
{
    while (1) {
        OSSemPend(...);
        OSTimeTick();
    }
}
```

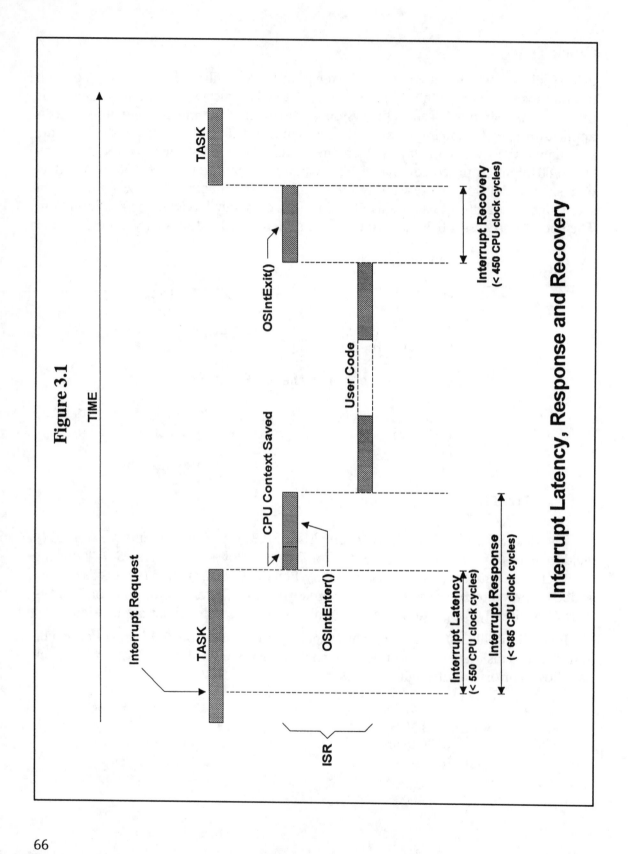

Figure 3.1

Interrupt Latency, Response and Recovery

Figure 3.2

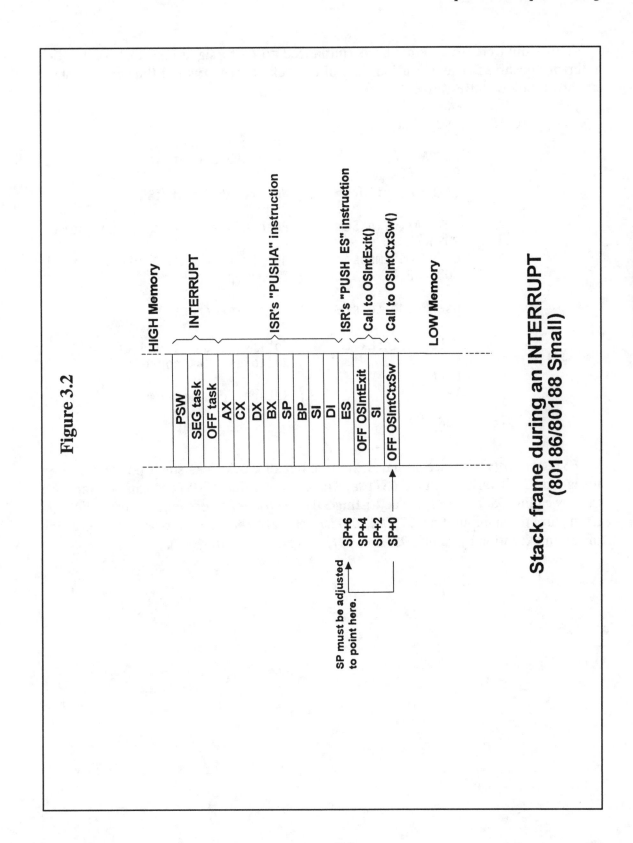

Stack frame during an INTERRUPT
(80186/80188 Small)

You would create a semaphore (initialized to *0*) to signal the task that a tick interrupt occurred. The execution time of the tick interrupt would thus be very short as shown below (80186/80188).

```
TickISR     PROC FAR
            STI                 ; Enable interrupts
            PUSHA               ; Save CPU's context
            PUSH ES
            CALL _OSIntEnter    ; Notify µC/OS of ISR
;
            MOV  AX,_TickSem    ; Push address of tick semaphore
            PUSH AX
            CALL _OSSemPost     ; Notify tick task (tick occurred)
            ADD  SP,2           ; Clean up stack
;
;           User code to clear the tick interrupt
;
            CALL _OSIntExit     ; Notify µC/OS of end of ISR
            POP  ES             ; Restore CPU's context
            POPA
            IRET                ; Return from interrupt

TickISR     ENDP
```

OSTimeTick() also accumulates the number of clock ticks since power up in an unsigned 32 bit variable called *OSTime*. The current value of *OSTime* can be read by a task by calling *OSTimeGet()*. (See Listing 3.4). *OSTimeGet()* prevents your application from directly manipulating *OSTime*. *OSTime* can also be forced to any value during program execution by calling *OSTimeSet()* (Again see Listing 3.4).

Listing 3.3

```
/*
*********************************************************************************
*                            PROCESS SYSTEM TICK
*********************************************************************************
*/
void OSTimeTick(void)
{
    register OS_TCB *ptcb;

    ptcb = OSTCBList;                                   /* Point at first TCB in TCB list          */
    while (ptcb->OSTCBPrio != OS_LO_PRIO) {            /* Go through all TCBs in TCB list          */
        OS_ENTER_CRITICAL();
        if (ptcb->OSTCBDly != 0) {                     /* Delayed or waiting for event with TO     */
            if (--ptcb->OSTCBDly == 0) {               /* Decrement nbr of ticks to end of delay   */
                OSRdyGrp             |= ptcb->OSTCBBitY; /* Make task ready to run (timer timed out) */
                OSRdyTbl[ptcb->OSTCBY] |= ptcb->OSTCBBitX;
            }
        }
        OS_EXIT_CRITICAL();
        ptcb = ptcb->OSTCBNext;                        /* Point at next TCB in TCB list            */
    }
    OS_ENTER_CRITICAL();
    OSTime++;
    OS_EXIT_CRITICAL();
}
```

Listing 3.4

```
/*
*********************************************************************************
*                          GET CURRENT SYSTEM TIME
*********************************************************************************
*/
ULONG OSTimeGet(void)
{
    ULONG ticks;

    OS_ENTER_CRITICAL();
    ticks = OSTime;
    OS_EXIT_CRITICAL();
    return (ticks);
}


/*
*********************************************************************************
*                              SET SYSTEM CLOCK
*********************************************************************************
*/
void OSTimeSet(ULONG ticks)
{
    OS_ENTER_CRITICAL();
    OSTime = ticks;
    OS_EXIT_CRITICAL();
}
```

3

Chapter 4

Communication, Synchronization & Coordination

μC/OS supports message mailboxes and queues for communication. μC/OS supports the semaphore for synchronization and coordination. Under μC/OS, these services are considered events; you either signal the occurrence of the event (*POST*) or you wait for the event to occur (*PEND*).

Only tasks are allowed to wait for events to occur, that is, an ISR must never *PEND* on an event. More than one task is allowed to wait for the same event to occur. When the event occurs, μC/OS makes the highest priority task waiting for the event ready to run. ISRs and tasks can signal the occurrence of events; more than one ISR or task is allowed to signal the occurrence of an event.

Event Control Blocks

A data structure called an Event Control Block (ECB) is used to maintain the state of an event. The state of an event consists of:

a) the event itself:

A counter for semaphores

A message for mailboxes

A message queue for queues

b) a waiting list for tasks waiting for the event to occur.

Each semaphore, mailbox and queue is assigned an Event Control Block. The data structure for an ECB is shown in Listing 4.1. An ECB contains four fields.

OSEventGrp is similar to *OSRdyGrp* except that it indicates when any task in a group of eight tasks is waiting for the event to occur (see the description later.)

OSEventTbl [8] is also similar to *OSRdyTbl []* except that it contains a bit map of the tasks waiting for the event (see the later description).

When the ECB is used for a semaphore, *OSEventCnt* is used to hold the semaphore count (see Semaphores).

When the ECB is used for either a mailbox or a queue, *OSEventPtr* contains the mailbox message or a pointer to the queue data structure respectively (see Mailboxes and Queues).

Each task that is waiting for an event to occur is placed in a waiting list which consists of two variables, *OSEventGrp* and *OSEventTbl [8]*. Task priorities are grouped (8 tasks

```
/*
******************************************************************************************
*                                  EVENT CONTROL BLOCK
******************************************************************************************
*/

typedef struct os_event {
    UBYTE  OSEventGrp;            /* Group corresponding to tasks waiting for event to occur   */
    UBYTE  OSEventTbl[8];         /* List of tasks waiting for event to occur                  */
    WORD   OSEventCnt;            /* Count of used when event is a semaphore                   */
    void  *OSEventPtr;            /* Pointer to message or queue structure                     */
} OS_EVENT;
```

Listing 4.1

per group) in *OSEventGrp*. Each bit in *OSEventGrp* is used to indicate whenever any task in a group is waiting for the event. When a task needs to wait for the event it also sets its corresponding bit in the waiting list, *OSEventTbl[8]*. The task that will be awakened when the event occurs is the highest priority task waiting for the event. This is done by determining the lowest priority number which has its bit set in *OSEvent-Tbl[8]*. The relationship between *OSEventGrp* and *OSEventTbl[8]* is shown in Figure 4.1 and is given by the following rules.

Bit 0 in *OSEventGrp* is 1 when any bit in *OSEventTbl[0]* is 1.

Bit 1 in *OSEventGrp* is 1 when any bit in *OSEventTbl[1]* is 1.

Bit 2 in *OSEventGrp* is 1 when any bit in *OSEventTbl[2]* is 1.

Bit 3 in *OSEventGrp* is 1 when any bit in *OSEventTbl[3]* is 1.

Bit 4 in *OSEventGrp* is 1 when any bit in *OSEventTbl[4]* is 1.

Bit 5 in *OSEventGrp* is 1 when any bit in *OSEventTbl[5]* is 1.

Bit 6 in *OSEventGrp* is 1 when any bit in *OSEventTbl[6]* is 1.

Bit 7 in *OSEventGrp* is 1 when any bit in *OSEventTbl[7]* is 1.

When a task needs to wait for an event to occur, it executes the following section of code:

```
OSEventGrp            |= OSMapTbl[p >> 3];
OSEventTbl[p >> 3]    |= OSMapTbl[p & 0x07];
```

where p is the task's priority.

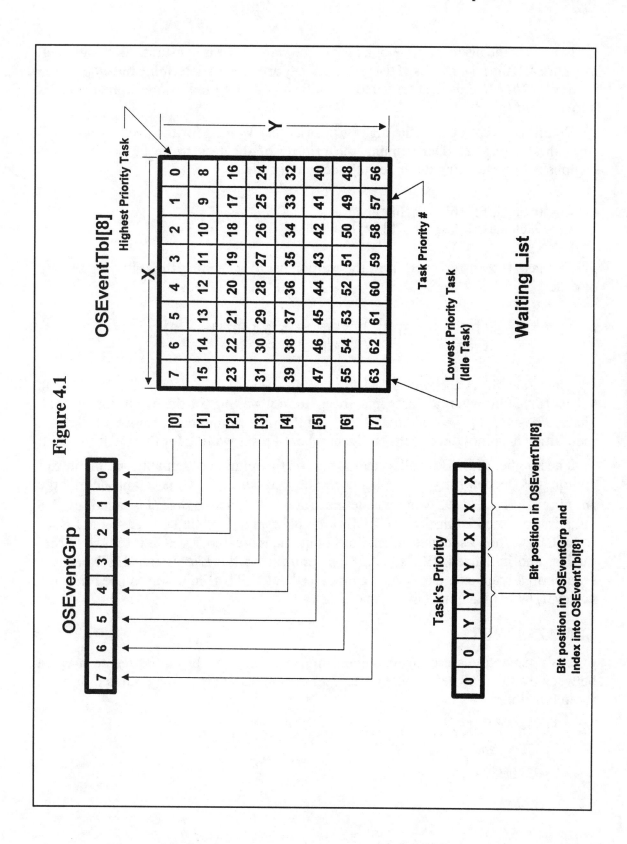

Figure 4.1

Note that the insertion time of a task in the waiting list is constant. As can be seen in Figure 4.1, the lower 3 bits of the task's priority are used to determine the bit position in *OSEventTbl [8]*. The next three most significant bits are used to determine the index into *OSEventTbl [8]*.

When the event occurs, the highest priority task waiting for the event is removed from the waiting list. Determining the priority of the task to be awakened is accomplished by executing the following section of code:

```
y = OSUnMapTbl[OSEventGrp];
x = OSUnMapTbl[OSEventTbl[y]];
p = (y << 3) + x;
```

The task is then removed from the waiting list by executing the following section of code:

```
if ((OSEventTbl[p >> 3] &= ~OSMapTbl[p & 0x07]) == 0)
        OSEventGrp      &= ~OSMapTbl[p >> 3];
```

This code clears the wait bit of the task in *OSEventTbl [8]* and clears the bit in *OSEventGrp*, but only if all tasks in a group are not waiting for the event, that is, if all bits in *OSEventTbl [p >> 3]* are 0. Note that the time required to remove a task from the waiting list is not dependent on the number of tasks waiting for the event to occur.

The number of ECBs to allocate depends on the number of semaphores, mailboxes and queues needed for your application. The number of ECBs is established by the *#define OS_MAX_EVENTS* which you define in *UCOS.H*. When *OSInit()* is called (µC/OS initialization, see Listing 5.1), all ECBs are linked in a singly linked list — the List of free ECBs. When a semaphore, mailbox or queue is created, an ECB is removed from this list and initialized. ECBs cannot be returned to the List of free ECB because semaphores, mailboxes and queues cannot be deleted. This limitation can be removed, however, by writing appropriate functions.

SEMAPHORES

µC/OS's semaphores are 16 bit signed integers that must be initialized to a value between 0 and 32767 before their use. A semaphore can only be manipulated through three functions:

1) *OSSemCreate()*

2) *OSSemPend()*

3) *OSSemPost()*

OSSemCreate() (see Listing 4.2) allocates an event control block for use by the semaphore. *OSSemCreate()* also sets the initial value of the semaphore. *OSSemCreate()* returns a pointer to the event control block allocated for the semaphore. This pointer will need to be assigned to a variable in your application because it is used as the semaphore's "handle". If all event control blocks are used, *OSSemCreate()* returns a NULL pointer. Once created, a semaphore cannot be deleted (that is, it cannot be deallocated). The *OSEventCnt* field of the Event Control Block contains the current value of the semaphore and can be between -63 and 32767. A positive value indicates how many tasks can access the resource at one time or how many times an event has

Listing 4.2

```
/*
*********************************************************************************************
*                                     INITIALIZE SEMAPHORE
*********************************************************************************************
*/

OS_EVENT *OSSemCreate(WORD cnt)
{
    register OS_EVENT *pevent;


    OS_ENTER_CRITICAL();
    pevent = OSEventFreeList;                            /* Get next free event control block      */
    if (OSEventFreeList != (OS_EVENT *)0) {             /* See if pool of free ECB pool was empty  */
        OSEventFreeList = (OS_EVENT *)OSEventFreeList->OSEventPtr;
    }
    OS_EXIT_CRITICAL();
    if (pevent != (OS_EVENT *)0) {                       /* Get an event control block             */
        if (cnt >= 0) {                                 /* Semaphore cannot start negative        */
            pevent->OSEventCnt    = cnt;                /* Set semaphore value                     */
            pevent->OSEventGrp    = 0x00;              /* Initialize rest of event control block  */
            pevent->OSEventTbl[0] = 0x00;
            pevent->OSEventTbl[1] = 0x00;
            pevent->OSEventTbl[2] = 0x00;
            pevent->OSEventTbl[3] = 0x00;
            pevent->OSEventTbl[4] = 0x00;
            pevent->OSEventTbl[5] = 0x00;
            pevent->OSEventTbl[6] = 0x00;
            pevent->OSEventTbl[7] = 0x00;
            return (pevent);
        } else {
            OS_ENTER_CRITICAL();                        /* Return event control block on error     */
            pevent->OSEventPtr = (void *)OSEventFreeList;
            OSEventFreeList    = pevent;
            OS_EXIT_CRITICAL();
            return ((OS_EVENT *)0);
        }
    } else {
        return ((OS_EVENT *)0);                          /* Ran out of event control blocks         */
    }
}
```

4

occurred. When the semaphore value is zero, the resource is not available or the event didn't occur. When the value is negative, it indicates how many tasks are waiting for the resource to become available or for the event to occur.

If a task calls *OSSemPend()* (see Listing 4.3) and the value of the semaphore is greater than zero, then *OSSemPend()* will decrement the semaphore count and return to its caller. If, however, the value of the semaphore is less than or equal to zero, *OSSemPend()* decrements the semaphore count and places the calling task in the waiting list for the semaphore. The task will thus wait until another task or an ISR releases the semaphore or signals the occurrence of the event. While the task is waiting for the semaphore, rescheduling occurs and the next highest priority task ready to run is given control of the CPU. An optional timeout may be specified when pending for a

Listing 4.3

```
/*
*********************************************************************************************
*                                    PEND ON SEMAPHORE
*********************************************************************************************
*/

void OSSemPend(OS_EVENT *pevent, UWORD timeout, UBYTE *err)
{
    OS_ENTER_CRITICAL();
    if (pevent->OSEventCnt-- > 0) {                    /* If semaphore is positive, resource available   */
        OS_EXIT_CRITICAL();
        *err = OS_NO_ERR;
    } else {                                          /* Otherwise, must wait until event occurs         */
        OSTCBCur->OSTCBStat = OS_STAT_SEM;            /* Resource not available, pend on semaphore       */
        OSTCBCur->OSTCBDly  = timeout;                /* Store pend timeout in TCB                       */
        if ((OSRdyTbl[OSTCBCur->OSTCBY] &= ~OSTCBCur->OSTCBBitX) == 0) {  /* Task no longer ready       */
            OSRdyGrp &= ~OSTCBCur->OSTCBBitY;
        }
        pevent->OSEventTbl[OSTCBCur->OSTCBY] |= OSTCBCur->OSTCBBitX;      /* Put task in waiting list */
        pevent->OSEventGrp                   |= OSTCBCur->OSTCBBitY;
        OS_EXIT_CRITICAL();
        OSSched();                                    /* Find next highest priority task ready to run    */
        OS_ENTER_CRITICAL();
        if (OSTCBCur->OSTCBStat == OS_STAT_SEM) {     /* Must have timed out if still waiting for event*/
            if ((pevent->OSEventTbl[OSTCBCur->OSTCBY] &= ~OSTCBCur->OSTCBBitX) == 0) {
                pevent->OSEventGrp &= ~OSTCBCur->OSTCBBitY;
            }
            OSTCBCur->OSTCBStat     = OS_STAT_RDY;    /* Set status to ready                             */
            OSTCBCur->OSTCBEventPtr = (OS_EVENT *)0;  /* Task is no longer waiting for the event         */
            OS_EXIT_CRITICAL();
            *err = OS_TIMEOUT;                        /* Indicate to caller that didn't get event within TO */
        } else {
            OSTCBCur->OSTCBEventPtr = (OS_EVENT *)0;
            OS_EXIT_CRITICAL();
            *err = OS_NO_ERR;
        }
    }
}
```

semaphore. This feature is useful to avoid waiting indefinitely for the semaphore. A low priority task may not gain access to the semaphore if higher priority tasks are waiting for it as well. A timeout can be treated as an error and appropriate actions can be taken. The timeout can be as long as 65535 clock ticks. A timeout value of zero indicates that the task will wait indefinitely for the semaphore. When the pending task resumes (*OSSched()* returns to *OSSemPend()*) the task status is examined to determine if the task is still waiting for the semaphore. A timeout condition is detected if *OSTCBStat* is still set to *OS_STAT_SEM*, the task is removed from the semaphore's waiting list and the caller is notified that a timeout occurred.

WARNING

OSSemPend() must never be called by an ISR.

A semaphore is signaled by calling *OSSemPost()* (see Listing 4.4). If the semaphore value is greater than or equal to zero, the semaphore count is incremented and *OSSemPost()* returns to its caller. If the semaphore count is negative then tasks are waiting for the semaphore to be signaled. In this case, *OSSemPost()* removes the highest

4

Listing 4.4

```
/*
*********************************************************************************************************
*                                          POST TO A SEMAPHORE
*********************************************************************************************************
*/

UBYTE OSSemPost(OS_EVENT *pevent)
{
    OS_ENTER_CRITICAL();
    if (pevent->OSEventCnt < 32766) {              /* Make sure semaphore will not overflow            */
        if (pevent->OSEventCnt++ >= 0) {
            OS_EXIT_CRITICAL();
        } else {                                   /* Negative semaphore value means task(s) pending   */
            if (pevent->OSEventGrp) {              /* See if any task pending on semaphore             */
                OS_EXIT_CRITICAL();
                OSEventTaskResume(pevent);         /* Resume highest priority task pending on semaphore */
                OSSched();                         /* Find highest priority task ready to run          */
            } else {
                OS_EXIT_CRITICAL();
            }
        }
        return (OS_NO_ERR);
    } else {
        OS_EXIT_CRITICAL();
        return (OS_SEM_OVF);
    }
}
```

priority task pending (waiting) for the semaphore from the waiting list and makes this task ready to run by *OSEventTaskResume()*. Note that the *OSTCBDly* field is cleared of the task's *OS_TCB* to prevent *OSTimeTick()* from readying this task. The scheduler is then called to determine if the awakened task is now the highest priority task ready to run.

MAILBOXES

µC/OS allows a task or an ISR to send a message, a pointer size variable (message) to one or more tasks through a mailbox. Your application decides what the pointer points to. A mailbox can be manipulated through three functions:

    1) *OSMboxCreate()*

    2) *OSMboxPend()*

    3) *OSMboxPost()*

    OSMboxCreate() (see Listing 4.5) allocates an event control block for use by the mailbox, and allows the contents of the mailbox to be initialized. *OSMboxCreate()* returns a pointer to the event control block allocated for the mailbox. This pointer will

---

Listing 4.5

```
/*
*********************************************************************************************************
*                                     INITIALIZE MESSAGE MAILBOX
*********************************************************************************************************
*/

OS_EVENT *OSMboxCreate(void *msg)
{
    OS_EVENT *pevent;


    OS_ENTER_CRITICAL();
    pevent = OSEventFreeList;                        /* Get next free event control block           */
    if (OSEventFreeList != (OS_EVENT *)0) {          /* See if pool of free ECB pool was empty      */
        OSEventFreeList = (OS_EVENT *)OSEventFreeList->OSEventPtr;
    }
    OS_EXIT_CRITICAL();
    if (pevent != (OS_EVENT *)0) {
        pevent->OSEventPtr    = msg;                 /* Deposit message in event control block      */
        pevent->OSEventGrp    = 0x00;               /* Initialize rest of event control block      */
        pevent->OSEventTbl[0] = 0x00;
        pevent->OSEventTbl[1] = 0x00;
        pevent->OSEventTbl[2] = 0x00;
        pevent->OSEventTbl[3] = 0x00;
        pevent->OSEventTbl[4] = 0x00;
        pevent->OSEventTbl[5] = 0x00;
        pevent->OSEventTbl[6] = 0x00;
        pevent->OSEventTbl[7] = 0x00;
    }
    return (pevent);                                 /* Return pointer to event control block       */
}
```

---

need to be assigned to a variable in your application because it is used as the mailbox's "handle". If all event control blocks are previously used, *OSMboxCreate()* returns a NULL pointer. Once created, a mailbox cannot be deleted (that is, it cannot be deallocated). The *OSEventPtr* field of the event control block contains the mailbox's message. When *OSEventPtr* points to NULL, the mailbox is considered empty and does not contain a message.

If a task calls *OSMboxPend()* and the mailbox contains a non-NULL pointer, then *OSMboxPend()* removes the message from the mailbox and clears the mailbox (see Listing 4.6). The removed message is returned to *OSMboxPend()*'s caller. If, however, the mailbox contains a NULL pointer, *OSMboxPend()* places the calling task in the waiting list for the mailbox. The task will thus wait until another task or an ISR deposits a message in the mailbox. When the current task is placed in the waiting list, rescheduling occurs and the next highest priority task ready to run is given control of the CPU. An optional timeout may be specified when pending for a mailbox. This feature is useful to avoid waiting indefinitely for a message to be received. A low priority task may not get a message if higher priority tasks are waiting for messages as well. A timeout can be treated as an error and appropriate actions taken. The timeout can be as long as 65535 clock ticks. A timeout value of zero indicates that the task will wait indefinitely for a message. When the pending task resumes (*OSSched()* returns to *OSMboxPend()*) the task status is examined to determine if the task is still waiting for a message. A timeout condition is detected if *OSTCBStat* is still set to *OS_STAT_MBOX*, the task is removed from the mailbox's waiting list and the caller is notified that a timeout occurred.

WARNING

OSMboxPend() must never be called by an ISR.

A message is sent to a task by calling *OSMboxPost()* (see Listing 4.7). An error occurs if the mailbox already contains a message, and *OSMboxPost()* returns an error code to its caller. If the mailbox is empty, the message is deposited in the mailbox and *OSMboxPost()* determines if any task is waiting for a message to arrive. If a task is waiting, *OSMboxPost()* removes the highest priority task from the waiting list and makes this task ready to run by calling *OSEventTaskResume()*. Note that *OSEventTaskResume()* also clears the *OSTCBDly* field of the task's *OS_TCB* to prevent *OSTimeTick()* from readying this task. The scheduler is then called to determine if the awakened task is now the highest priority task ready to run.

Listing 4.6

```
/*
*********************************************************************************************
*                              PEND ON MAILBOX FOR A MESSAGE
*********************************************************************************************
*/

void *OSMboxPend(OS_EVENT *pevent, UWORD timeout, UBYTE *err)
{
    void  *msg;


    OS_ENTER_CRITICAL();
    if ((msg = pevent->OSEventPtr) != (void *)0) {    /* See if there is already a message      */
        pevent->OSEventPtr = (void *)0;               /* Clear the mailbox                      */
        OS_EXIT_CRITICAL();
        *err = OS_NO_ERR;
    } else {
        OSTCBCur->OSTCBStat = OS_STAT_MBOX;           /* Message not available, task will pend  */
        OSTCBCur->OSTCBDly  = timeout;                /* Load timeout in TCB                    */
        if ((OSRdyTbl[OSTCBCur->OSTCBY] &= ~OSTCBCur->OSTCBBitX) == 0) {  /* Task no longer ready  */
            OSRdyGrp &= ~OSTCBCur->OSTCBBitY;
        }
        pevent->OSEventTbl[OSTCBCur->OSTCBY] |= OSTCBCur->OSTCBBitX;      /* Put task in waiting list */
        pevent->OSEventGrp                   |= OSTCBCur->OSTCBBitY;
        OS_EXIT_CRITICAL();
        OSSched();                                    /* Find next highest priority task ready to run */
        OS_ENTER_CRITICAL();
        if (OSTCBCur->OSTCBStat == OS_STAT_MBOX) {    /* If status is not OS_STAT_RDY, timeout occured */
            if ((pevent->OSEventTbl[OSTCBCur->OSTCBY] &= ~OSTCBCur->OSTCBBitX) == 0) {
                pevent->OSEventGrp &= ~OSTCBCur->OSTCBBitY;
            }
            OSTCBCur->OSTCBStat     = OS_STAT_RDY;    /* Set status to ready                    */
            OSTCBCur->OSTCBEventPtr = (OS_EVENT *)0;
            msg                     = (void *)0;      /* Set message contents to NULL           */
            OS_EXIT_CRITICAL();
            *err                    = OS_TIMEOUT;     /* Indicate that a timeout occured        */
        } else {
            msg                     = pevent->OSEventPtr; /* Message received                   */
            pevent->OSEventPtr      = (void *)0;      /* Clear the mailbox                      */
            OS_EXIT_CRITICAL();
            *err                    = OS_NO_ERR;
        }
    }
    return (msg);                                     /* Return the message received (or NULL)  */
}
```

Listing 4.7

```
/*
*******************************************************************************************
*                                POST MESSAGE TO A MAILBOX
*******************************************************************************************
*/

UBYTE OSMboxPost(OS_EVENT *pevent, void *msg)
{
    OS_ENTER_CRITICAL();
    if (pevent->OSEventPtr != (void *)0) {      /* Make sure mailbox doesn't already contain a msg   */
        OS_EXIT_CRITICAL();
        return (OS_MBOX_FULL);
    } else {
        pevent->OSEventPtr = msg;               /* Place message in mailbox                          */
        if (pevent->OSEventGrp) {               /* See if any task pending on mailbox                */
            OS_EXIT_CRITICAL();
            OSEventTaskResume(pevent);          /* Resume highest priority task pending on mailbox   */
            OSSched();                          /* Find highest priority task ready to run           */
        } else {
            OS_EXIT_CRITICAL();
        }
        return (OS_NO_ERR);
    }
}
```

QUEUES

Queues are similar to mailboxes. A mailbox allows a task or an ISR to send a single pointer size message to one or more tasks. Queues are used to send a user definable number of messages to one or more tasks. As with the mailbox, the contents of the messages sent are application specific. A queue can be manipulated through three functions:

　　1) *OSQCreate()*

　　2) *OSQPend()*

　　3) *OSQPost()*

　　OSQCreate() (see Listing 4.8) allocates an event control block for use by the queue. *OSQCreate()* returns a pointer to the event control block allocated to the queue. This pointer will need to be assigned to a variable in your application because it is used as the queue's "handle". If all event control blocks are used, *OSQCreate()* returns a NULL pointer. Once created, a queue cannot be deleted (that is, it cannot be deallocated). *OSQCreate()* also allocates a queue control block which is linked to the Event Control Block as shown in Figure 4.2. Note that *OSQCreate()* is called with two arguments. *start* is a pointer to the start of the storage area where the messages will be placed and is declared as an array of pointers to *void* as shown in Figure 4.2. *size* is the size of this array. Note that *OSQCreate()* always creates an empty message queue.

Listing 4.8

```
/*
*********************************************************************************************
*                                  INITIALIZE MESSAGE QUEUE
*********************************************************************************************
*/

OS_EVENT *OSQCreate(void **start, UBYTE size)
{
    OS_EVENT *pevent;
    OS_Q     *pq;


    OS_ENTER_CRITICAL();
    pevent = OSEventFreeList;                        /* Get next free event control block          */
    if (OSEventFreeList != (OS_EVENT *)0) {          /* See if pool of free ECB pool was empty      */
        OSEventFreeList = (OS_EVENT *)OSEventFreeList->OSEventPtr;
    }
    OS_EXIT_CRITICAL();
    if (pevent != (OS_EVENT *)0) {                   /* See if we have an event control block        */
        OS_ENTER_CRITICAL();                         /* Get a free queue control block               */
        pq = OSQFreeList;
        if (OSQFreeList != (OS_Q *)0) {
            OSQFreeList = OSQFreeList->OSQPtr;
        }
        OS_EXIT_CRITICAL();
        if (pq != (OS_Q *)0) {                       /* See if we were able to get a queue control block */
            pq->OSQStart        = start;             /* Yes, initialize the queue                    */
            pq->OSQEnd          = &start[size];
            pq->OSQIn           = start;
            pq->OSQOut          = start;
            pq->OSQSize         = size;
            pq->OSQEntries      = 0;
            pevent->OSEventPtr  = pq;
            pevent->OSEventGrp  = 0x00;              /* Initialize rest of event control block       */
            pevent->OSEventTbl[0] = 0x00;
            pevent->OSEventTbl[1] = 0x00;
            pevent->OSEventTbl[2] = 0x00;
            pevent->OSEventTbl[3] = 0x00;
            pevent->OSEventTbl[4] = 0x00;
            pevent->OSEventTbl[5] = 0x00;
            pevent->OSEventTbl[6] = 0x00;
            pevent->OSEventTbl[7] = 0x00;
        } else {                                     /* No,  since we couldn't get a queue control block */
            OS_ENTER_CRITICAL();                     /* Return event control block on error          */
            pevent->OSEventPtr = (void *)OSEventFreeList;
            OSEventFreeList    = pevent;
            OS_EXIT_CRITICAL();
            pevent = (OS_EVENT *)0;
        }
    }
    return (pevent);
}
```

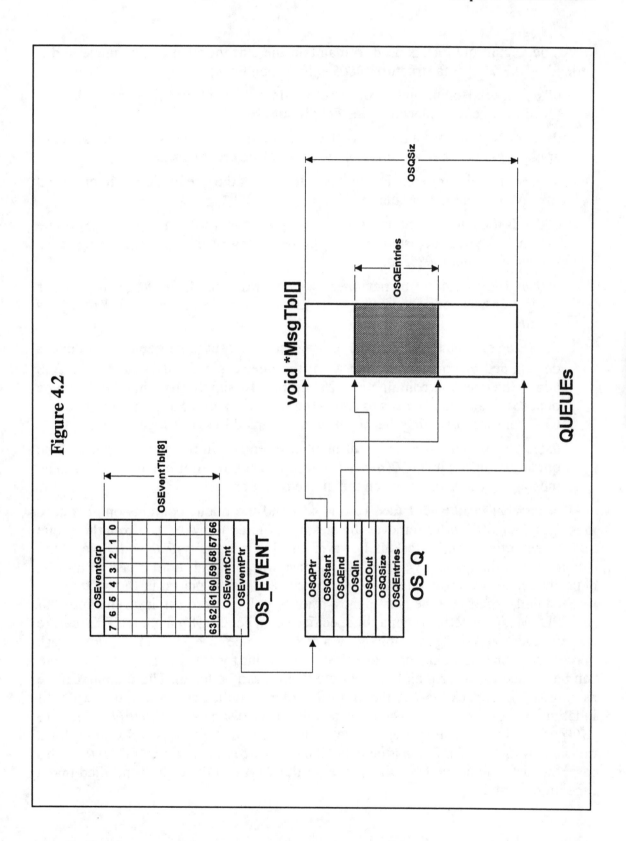

Figure 4.2

A queue control block is used to maintain the current state of the queue and is defined by the *OS_Q* data structure (*UCOS.H* in Appendix A).

OSQPtr is used to link queue control blocks in the list of free queue control blocks. Once the queue is allocated, this field is not used.

OSQStart contains a pointer to the start of the message storage area. Your application must declare this storage area before creating the queue.

OSQEnd is a pointer to one location past the end of the queue. This pointer is used to make the queue a circular buffer.

OSQIn is a pointer to the location in the queue where the next message will be inserted. *OSQIn* is adjusted back to the beginning of the message storage area when *OSQIn* equals *OSQEnd*.

OSQOut is a pointer to the next message to be extracted from the queue. *OSQOut* is adjusted back to the beginning of the message storage area when *OSQOut* equals *OSQEnd*.

OSQSize contains the size of the message storage area. The size of the queue is determined by your application when the queue is created. Note that µC/OS allows the queue to contain up to 254 entries. By simply changing the data type of *OSQSize* and *OSQEntries* to *UWORD* the size of a queue can support as many as 65534 entries (assuming that the processor can address this many entries).

OSQEntries contains the current number of entries in the message queue. The queue is empty when *OSQEntries* is zero and full when it equals *OSQSize*. The message queue is empty when the queue is created.

If a task calls *OSQPend()* (see Listing 4.9) and the queue contains one or more messages, then *OSQPend()* removes the message pointed to by *OSQOut* from the queue and returns it to the calling task. If, however, the queue is empty, *OSQPend()* places the calling task in the queue's waiting list. The task will thus wait until a task or an ISR deposits a message in the queue. When the current task is placed in the waiting list, rescheduling occurs and the next highest priority task ready to run is given control of the CPU. An optional timeout may be specified when pending for a queue. This feature is useful to avoid waiting indefinitely for a message to be received. A low priority task may not get a message if higher priority tasks are waiting for messages as well. A timeout can be treated as an error and appropriate actions can be taken. The timeout can be as long as 65535 clock ticks. A timeout value of zero indicates that the task will wait indefinitely for a message. When the pending task resumes (*OSSched()* returns to *OSQPend()*) the task status is examined to determine if the task is still waiting for a message. A timeout condition is detected if *OSTCBStat* is still set to *OS_STAT_Q*. In this case, the task is removed from the queue's waiting list and the caller is notified that a timeout occurred.

Listing 4.9

```
/*
*********************************************************************************************
*                              PEND ON A QUEUE FOR A MESSAGE
*********************************************************************************************
*/

void *OSQPend(OS_EVENT *pevent, UWORD timeout, UBYTE *err)
{
    void  *msg;
    OS_Q  *pq;


    OS_ENTER_CRITICAL();
    pq = pevent->OSEventPtr;                     /* Point at queue control block                */
    if (pq->OSQEntries != 0) {                   /* See if any messages in the queue            */
        msg = *pq->OSQOut++;                      /* Yes, extract oldest message from the queue  */
        pq->OSQEntries--;                        /* Update the number of entries in the queue   */
        if (pq->OSQOut == pq->OSQEnd) {          /* Wrap OUT pointer if we are at the end of the queue */
            pq->OSQOut = pq->OSQStart;
        }
        OS_EXIT_CRITICAL();
        *err = OS_NO_ERR;
    } else {
        OSTCBCur->OSTCBStat = OS_STAT_Q;         /* Task will have to pend for a message to be posted */
        OSTCBCur->OSTCBDly  = timeout;           /* Load timeout into TCB                        */
        if ((OSRdyTbl[OSTCBCur->OSTCBY] &= ~OSTCBCur->OSTCBBitX) == 0) {  /* Task no longer ready */
            OSRdyGrp &= ~OSTCBCur->OSTCBBitY;
        }
        pevent->OSEventTbl[OSTCBCur->OSTCBY] |= OSTCBCur->OSTCBBitX;      /* Put task in waiting list */
        pevent->OSEventGrp                   |= OSTCBCur->OSTCBBitY;
        OS_EXIT_CRITICAL();
        OSSched();                               /* Find next highest priority task ready to run */
        OS_ENTER_CRITICAL();
        if (OSTCBCur->OSTCBStat == OS_STAT_Q) {  /* Timeout occured if status indicates pending on Q */
            if ((pevent->OSEventTbl[OSTCBCur->OSTCBY] &= ~OSTCBCur->OSTCBBitX) == 0) {
                pevent->OSEventGrp &= ~OSTCBCur->OSTCBBitY;
            }
            OSTCBCur->OSTCBStat     = OS_STAT_RDY;   /* Set status to ready                      */
            OSTCBCur->OSTCBEventPtr = (OS_EVENT *)0; /* No longer waiting for event              */
            msg                     = (void *)0;     /* No message received                      */
            OS_EXIT_CRITICAL();
            *err                    = OS_TIMEOUT;    /* Indicate a timeout occured               */
        } else {
            msg = *pq->OSQOut++;                  /* Message received, extract from queue         */
            pq->OSQEntries--;                    /* Update the number of entries in the queue    */
            if (pq->OSQOut == pq->OSQEnd) {      /* Wrap OUT pointer if we are at the end of the queue */
                pq->OSQOut = pq->OSQStart;
            }
            OS_EXIT_CRITICAL();
            *err = OS_NO_ERR;
        }
    }                                            /* Return message received (or NULL)            */
    return (msg);
}
```

4

WARNING

OSQPend() must never be called by an ISR.

A message is sent to a task by calling *OSQPost()* (see Listing 4.10). An error occurs if the queue is full. In this case, *OSQPost()* returns an error code to its caller. If the queue is not full, the message is deposited in the queue and *OSQPost()* determines if any task is waiting for a message to arrive. In this case, *OSQPost()* removes the highest priority task waiting for a message from the waiting list and makes this task ready to run by calling *OSEventTaskResume()*. Note that *OSEventTaskResume()* also clears the *OSTCBDly* field of the task's *OS_TCB* to prevent *OSTimeTick()* from readying this task. The scheduler is then called to determine if the awakened task is now the highest priority task ready to run.

Listing 4.10

```
/*
********************************************************************************************************
*                                     POST MESSAGE TO A QUEUE
********************************************************************************************************
*/

UBYTE OSQPost(OS_EVENT *pevent, void *msg)
{
    OS_Q  *pq;


    OS_ENTER_CRITICAL();
    pq = pevent->OSEventPtr;                    /* Point to queue control block                    */
    if (pq->OSQEntries >= pq->OSQSize) {        /* Make sure queue is not full                     */
        OS_EXIT_CRITICAL();
        return (OS_Q_FULL);
    } else {
        *pq->OSQIn++ = msg;                     /* Insert message into queue                       */
        pq->OSQEntries++;                       /* Update the number of entries in the queue       */
        if (pq->OSQIn == pq->OSQEnd) {          /* Wrap IN pointer if we are at the end of the queue */
            pq->OSQIn = pq->OSQStart;
        }
        if (pevent->OSEventGrp) {               /* See if any task pending on queue                */
            OS_EXIT_CRITICAL();
            OSEventTaskResume(pevent);          /* Yes, resume highest priority task pending on queue */
            OSSched();                          /* Find highest priority task ready to run         */
        } else {
            OS_EXIT_CRITICAL();
        }
        return (OS_NO_ERR);
    }
}
```

Chapter 5

Initialization & Configuration

Initialization

μC/OS is initialized by calling *OSInit()* (see Listing 5.1). μC/OS assumes that you have declared the following #*defines* in *UCOS.H* (see Appendix A).

OS_IDLE_TASK_STK_SIZE declares the size of the idle task in number of bytes. Sufficient stack space must be allocated to accommodate for maximum interrupt nesting.

OS_MAX_TASKS defines the maximum number of tasks that you wish μC/OS to manage. For example if your application has 20 tasks, *OS_MAX_TASKS* would be set to at least 20. You may allocate more tasks than you currently have for future expansion.

OS_MAX_EVENTS defines the maximum number of event control blocks that your application will create. Each semaphore, mailbox and queue requires an event control block.

OS_MAX_QS defines the maximum number of message queues that your application will create.

Figure 5.1 shows the different data structures in μC/OS and their state after calling *OSInit()*.

5

Multitasking starts when you call *OSStart()* (see Listing 5.2). *OSInit()* must be called before *OSStart()* and you must create at least one of your tasks prior to calling *OSStart()*. *OSStart()* determines the highest priority task that you created and sets *OSTCBHighRdy* accordingly. The flag *OSRunning* is set to *TRUE* indicating that multitasking has started. *OSRunning* allows you to create tasks prior to giving control to μC/OS and starting multitasking. *OSStart()* calls the assembly language function *OSStartHighRdy()* (see Listing 5.3) to load the context of the highest priority task into the processor and actually start executing its code. *OSStartHighRdy()* never returns to *OSStart()*.

Configuration

µC/OS is very easy to configure, and requires the following steps:

1) Change the following #defines in UCOS.H for your application:

   OS_IDLE_TASK_STACK_SIZE

   OS_MAX_TASKS

   OS_MAX_EVENTS

   OS_MAX_QS

   uCOS

2) Write an ISR which calls OSTimeTick()

3) Allocate and set an interrupt vector for the context switch code OS_TASK_SW().
   The interrupt vector number is specified to µC/OS through the #define uCOS
   in UCOS.H.

4) Allocate and set an interrupt vector for the tick ISR

5) Call OSInit() in main() before calling OSStart()

6) Create all your Semaphores, Mailboxes and Queues

7) Allocate storage for your task stacks

8) Create at least one of your tasks.

9) Call OSStart() when you are ready to start multitasking.

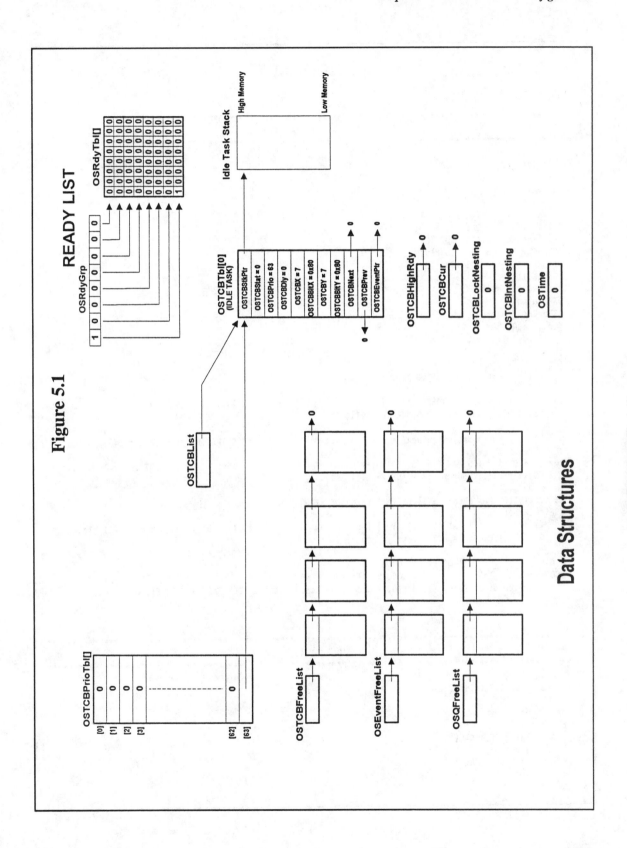

Figure 5.1

Data Structures

Listing 5.1

```
/*
*******************************************************************************************************
*                                    uCOS INITIALIZATION
*******************************************************************************************************
*/
void OSInit(void)
{
    UBYTE i;


    OSTime        = 0L;
    OSTCBHighRdy  = (OS_TCB *)0;
    OSTCBCur      = (OS_TCB *)0;
    OSTCBList     = (OS_TCB *)0;
    OSIntNesting  = 0;
    OSLockNesting = 0;
    OSRunning     = 0;
    OSRdyGrp      = 0;
    for (i = 0; i < 8; i++) {
        OSRdyTbl[i] = 0;
    }
    for (i = 0; i < 64; i++) {
        OSTCBPrioTbl[i] = (OS_TCB *)0;
    }
    for (i = 0; i < OS_MAX_TASKS; i++) {                     /* Init. list of free TCBs           */
        OSTCBTbl[i].OSTCBNext = &OSTCBTbl[i+1];
    }
    OSTCBTbl[OS_MAX_TASKS].OSTCBNext = (OS_TCB *)0;          /* Last OS_TCB is for OSTaskIdle()    */
    OSTCBFreeList                    = &OSTCBTbl[0];
    for (i = 0; i < (OS_MAX_EVENTS - 1); i++) {              /* Init. list of free EVENT control blocks */
        OSEventTbl[i].OSEventPtr = &OSEventTbl[i+1];
    }
    OSEventTbl[OS_MAX_EVENTS - 1].OSEventPtr = (OS_EVENT *)0;
    OSEventFreeList                          = &OSEventTbl[0];
    for (i = 0; i < (OS_MAX_QS - 1); i++) {                  /* Init. list of free QUEUE control blocks */
        OSQTbl[i].OSQPtr = &OSQTbl[i+1];
    }
    OSQTbl[OS_MAX_QS - 1].OSQPtr = (OS_Q *)0;
    OSQFreeList                  = &OSQTbl[0];
    OSTaskCreate(OSTaskIdle, (void *)0, (void *)&OSTaskIdleStk[OS_IDLE_TASK_STK_SIZE], OS_LO_PRIO);
}

/*
*******************************************************************************************************
*                                        IDLE TASK
*******************************************************************************************************
*/
static void far OSTaskIdle(void *data)
{
    data = data;
    while (1) {
        OS_ENTER_CRITICAL();
        OSIdleCtr++;
        OS_EXIT_CRITICAL();
    }
}
```

Listing 5.2

```c
/*
*********************************************************************************************
*                                    START MULTITASKING
*********************************************************************************************
*/

void OSStart(void)
{
    UBYTE y;
    UBYTE x;
    UBYTE p;


    y           = OSUnMapTbl[OSRdyGrp];        /* Find highest priority's task priority number   */
    x           = OSUnMapTbl[OSRdyTbl[y]];
    p           = (y << 3) + x;
    OSTCBHighRdy = OSTCBPrioTbl[p];            /* Point to highest priority task ready to run    */
    OSRunning   = 1;
    OSStartHighRdy();
}
```

Listing 5.3

```asm
;*********************************************************************************************
;                                    START MULTITASKING
;                                 void OSStartHighRdy(void)
;
; Total execution time : 123 bus cycles
;*********************************************************************************************

_OSStartHighRdy    PROC NEAR

        MOV     BX,[_OSTCBHighRdy]      ;  9~, Point to TCB of highest priority task ready to run
        MOV     [_OSTCBCur],BX          ; 12~
        MOV     AX,[BX]                 ;  9~, Point to task's top of stack
        MOV     SP,AX                   ;  2~
        MOV     AX,DS                   ;  2~, Stacks are in DATA segment thus set SS to DS
        MOV     SS,AX                   ;  2~
        POP     ES                      ;  8~
        POPA                            ; 51~
        IRET                            ; 28~, Run task

_OSStartHighRdy    ENDP
```

Chapter 6

Reference Manual and Timing Reference

Introduction

This chapter provides a user's guide to μC/OS's services. Each of the user accessible kernel services is presented in alphabetical order and the following information is provided for each of the services:

1) A brief description
2) The file name where the source code is found
3) The function prototype
4) A description of the arguments passed to the function
5) A description of the return value(s)
6) Specific notes and warning on the usage of the service
7) An example on how to invoke the function
8) The execution time based on different scenarios

The 80186/80188 microprocessor (Small memory model) is assumed throughout. The code was compiled using the Borland International C++ Version 3.0 Compiler running under the MS-DOS operating system Version 5.0. Code was compiled under the Borland Integrated Development Environment (IDE). The IDE allows projects to be created. When a project is compiled, Borland's C++ performs an intelligent product build, that is, it compiles only the files that were changed since the last build.

6

The following compiler options were selected to provide maximum speed optimization:

```
Compiler:
    Code generation:
        Model              : Small
        Options            : Treat enums as ints
                             Pre-compiled headers
        Assume SS Equals DS: Default for memory model

    Advance code generation :
        Floating point     : Emulation
        Instruction set    : 80186
        Options            : Generate underbars
                             Debug info in OBJs
                             Fast floating point

    Optimization:
        Optimization:
            Global register allocation
            Invariant code motion
            Induction variables
            Loop optimization
            Supress redundant loads
            Copy propagation
            Dead code elimination
            Jump optimization
            Inline intrinsic functions
        Register variables:
            Automatic
        Common subexpressions
            Optimize globally
        Optimize for:
            Speed
```

The execution time for each function was obtained by having the compiler generate an assembly language file. From the assembly language output, the number of cycles for each instruction was then added for the different execution scenarios.

The file *INCLUDES.H* is assumed to include all header files required for your application and will include *UCOS.H* and *80186S_C.H*.

Memory Usage

Program Memory

The code in *UCOS.C*, *80186S_A.ASM* and *80186S_C.C* require less than 3150 bytes of program memory space. Program memory can be reduced if your application doesn't require some of the services provided by µC/OS as shown below. A minimum µC/OS configuration would thus require about 1600 bytes.

```
Kernel Service          Delete Function(s)      #Bytes Saved
--------------------    --------------------    ------------
Change task priority    OSTaskChangePrio()          375

Delete a task           OSTaskDel()                 200

Semaphores              OSSemCreate()               300
                        OSSemPend()
                        OSSemPost()

Mailboxes               OSMboxCreate()              275
                        OSMboxPend()
                        OSMboxpost()

Queues                  OSQCreate()                 400
                        OSQPend()
                        OSQPost()
```

Data Memory

The data memory (RAM) requirements for a small memory model 80186/80188 implementation of µC/OS is given below. Note that this does not account for the memory requirements of your application.

```
RAM = 200
    + ((1 + OS_MAX_TASKS) * 16)
    + (OS_MAX_EVENTS * 13)
    + (OS_MAX_QS * 13)
    + SUM(Storage requirements for each message queue)
    + SUM(Storage requirements for each task stack)
    + (OS_IDLE_TASK_STK_SIZE)
```

6

For example, a 20 task application using 256 bytes for each task stack, 10 semaphores, 5 mailboxes and 5 queues of 10 entries would require:

```
RAM = 200
    + (1 + 20) * 16
    + (10 semaphores + 5 mailboxes + 5 queues) * 13
    + 5 * 13 queues
    + 5 queues * 10 messages/queue * 2 bytes/message
    + 20 tasks * 256 bytes/task stack
    + 256 bytes for the idle task stack
```

thus,

```
RAM =   200
    +   336
    +   260
    +    65
    +   100
    + 5120
    +   256
    ------
      6337 bytes
```

Kernel Services

OSInit()	Initialize μC/OS
OSIntEnter()	Signal ISR entry
OSIntExit()	Signal ISR exit
OSMboxCreate()	Create a mailbox
OSMboxPend()	Pend for message from mailbox
OSMboxPost()	Post a message to mailbox
OSQCreate()	Create a queue
OSQPend()	Pend for message from queue
OSQPost()	Post a message to queue
OSSchedLock()	Prevent rescheduling
OSSchedUnlock()	Allow rescheduling
OSSemCreate()	Create a semaphore
OSSemPend()	Wait on semaphore
OSSemPost()	Signal semaphore
OSStart()	Start multitasking
OSTaskChangePrio()	Change a task's priority
OSTaskCreate()	Create a task
OSTaskDel()	Delete a task
OSTimeDly()	Delay a task for *n* system ticks
OSTimeGet()	Get current system time
OSTimeSet()	Set system time
OSTimeTick()	Process a system tick

MACROS

OS_ENTER_CRITICAL()
OS_EXIT_CRITICAL()

#DEFINEs

OS_MAX_TASKS
OS_MAX_EVENTS
OS_MAX_QS
OS_IDLE_TASK_STK_SIZE
uCOS

6

OSInit()

Description:

   OSInit() is used to initialize μC/OS. *OSInit()* must be called prior to calling *OSStart()* which will actually start multitasking.

File:
   UCOS.C

Function Prototype:
   void OSInit(void);

Arguments:
   NONE

Returned Value:
   NONE

Notes/Warnings:
   OSInit() must be called before *OSStart()*.

Example:

```
void main(void)
{
            .            /* User Code           */
            .
    OSInit();            /* Initialize μC/OS    */
            .            /* User Code           */
            .
    OSStart();           /* Start Multitasking  */
}
```

Execution Time:

   The execution time for this function is not specified since it is not assumed to be time critical.

OSIntEnter()

Description:

OSIntEnter() is used to notify µC/OS that an ISR is being processed. This allows µC/OS to keep track of interrupt nesting. *OSIntEnter()* is used in conjunction with *OSIntExit()*.

File:
```
UCOS.C
```

Function Prototype:
```
void OSIntEnter(void);
```

Arguments:

NONE

Returned Value:

NONE

Notes/Warnings:

This function must not be called at the task level.

Example:

```
ISRx      PROC       FAR
          STI
          PUSHA
          PUSH       ES
          CALL       _OSIntEnter    ; Notify µC/OS of start of ISR
            .                       ; User Code
            .
          POP        ES
          POPA
ISRx      ENDP
```

Execution Time:

This function executes in less than 50 CPU clock cycles and will not disable interrupts for more than 25 CPU clock cycles.

OSIntExit()

Description:

OSIntExit() is used to notify µC/OS that an ISR has completed. This allows µC/OS to keep track of interrupt nesting. *OSIntExit()* is used in conjunction with *OSInt-Enter()*. When the last nested interrupt completes, µC/OS will call the scheduler to determine if a higher priority task has been made ready to run. In this case, the interrupt will return to the higher priority interrupt instead of the interrupted task.

File:
    UCOS.C

Function Prototype:
    void OSIntEnter(void);

Arguments:
    NONE

Returned Value:

    NONE

Notes/Warnings:

    This function must not be called at the task level.

Example:
```
ISRx        PROC        FAR
            STI
            PUSHA
            PUSH        ES
                .                       ; User Code
                .
            CALL        _OSIntExit      ; Notify µC/OS of end of ISR
            POP         ES
            POPA
ISRx        ENDP
```

Execution Time:

If the ISR which calls *OSIntExit()* is not the last nested interrupt or scheduling has been disabled (that is, *OSLockNesting != 0*), *OSIntExit()* executes in less than 100 CPU clock cycles. When the ISR is the last nested interrupt, *OSIntExit()* determines if a higher priority task has been made ready to run. If a higher priority task is made ready to run, *OSIntExit()* returns to this task in less than 450 CPU clock cycles. If no higher priority tasks are ready to run, *OSIntExit()* returns to the interrupted task in less than 275 CPU clock cycles. *OSIntExit()* will not disable interrupts for more than 375 CPU clock cycles.

OSMboxCreate()

Description:

OSMboxCreate() is used to create and initialize a mailbox. A mailbox is used to allow tasks or ISRs to send a pointer sized variable (message) to one or more tasks.

File:
    UCOS.C

Function Prototype:
    OS_EVENT *OSMboxCreate(void *msg);

Arguments:

msg is used to initialize the contents of the mailbox. The mailbox is empty when *msg* is a NULL pointer. The mailbox will initially contain a message when *msg* is non NULL.

Returned Value:

A pointer to the event control block allocated to the mailbox. If no event control block is available, *OSMboxCreate()* will return a NULL pointer.

Notes/Warnings:

Mailboxes must be created before they are used. This function cannot be called from an ISR.

Example:
    OS_EVENT *CommMbox;

```
void main(void)
{
        .                                   /* User Code             */
        .
    OSInit();                               /* Initialize µC/OS      */
        .                                   /* User Code             */
        .
    CommMbox = OSMboxCreate((void *)0);   /* Create COMM Mbox      */
    OSStart();                              /*  Start Multitasking   */
}
```

Execution Time:

If an event control block is available, *OSMboxCreate()* executes in less than 475 CPU clock cycles and disables interrupts for a maximum of 75 CPU clock cycles.

OSMboxPend()

Description:

OSMboxPend() is used when a task desires to receive a message. The message is sent to the task either by an ISR or by another task. The message received is a pointer size variable and its use is application specific.

File:
    UCOS.C

Function Prototype:
    void *OSMboxPend(OS_EVENT *pevent, UWORD timeout, UBYTE *err);

Arguments:

pevent is a pointer to the mailbox where the message is to be received from. This pointer is returned to your application when the mailbox is created (see *OSMbox-Create()*).

timeout is used to allow the task to resume execution if a message is not received from the mailbox within the specified number of clock ticks. A *timeout* value of 0 indicates that the task desires to wait forever for the message. The maximum *timeout* is 65535 clock ticks.

err is a pointer to a variable which will be used to hold an error code. *OSMboxPend()* sets *err to either:

    1) OS_NO_ERR, a message was received

    2) OS_TIMEOUT, a timeout occurred

Returned Value:

OSMboxPend() returns the message sent by either a task or an ISR and *err is set to *OS_NO_ERR*. If a timeout occurred, the returned message is a *NULL* pointer and *err is set to *OS_TIMEOUT*.

Notes/Warnings:

Mailboxes must be created before they are used. This function cannot be called from an ISR.

Example:

```
OS_EVENT *CommMbox;


void far CommTask(void *data)
{
    UBYTE  err;
    void  *msg;


    while (1) {
                    .              /* User Code              */
                    .
            msg = OSMboxPend(CommMbox, 10, &err);
                    .              /* User Code              */
                    .
    }
}
```

Execution Time:

If a message is already available in the mailbox, *OSMboxPend()* returns in less than 200 CPU clock cycles. If a message is not available, the calling task will be suspended until an ISR or a task sends a message. In this case, µC/OS will resume execution of the next highest priority interrupt within 850 CPU clock cycles. *OSMboxPend()* disables interrupts for a maximum of 400 CPU clock cycles.

6

OSMboxPost()

Description:

OSMboxPost() is used to send a message to a task through a mailbox. A message can either be sent by an ISR or another task.

File:
   UCOS.C

Function Prototype:

   UBYTE OSMboxPost(OS_EVENT *pevent, void *msg);

Arguments:

pevent is a pointer to the mailbox where the message is to be deposited into. This pointer is returned to your application when the mailbox is created (see *OSMbox-Create()*).

msg is the actual message sent to the task. *msg* is a pointer size variable and is application specific.

Returned Value:

OSMboxPost() returns one of these two error codes:

   1) *OS_NO_ERR*, if the message was deposited in the mailbox

   2) *OS_MBOX_FULL*, if the mailbox already contained a message

Notes/Warnings:

Mailboxes must be created before they are used.

Example:

```
OS_EVENT *CommMbox;
UBYTE    CommRxBuf[100];


void far CommTaskRx(void *data)
{
    UBYTE  err;


    while (1) {
            .                    /* User Code                    */
            .
        err = OSMboxPost(CommMbox, (void *)&CommRxBuf[0]);
            .                    /* User Code                    */
            .
    }
}
```

Execution Time:

If the mailbox already contains a message, *OSMboxPost ()* returns to its caller is less than 125 CPU clock cycles. If *OSMboxPost ()* is called by a task and a higher priority task was waiting for a message, *OSMboxPost ()* returns to the higher priority task is less than 550 CPU clock cycles. If the calling task is still the highest priority task, *OSMbox-Post ()* returns to its caller in less than 1050 CPU clock cycles. *OSMboxPost ()* disables interrupts for a maximum of 400 CPU clock cycles.

6

OSQCreate()

Description:

OSQCreate() is used to create a message queue. A message queue is used to allow tasks or ISRs to send pointer sized variables (messages) to one or more tasks. The meaning of the messages sent are application specific.

File:
    UCOS.C

Function Prototype:

    OS_EVENT *OSQCreate(void **start, UBYTE size);

Arguments:

start is the base address of the message storage area. A message storage area is declared as an array of pointers to voids.

size is the size (in number of entries) of the message storage area.

Returned Value:

OSQcreate() returns a pointer to the event control block allocated to the queue. If no event control block is available, *OSQCreate()* will return a NULL pointer.

Notes/Warnings:

Queues must be created before they are used. This function cannot be called from an ISR.

Example:

```
OS_EVENT *CommQ;

void main(void)
{
        .                               /* User Code               */
        .
    OSInit();                           /* Initialize µC/OS        */
        .                               /* User Code               */
        .
    CommQ = OSQCreate((void *)0); /* Create COMM Q           */
    OSStart();                          /* Start Multitasking      */
}
```

Execution Time:

If an event control block is available, *OSQCreate()* executes in less than 800 CPU clock cycles and disables interrupts for a maximum of 75 CPU clock cycles.

6

OSQPend()

Description:

OSQPend() is used when a task desires to receive messages from a queue. The messages are sent to the task either by an ISR or by another task. The messages received are pointer size variables and their use is application specific.

File:
    UCOS.C

Function Prototype:
    void *OSQPend(OS_EVENT *pevent, UWORD timeout, UBYTE *err);

Arguments:

pevent is a pointer to the queue where the messages are to be received from. This pointer is returned to your application when the queue is created (see *OSQCreate()*).

timeout is used to allow the task to resume execution if no message is received from the queue within the specified number of clock ticks. A *timeout* value of 0 indicates that the task desires to wait forever for a message. The maximum *timeout* is 65535 clock ticks.

err is a pointer to a variable which will be used to hold an error code. *OSQPend()* sets *err to either:

    1) *OS_NO_ERR, a message was received*

    2) *OS_TIMEOUT, a timeout occurred*

Returned Value:

OSQPend() returns a message sent by either a task or an ISR and *err is set to *OS_NO_ERR*. If a timeout occurred, *OSQPend()* returns a NULL pointer and sets *err to *OS_TIMEOUT*.

Notes/Warnings:

Queues must be created before they are used. This function cannot be called from an ISR.

Example:

```
OS_EVENT *CommQ;

void far CommTask(void *data)
{
    UBYTE  err;
    void   *msg;

    while (1) {
        .                       /* User Code               */
        .
    msg = OSQPend(CommQ, 100, &err);
        .                       /* User Code               */
        .
    }
}
```

Execution Time:

If a message is available in the queue, *OSQPend()* returns in less than 250 CPU clock cycles. If a message is not available, the calling task will be suspended until an ISR or a task sends a message. In this case, µC/OS will resume execution of the next highest priority interrupt within 850 CPU clock cycles. *OSQPend()* disables interrupts for a maximum of 400 CPU clock cycles.

6

OSQPost()

Description:

OSQPost() is used to send a message to a task through a queue. A message can either be sent by an ISR or another task.

File:
    UCOS.C

Function Prototype:

    UBYTE OSQPost(OS_EVENT *pevent, void *msg);

Arguments:

pevent is a pointer to the queue where the message is to be deposited into. This pointer is returned to your application when the queue is created (see *OSQCreate()*).

msg is the actual message sent to the task. *msg* is a pointer size variable and is application specific.

Returned Value:

OSQPost() returns one of these two error codes:
    1) *OS_NO_ERR*, if the message was deposited in the queue
    2) *OS_Q_FULL*, if the queue is already full

Notes/Warnings:

Queues must be created before they are used.

Example:

```
OS_EVENT *CommQ;
UBYTE     CommRxBuf[100];


void far CommTaskRx(void *data)
{
    UBYTE  err;


    while (1) {
            .                     /* User Code                */
            .
         err = OSQPost(CommQ, (void *)&CommRxBuf[0]);
            .                     /* User Code                */
            .
    }
}
```

Execution Time:

If the queue is full, *OSQPost ()* returns to its caller is less than 150 CPU clock cycles otherwise, if *OSQPost ()* is called by a task and a higher priority task was waiting for a message, *OSQPost ()* returns to the higher priority task is less than 1050 CPU clock cycles. If the calling task is still the highest priority task, *OSQPost ()* returns to its caller in less than 1150 CPU clock cycles. *OSQPost ()* disables interrupts for a maximum of 400 CPU clock cycles.

6

OSSchedLock()

Description:

The *OSSchedLock()* function is used to prevent task rescheduling until its counterpart, *OSSchedUnlock()*, is called. The task which calls *OSSchedLock()* keeps control of the CPU even though other higher priority tasks are ready to run. However, interrupts will still be recognized and serviced (assuming interrupts are enabled). *OSSchedLock()* and *OSSchedUnlock()* must be used in pair. µC/OS allows *OSSchedLock()* to be nested up to 254 levels deep. Scheduling is enabled when an equal number of *OSSchedUnlock()* calls have been made.

File:

    UCOS.C

Function Prototype:

    void OSSchedLock(void);

Arguments:
    NONE

Returned Value:
    NONE

Notes/Warnings:

After calling *OSSchedLock()*, you application must not make any system call which will suspend execution of the current task i.e., your application cannot call *OSTimeDly()*, *OSSemPend()*, *OSMboxPend()* or *OSQPend()*. Since the scheduler is locked out, no other task will be allowed to run and your system will lock up.

Example:

```
double ValueX;

void far TaskX(void *data)
{
    while (1) {
                            /* User Code            */
            .
        OSSchedLock();
        ValueX = (double)0.0;
        OSSchedUnlock();
                            /* User Code            */
        .
        .
    }
}
```

Execution Time:

OSSchedLock() executes in less than 50 CPU clock cycles. Interrupts are disabled for less than 25 CPU clock cycles.

6

OSSchedUnlock()

Description:

The *OSSchedUnlock()* function is used to re-enable task scheduling. *OSSched-Unlock()* is used with *OSSchedLock()* in pair. Scheduling is enabled when an equal number of *OSSchedUnlock()* as *OSSchedLock()* have been made.

File:
   UCOS.C

Function Prototype:
   void OSSchedUnlock(void);

Arguments:
   NONE

Returned Value:
   NONE

Notes/Warnings:

After calling *OSSchedLock()*, you application must not make any system call which will suspend execution of the current task i.e., your application cannot call *OSTimeDly*, *OSSemPend()*, *OSMboxPend()* or *OSQPend()*. Since the scheduler is locked out, no other task will be allowed to run and your system will lock up.

Example:

```
double ValueX;

void far TaskX(void *data)
{
    while (1) {
        .                        /* User Code                */
        .
        OSSchedLock();
        ValueX = (double)0.0;
        OSSchedUnlock();
        .                        /* User Code                */
        .
    }
}
```

Execution Time:

If *OSLockNesting* is decremented to *0*, *OSSchedUnlock()* resumes a higher priority task within 500 CPU clock cycles and interrupts are disabled for less than 375 CPU clock cycles. If *OSLockNesting* is non zero *OSSchedUnlock()* returns to its caller within 100 CPU clock cycles.

6

OSSemCreate()

Description:

OSSemCreate() is used to create and initialize a semaphore. A semaphore is used to:

    1) Allow a task to synchronize with either an ISR or a task

    2) Gain exclusive access to a resource

    3) Signal the occurrence of an event

File:
```
UCOS.C
```

Function Prototype:
```
OS_EVENT *OSSemCreate(WORD value);
```

Arguments:

value is the initial value of the semaphore. The initial *value* of the semaphore is allowed to be between 0 and 32767.

Returned Value:

A pointer to the event control block allocated to the semaphore. If no event control block is available, *OSSemCreate()* will return a NULL pointer.

Notes/Warnings:

Semaphores must be created before they are used. This function cannot be called from an ISR.

Example:

```
OS_EVENT *DispSem;

void main(void)
{
        .                       /* User Code                */
        .
    OSInit();                   /* Initialize µC/OS         */
        .                       /* User Code                */
        .
    DispSem = OSSemCreate(1);   /* Create Display Semaphore  */
    OSStart();                  /* Start Multitasking        */
}
```

Execution Time:

If an event control block is available, *OSSemCreate ()* executes in less than 400 CPU clock cycles and disables interrupts for a maximum of 75 CPU clock cycles.

6

OSSemPend()

Description:

OSSemPend() is used when a task desires to get exclusive access to a resource, synchronize its activities with an ISRor wait until an event occurs. If a task calls *OSSemPend()* and the value of the semaphore is greater than 0, then *OSSemPend()* will decrement the semaphore and return to its caller. However, if the value of the semaphore is less than or equal to zero, *OSSemPend()* decrements the semaphore value and places the calling task in the waiting list for the semaphore. The task will thus wait until a task or an ISR releases the semaphore or signals the occurence of the event. In this case, rescheduling occurs and the next highest priority task ready to run is given control of the CPU. An optional timeout may be specified when pending for a semaphore.

File:
    UCOS.C

Function Prototype:
    void OSSemPend(OS_EVENT *pevent, UWORD timeout, UBYTE *err);

Arguments:

pevent is a pointer to the semaphore. This pointer is returned to your application when the semaphore is created (see *OSSemCreate()*).

timeout is used to allow the task to resume execution if the semaphore is not acquired within the specified number of clock ticks. A *timeout* value of 0 indicates that the task desires to wait forever for the semaphore. The maximum *timeout* is 65535 clock ticks.

err is a pointer to a variable which will be used to hold an error code. *OSSemPend()* sets *err to either:

    1) *OS_NO_ERR*, the semaphore is available

    2) *OS_TIMEOUT*, a timeout occurred

Returned Value:

    NONE

Notes/Warnings:

Semaphores must be created before they are used. This function cannot be called from an ISR.

Example:

```
OS_EVENT *DispSem;

void far DispTask(void *data)
{
    UBYTE  err;

    while (1) {
                .                   /* User Code                  */
                .
            OSSemPend(DispSem, 0, &err);
                .                   /* User Code                  */
                .
    }
}
```

Execution Time:

If the semaphore is available, *OSSemPend()* returns in less than 125 CPU clock cycles. If the semaphore is not available, the calling task will be suspended until an ISR or a task makes the semaphore available. In this case, μC/OS will resume execution of the next highest priority interrupt within 650 CPU clock cycles. *OSSemPend()* disables interrupts for a maximum of 400 CPU clock cycles.

6

OSSemPost()

Description:

A semaphore is signaled by calling *OSSemPost()*. If the semaphore value is greater than or equal to zero, the semaphore is incremented and *OSSemPost()* returns to its caller. If the semaphore value is negative then tasks are waiting for the semaphore to be signaled. In this case, *OSSemPost()* removes the highest priority task pending (waiting) for the semaphore from the waiting list and makes this task ready to run. The scheduler is then called to determine if the awakened task is now the highest priority task ready to run.

File:

    UCOS.C

Function Prototype:

    UBYTE OSSemPost(OS_EVENT *pevent);

Arguments:

pevent is a pointer to the semaphore. This pointer is returned to your application when the semaphore is created (see *OSSemCreate()*).

Returned Value:

OSSemPost() returns one of these two error codes:

  1) `OS_NO_ERR, if the message was deposited in the mailbox`
  2) `OS_SEM_OVF, if the semaphore count overflowed`

Notes/Warnings:

Semaphores must be created before they are used.

Example:

```
OS_EVENT *DispSem;

void far TaskX(void *data)
{
    UBYTE  err;

    while (1) {
                            /* User Code                 */
            .
        err = OSSemPost(DispSem);
            .               /* User Code                 */
            .
    }
}
```

Execution Time:

If the semaphore count is greater than or equal to zero, *OSSemPost()* returns to its caller is less than 150 CPU clock cycles. If *OSSemPost()* is called by a task and a higher priority task was waiting for the semaphore, *OSSemPost()* returns to the higher priority task is less than 1000 CPU clock cycles. If the calling task is still the highest priority task, *OSSemPost()* returns to its caller in less than 1050 CPU clock cycles. *OSSemPost()* disables interrupts for a maximum of 400 CPU clock cycles.

6

OSStart()

Description:

OSStart() is used to start multitasking under µC/OS.

File:

UCOS.C

Function Prototype:

```
void OSStart(void);
```

Arguments:
NONE

Returned Value:
NONE

Notes/Warnings:

OSInit() must be called prior to calling OSStart(). OSStart() will never return to its caller.

Example:

```
void main(void)
{
            .              /* User Code           */
            .
    OSInit();              /* Initialize µC/OS    */
            .              /* User Code           */
            .
    OSStart();             /* Start Multitasking  */
}
```

Execution Time:

The execution time for this function is not specified since it is not assumed to be time critical.

6

OSTaskChangePrio()

Description:

OSTaskChangePrio() allows you to change the priority of a task.

File:

UCOS.C

Function Prototype:

UBYTE OSTaskChangePrio(UBYTE oldp, UBYTE newp);

Arguments:

oldp is the priority number of the task to change.

newp is the new task's priority.

Returned Value:

OSTaskChangePrio() returns one of these error codes:

1) *OS_NO_ERR*, the task's priority was changed

2) *OS_PRIO_EXIST*, if newp already existed

3) *OS_PRIO_ERR*, the task to change priority doesn't exist

Notes/Warnings:

The desired priority must not have already been assigned, otherwise, an error code is returned. Also, *OSChangePrio()* verifies that the task to change exist. *OSTaskChangePrio()* disables interrupts for the longest amount of time.

Example:

```
void far TaskX(void *data)
{
    UBYTE  err;


    while (1) {
                .                    /* User Code                */
                .
        err = OSTaskChangePrio(10, 15);
                .                    /* User Code                */
                .
    }
}
```

Execution Time:

OSTaskChangePrio() executes in less than 1425 CPU clock cycles when the new task's priority is lower that the running task. When the new priority is higher than the running task, scheduling is required and the new task's code executes within 1600 CPU clock cycles. Interrupts are disabled for less than 500 CPU clock cycles.

6

OSTaskCreate()

Description:

This function allows an application to create a task. The task is managed by µC/OS. Tasks can either be created prior to the start of multitasking or by a running task. A task cannot be created by an ISR.

File:
80186S_C.C

Function Prototype:
```
UBYTE OSTaskCreate(void (far *task)(void *pd),
                   void *pdata,
                   void *pstk,
                   UBYTE prio);
```

Arguments:

task is a pointer to the task's code.

pdata is a pointer to an optional data area which can be used to pass parameters to the task when it is created.

pstk is a pointer to the task's top of stack. The stack is used to store local variables, function parameters and return addresses and CPU registers during an interrupt. The size of this stack is defined by the task requirements and the anticipated interrupt nesting. Determining the size of the stack involves knowing how many bytes are required for storage of local variables for the task itself, all nested functions, as well as requirements for interrupts (accounting for nesting).

p is the task priority. A unique priority number must be assigned to each task and the lower the number, the higher the priority.

Returned Value:

OSTaskCreate() returns one of the following error codes:

  1) *OS_PRIO_EXIST* if the requested priority already exist.

  2) *OS_NO_ERR,*   if the function was successful.

Notes/Warnings:

A task cannot be created by an ISR.

Example:

```
UBYTE *Task1Stk[1000];
UBYTE  Task1Data;



void main(void)
{
    UBYTE err;


          .                 /* User Code           */
          .
    OSInit();               /* Initialize µC/OS    */
          .                 /* User Code           */
          .
    OSTaskCreate(Task1,
                (void *)&Task1Data,
                (void *)&Task1Stk[1000],
                25);
    OSStart();              /* Start Multitasking  */
}


void far Task1(void *data)
{
    while (1) {
          .                 /* User Code           */
          .
          .
    }
}
```

Execution Time:

OSTaskCreate() executes in less than 1500 CPU clock cycles if multitasking has started and a higher priority task is being created. *OSTaskCreate()* executes in less than 850 CPU clock cycles if mustitasking has started and a lower priority task is being created. *OSTaskCreate()* disables interrupts for a maximum of 400 CPU clock cycles.

OSTaskDel()

Description:

OSTaskDel() allows your application to delete a task by specifying the priority number of the task to delete. The calling task can be deleted by specifying its own priority number. The deleted task is returned to the dormant state. The deleted task may be created to make the deleted task active again.

File:

UCOS.C

Function Prototype:

UBYTE OSTaskDel(UBYTE prio);

Arguments:

prio is the task's priority number to delete.

Returned Value:

OSTaskDel() returns one of the following error codes:

1) *OS_TASK_DEL_IDLE*, you tried to delete the idle task

2) *OS_TASK_DEL_ERR*, the task to delete does not exist

3) *OS_NO_ERR*, if the task was deleted

Notes/Warnings:

An ISR cannot delete a task. *OSTaskDel()* will verify that you are not attempting to delete the µC/OS's idle task.

Example:

```
void far TaskX(void *data)
{
    UBYTE err;


    while (1) {
                .                   /* User Code                    */
                .
            err = OSTaskDel(10);/* Delete task with priority 10 */
                .                   /* User Code                    */
                .
    }
}
```

Execution Time:

OSTaskDel() executes in 725 CPU clock cycles if the task is not deleting itself. If the task is deleting itself, scheduling will occur and the next highest priority task will execute within 900 CPU clock cycles. Interrupts are disabled for less than 400 CPU clock cycles.

6

OSTimeDly()

Description:

OSTimeDly() allows a task to delay itself for a number of clock ticks. Rescheduling always occurs when the number of clock ticks is greater than zero. Valid delays range from 1 to 65535 ticks. Note that calling this function with a delay of 0 results in no delay and thus the function returns to the caller.

File:

```
UCOS.C
```

Function Prototype:

```
void OSTimeDly(UWORD ticks);
```

Arguments:

ticks is the number of clock ticks to delay the current task.

Returned Value:

NONE

Notes/Warnings:

OSTimeDly() cannot be called from an ISR.

Example:

```
void far TaskX(void *data)
{
    UBYTE err;

    while (1) {
        .                       /* User Code                    */
        .
        err = OSTimeDly(10);/* Delay task for 10 clock ticks*/
        .                       /* User Code                    */
        .
    }
}
```

Execution Time:

The next highest priority task will execute in less than 625 CPU clock cycles. Interrupts are disabled for less than 400 CPU clock cycles.

6

OSTimeGet()

Description:

OSTimeGet () allows a task obtain the current value of the system clock. The system clock is a 32 bit counter which counts the number of clock ticks since power was applied or since the system clock was last set.

File:
UCOS.C

Function Prototype:
ULONG OSTimeGet(void);

Arguments:

NONE

Returned Value:

The current system clock value.

Notes/Warnings:

NONE

Example:
```
void far TaskX(void *data)
{
    ULONG clk;


    while (1) {
                .                   /* User Code                */
                .
        clk = OSTimeGet();  /* Get current value of clock   */
                .           /* User Code                */
                .
    }
}
```

Execution Time:

OSTimeGet () always executes in less than 125 CPU clock cycles. Interrupts are disabled for less than 50 CPU clock cycles.

OSTimeSet()

Description:

OSTimeSet() allows a task to set the system clock. The system clock is a 32 bit counter which counts the number of clock ticks since power was applied or since the system clock was last set.

File:
    UCOS.C

Function Prototype:
    void OSTimeSet(ULONG value);

Arguments:

value is the desired value for the system clock.

Returned Value:

    NONE

Notes/Warnings:

    NONE

Example:
```
void far TaskX(void *data)
{
    while (1) {
        .                    /* User Code               */
        .
        OSTimeSet(0L);       /* Reset the system clock  */
        .                    /* User Code               */
        .
    }
}
```

Execution Time:

OSTimeSet() always executes in less than 100 CPU clock cycles. Interrupts are disabled for less than 50 CPU clock cycles.

6

OSTimeTick()

Description:

   OSTimeTick() is used to process a clock tick.

File:

   UCOS.C

Function Prototype:

   void OSTimeTick(void);

Arguments:

   NONE

Returned Value:

   NONE

Notes/Warnings:

   The execution time of *OSTimeTick()* is directly proportional to the number of tasks created in an application. *OSTimeTick()* can be called by either an ISR or a task. If called by a task, the task priority should be high.

Example:

```
TickISR    PROC       FAR
           STI
           PUSHA
           PUSH       ES
           CALL       _OSIntEnter    ; Notify µC/OS of start of ISR
           CALL       _OSTimeTick    ; Process clock tick
             .                       ; User Code to clear interrupt
             .
           CALL       _OSIntExit
           POP        ES
           POPA
TickISR    ENDP
```

Execution Time:

The minimum execution time is given by (N is the number of tasks created) and assumes that none of the tasks created are delayed or pending on an event with timeout:

$70 * N + 100$ (CPU clock cycles)

The maximum execution time is given below and assumes that all of created tasks are delayed or pending on an event with timeout:

$170 * N + 100$ (CPU clock cycles)

The actual execution time is difficult to determine because of the dynamic nature of multitasking. Interrupts are disabled for a maximum of 150 CPU clock cycles.

6

OS_ENTER_CRITICAL() & OS_EXIT_CRITICAL()

Description:

OS_ENTER_CRITICAL() and *OS_EXIT_CRITICAL()* are macros which are used to disable and enable the processor's interrupts, respectively.

File:

80186S_C.H

Function Prototype:

N/A

Arguments:

NONE

Returned Value:

NONE

Notes/Warnings:

These macros must be used in pairs.

Example:

```
UWORD Val;


void far TaskX(void *data)
{
    while (1) {
            .                       /* User Code                  */
            .
        OS_ENTER_CRITICAL();/* Disable interrupts         */
        Val = 10;
        OS_EXIT_CRITICAL(); /* Enable  interrupts         */
            .                   /* User Code                  */
            .
    }
}
```

Execution Time:

Both these macros execute in about 5 CPU clock cycles.

#DEFINEs

OS_IDLE_TASK_STK_SIZE:

This #define specifies the number of bytes allocated for μC/OS's idle task. The size of the idle task's stack must be large enough to accomodate for maximum interrupt nesting.

OS_MAX_TASKS:

This #define specifies the maximum number of tasks that you are allowed to create in your application. The maximum value is 63. μC/OS will allocate storage for one more *OS_TCB*, for the idle task.

OS_MAX_EVENTS:

This #define specifies the maximum number of event control blocks required in your application. Each semaphore, mailbox and queue requires one event control block. You must declare at least 1 event control block event if your application does not use semaphores, mailboxes or queues.

OS_MAX_QS:

This #define specifies the maximum number of message queue created in your application. Not only does a queue require an event control block but it also requires a queue control block. You must declare at least 1 queue control block even if your application does not use message queues.

uCOS:

This #define specifies the vector number used by μC/OS to perform a context switch. Your application must setup the Interrupt Vector Table (IVT) for this interrupt to vector to the context switch code, *OSCtxSw*.

6

Execution Time Summary

Table 6.1 shows the execution time of each of the kernel services in terms of CPU clock cycles. The INT. DIS. column indicates the amount of time interrupts are disabled. The MINIMUM column indicates the minimum execution for the function. This minimum assumes that the function executed normally (that is, without any error). The MAXIMUM column indicates the worst case execution time of the function. Finally, the NEW TASK column indicates the time it will take the function to start executing a different task if the current task is suspended (task delayed or pending for an event) or a higher priority task has been made ready to run.

Table 6.2 through 6.5 show the same data but this time in microsecond (uS) for different 80186/80188 CPU clock rates.

Table 6.1

| KERNEL SERVICE | 80186/80188 (Small Memory Model) | | | |
	INT. DIS. (CPU Clock Cycles)	MINIMUM (CPU Clock Cycles)	MAXIMUM (CPU Clock Cycles)	NEW TASK (CPU Clock Cycles)
OSIntEnter()	25	50	50	-
OSIntExit()	375	275	450	400
OSMboxCreate()	75	250	475	-
OSMboxPend()	400	200	1,300	850
OSMboxPost()	400	125	1,050	550
OSQCreate()	75	250	800	-
OSQPend()	400	250	1,250	850
OSQPost()	400	150	1,150	1,050
OSSchedLock()	25	50	50	-
OSSchedUnlock()	400	100	575	500
OSSemCreate()	75	400	400	-
OSSemPend()	400	125	1,225	650
OSSemPost()	400	150	1,050	1,000
OSTaskChangePrio()	500	1,425	1,650	1,600
OSTaskCreate()	400	850	1,500	-
OSTaskDel()	400	725	950	900
OSTimeDly()	400	425	650	625
OSTimeGet()	50	125	125	-
OSTimeSet()	50	100	100	-
OSTimeTick()	150	4,510	10,810	-

**Kernel Services Execution Times
in CPU Clock Cycles**

6

Table 6.2

KERNEL SERVICE	INT. DIS.	80186/80188 (Small Memory Model)									
	(CPU Clock Cycles)	8 MHz		10 MHz		12.5 MHz		16 MHz		20 MHz	
		(uS)		(uS)		(uS)		(uS)		(uS)	
OSIntEnter()	25	3		3		2		2		1	
OSIntExit()	375	47		38		30		23		19	
OSMboxCreate()	75	9		8		6		5		4	
OSMboxPend()	400	50		40		32		25		20	
OSMboxPost()	400	50		40		32		25		20	
OSQCreate()	75	9		8		6		5		4	
OSQPend()	400	50		40		32		25		20	
OSQPost()	400	50		40		32		25		20	
OSSchedLock()	25	3		3		2		2		1	
OSSchedUnlock()	400	50		40		32		25		20	
OSSemCreate()	75	9		8		6		5		4	
OSSemPend()	400	50		40		32		25		20	
OSSemPost()	400	50		40		32		25		20	
OSTaskChangePrio()	500	63		50		40		31		25	
OSTaskCreate()	400	50		40		32		25		20	
OSTaskDel()	400	50		40		32		25		20	
OSTimeDly()	400	50		40		32		25		20	
OSTimeGet()	50	6		5		4		3		3	
OSTimeSet()	50	6		5		4		3		3	
OSTimeTick()	150	19		15		12		9		8	

Interrupt Disable Times in CPU
Clock Cycles & μSeconds

Table 6.3

KERNEL SERVICE	MINIMUM	80186/80188 (Small Memory Model)				
	(CPU Clock Cycles)	8 MHz	10 MHz	12.5 MHz	16 MHz	20 MHz
		(uS)	(uS)	(uS)	(uS)	(uS)
OSIntEnter()	50	6	5	4	3	3
OSIntExit()	100	13	10	8	6	5
OSMboxCreate()	250	31	25	20	16	13
OSMboxPend()	200	25	20	16	13	10
OSMboxPost()	125	16	13	10	8	6
OSQCreate()	250	31	25	20	16	13
OSQPend()	250	31	25	20	16	13
OSQPost()	150	19	15	12	9	8
OSSchedLock()	50	6	5	4	3	3
OSSchedUnlock()	100	13	10	8	6	5
OSSemCreate()	400	50	40	32	25	20
OSSemPend()	125	16	13	10	8	6
OSSemPost()	150	19	15	12	9	8
OSTaskChangePrio()	1425	178	143	114	89	71
OSTaskCreate()	850	106	85	68	53	43
OSTaskDel()	725	91	73	58	45	36
OSTimeDly()	425	53	43	34	27	21
OSTimeGet()	125	16	13	10	8	6
OSTimeSet()	100	13	10	8	6	5
OSTimeTick()*	70*N + 100	564	451	361	282	226

*Note: The times given for OSTimeTick() assumes that no task is delayed

Minimum Execution Times in CPU
Clock Cycles & μSeconds

6

Table 6.4

KERNEL SERVICE	80186/80188 (Small Memory Model)						
	MAXIMUM (CPU Clock Cycles)	8 MHz (uS)	10 MHz (uS)	12 MHz (uS)	16 MHz (uS)	20 MHz (uS)	
OSIntEnter()	50	6	5	4	3	3	
OSIntExit()	450	56	45	38	28	23	
OSMboxCreate()	475	59	48	40	30	24	
OSMboxPend()	1300	163	130	108	81	65	
OSMboxPost()	1050	131	105	88	66	53	
OSQCreate()	800	100	80	67	50	40	
OSQPend()	1250	156	125	104	78	63	
OSQPost()	1150	144	115	96	72	58	
OSSchedLock()	50	6	5	4	3	3	
OSSchedUnlock()	575	72	58	48	36	29	
OSSemCreate()	400	50	40	33	25	20	
OSSemPend()	1225	153	123	102	77	61	
OSSemPost()	1050	131	105	88	66	53	
OSTaskChangePrio()	1650	206	165	138	103	83	
OSTaskCreate()	1500	188	150	125	94	75	
OSTaskDel()	950	119	95	79	59	48	
OSTimeDly()	650	81	65	54	41	33	
OSTimeGet()	125	16	13	10	8	6	
OSTimeSet()	100	13	10	8	6	5	
OSTimeTick()*	170*N + 100	1351	1081	865	676	541	

*Note: The time given for OSTimeTick() assumes that all tasks are delayed

**Maximum Execution Times in CPU
Clock Cycles & μSeconds**

Table 6.5

KERNEL SERVICE	NEW TASK	80186/80188 (Small Memory Model)					
	(CPU Clock Cycles)	8 MHz	10 MHz	12.5 MHz	16 MHz	20 MHz
		(uS)	(uS)	(uS)	(uS)	(uS)
OSIntEnter()	-	-	-	-	-	-
OSIntExit()	400	50	40	32	25	20
OSMboxCreate()	-	-	-	-	-	-
OSMboxPend()	850	106	85	68	53	43
OSMboxPost()	550	69	55	44	34	28
OSQCreate()	-	-	-	-	-	-
OSQPend()	850	106	85	68	53	43
OSQPost()	1,050	131	105	84	66	53
OSSchedLock()	-	-	-	-	-	-
OSSchedUnlock()	500	63	50	40	31	25
OSSemCreate()	-	-	-	-	-	-
OSSemPend()	650	81	65	52	41	33
OSSemPost()	1,000	125	100	80	63	50
OSTaskChangePrio()	1,600	200	160	128	100	80
OSTaskCreate()	-	-	-	-	-	-
OSTaskDel()	900	113	90	72	56	45
OSTimeDly()	625	78	63	50	39	31
OSTimeGet()	-	-	-	-	-	-
OSTimeSet()	-	-	-	-	-	-
OSTimeTick()	-	-	-	-	-	-

**Time to New Task Execution in CPU
Clock Cycles & µSeconds**

6

Chapter 7

Examples

The code presented in the following examples was compiled using Borland International C++ version 3.x. The examples are written for an IBM-PC/AT or compatible running under the IBM PC-DOS or MS-DOS operating system (Version 3.3 or later).

Example #1

Listing 7.1 presents the code for our first example (*EX1.C*). This code creates ten identical tasks. Each task delays for 1 clock tick and then displays its I.D. number (i.e. *0* to *9*) at random positions on the screen. Another task is created that is responsible for maintaining statistics and determining if the user wishes to abort the program.

Like any other program, the code starts execution from *main()*. The screen is first cleared and then the current value of the stack pointer and base pointers are saved to allow for the program to cleanly return to DOS with the same state it had prior to multitasking.

μC/OS will use the PC's periodic time base (18.20648 Hz or a period of 54.925 mS) as a system tick. To maintain services provided by the old tick interrupt, μC/OS will call the BIOS's tick interrupt from μC/OS's tick ISR (see *TICK.ASM*, Listing 7.2). For this reason, a pointer to the BIOS's tick ISR is saved in *OldTickISR*. The BIOS's tick ISR is then relocated to *INT 81H* where it will be called by μC/OS's tick ISR. *INT 81H* was used in the past by the PC's ROM BASIC. Very few systems use ROM BASIC nowadays and it is thus safe to use this vector. The context switch vector is then installed at *INT 80H* (which was also formerly used by ROM BASIC). The definition of the constant for *uCOS* is found in *UCOS.H* (see Apendix A). The next step is to initialize μC/OS by calling *OSInit()*. *UCOS.H* is set to allow up to 20 Tasks, 20 Event Control Blocks (ECBs) and 5 Queues. However, these limits can be changed by editing *UCOS.H*. μC/OS objects can be created once μC/OS is initialized.

Because the PC's BIOS is non-reentrant, a display semaphore is created to provide exclusive access to this resource. The semaphore is initialized to *1* to indicate that only one task may access the display at any given time. Similarly, a semaphore is created to provide exclusive access to a Borland function which could be non-reentrant. Again, only one task will be allowed to access this resource.

As you know, at least one task must be created before calling *OSStart()*. I decided to create a task which will create all other tasks. I called this task *Stat()* because it will be responsible for displaying run-time statistics. The task is given the lowest priority, i.e. 62. Once the *Stat()* task is created, *OSStart()* is called to start the

7

Listing 7.1

```
/*
*********************************************************************************************
*                                    uCOS, The Real-Time Kernel
*
*                                         EXAMPLE #1
*********************************************************************************************
*/

#include "INCLUDES.H"

/*
*********************************************************************************************
*                                        CONSTANTS
*********************************************************************************************
*/

#define        TASK_STK_SIZE    1024                /* Size of each task's stacks (# of bytes)    */
/*
*********************************************************************************************
*                                        VARIABLES
*********************************************************************************************
*/

UBYTE          TaskStk[10][TASK_STK_SIZE];          /* Tasks stacks                               */
UBYTE          StatStk[TASK_STK_SIZE];
char           TaskData[10];                         /* Parameters to pass to each task            */
UBYTE          StatData;
OS_EVENT       *DispSem;                             /* Pointer to display semaphore               */
OS_EVENT       *RandomSem;
UWORD          OldSP;
UWORD          OldBP;
void interrupt (*OldTickISR)(void);

/*
*********************************************************************************************
*                                    FUNCTION PROTOTYPES
*********************************************************************************************
*/
void far       Task(void *data);                    /* Function prototypes of tasks               */
void far       Stat(void *data);                    /* Function prototypes of Statistics task     */
void           DispChar(UBYTE x, UBYTE y, char c);
void           DispStr(UBYTE x, UBYTE y, char *s);
void far       NewTickISR(void);

/*$PAGE*/
```

Listing 7.1 *continued*

```
/*
*********************************************************************************
*                                    MAIN
*********************************************************************************
*/
void main(void)
{
    clrscr();                                          /* Clear the screen                       */
    OldBP    = _BP;                                    /* Save current SP and BP                 */
    OldSP    = _SP;
    OldTickISR = getvect(0x08);                        /* Get MS-DOS's tick vector               */
    setvect(0x81, OldTickISR);                         /* Store MS-DOS's tick to chain           */

    setvect(uCOS, (void interrupt (*)(void))OSCtxSw);  /* uCOS's context switch vector           */
    OSInit();
    DispSem  = OSSemCreate(1);                         /* Display semaphore                      */
    RandomSem = OSSemCreate(1);                        /* Random number semaphore                */
    OSTaskCreate(Stat, (void *)&StatData, (void *)&StatStk[TASK_STK_SIZE], 62);
    OSStart();                                         /* Start multitasking                     */
}
/*$PAGE*/
/*
*********************************************************************************
*                                STATISTICS TASK
*********************************************************************************
*/
void far Stat(void *data)
{
    UBYTE  i;
    char   s[100];
    double max;
    double usage;

    data = data;                                       /* Prevent compiler warning              */
    OS_ENTER_CRITICAL();                               /* Install uCOS's clock tick ISR         */
    setvect(0x08, (void interrupt (*)(void))NewTickISR);
    OS_EXIT_CRITICAL();
    DispStr(0, 22, "Determining  CPU's capacity ...");  /* Determine maximum count for OSIdleCtr */
    OSTimeDly(1);                                      /* Synchronize to clock tick             */
    OSIdleCtr = 0L;                                    /* Determine MAX. idle counter value ... */
    OSTimeDly(18);                                     /* ... for 18 clock ticks                */
    max      = (double)OSIdleCtr;
    for (i = 0; i < 10; i++) {                         /* Create 10 identical tasks             */
        TaskData[i] = '0' + i;
        OSTaskCreate(Task, (void *)&TaskData[i], (void *)&TaskStk[i][TASK_STK_SIZE], i + 10);
    }
    DispStr(0, 23, "Press any key to quit.");
    OSIdleCtr = 0L;
```

7

Listing 7.1 *continued*

```
    while (1) {
        usage = 100.0 - (100.0 * (double)OSIdleCtr / max); /* Compute and display statistics    */
        sprintf(s, "Task Switches/sec: %d   CPU Usage: %5.2f %%   Idle Ctr: %7.0f / %7.0f   ",
                OSCtxSwCtr,
                usage,
                (double)OSIdleCtr,
                max);
        DispStr(0, 22, s);
        if (kbhit()) {                                    /* Exit if any key pressed            */
            OS_ENTER_CRITICAL();
            setvect(0x08, OldTickISR);
            OS_EXIT_CRITICAL();
            clrscr();
            _BP = OldBP;                                  /* Restore old SP and BP              */
            _SP = OldSP;
            exit(0);
        }
        OS_ENTER_CRITICAL();
        OSCtxSwCtr = 0;                                   /* Reset statistics counters          */
        OSIdleCtr  = 0L;
        OS_EXIT_CRITICAL();
        OSTimeDly(18);                                    /* Wait one second                    */
    }
}
/*$PAGE*/
/*
*********************************************************************************************************
*                                          TASKS
*********************************************************************************************************
*/

void far Task(void *data)
{
    UBYTE x;
    UBYTE y;
    UBYTE err;


    while (1) {
        OSTimeDly(1);                          /* Delay 1 clock tick                            */
        OSSemPend(RandomSem, 0, &err);         /* Acquire semaphore to perform random numbers   */
        x = random(79);                        /* Find X position where task number will appear */
        y = random(21);                        /* Find Y position where task number will appear */
        OSSemPost(RandomSem);                  /* Release semaphore                             */
        DispChar(x, y, *(char *)data);         /* Display the task number on the screen         */
    }
}


/*$PAGE*/
```

Listing 7.1 *continued*

```
/*
********************************************************************************************
*                                    DISPLAY FUNCTIONS
********************************************************************************************
*/

void DispChar(UBYTE x, UBYTE y, char c)
{
    UBYTE err;


    OSSemPend(DispSem, 0, &err);
    gotoxy(x + 1, y + 1);
    putchar(c);
    OSSemPost(DispSem);
}

void DispStr(UBYTE x, UBYTE y, char *s)
{
    UBYTE err;


    OSSemPend(DispSem, 0, &err);
    gotoxy(x + 1, y + 1);
    puts(s);
    OSSemPost(DispSem);
}
```

7

Listing 7.2

```
;************************************************************************************************
;                                        uCOS
;                    Microcomputer Real-Time Multitasking Operating System
;                                        KERNEL
;
;                        (c) Copyright 1992, Jean J. Labrosse, Plantation, FL
;                                    All Rights Reserved
;
;
;                                        TICK ISR
;                                    SMALL MEMORY MODEL
;
; File : TICK.ASM
; By   : Jean J. Labrosse
;************************************************************************************************

           PUBLIC  _NewTickISR

           EXTRN   _OSIntEnter:NEAR
           EXTRN   _OSIntExit:NEAR
           EXTRN   _OSTimeTick:NEAR

.MODEL     SMALL
.CODE
.186


;************************************************************************************************
;                                    HANDLE TICK ISR
;************************************************************************************************

_NewTickISR PROC   FAR

           STI
           PUSHA
           PUSH  ES
           CALL  _OSIntEnter
           CALL  _OSTimeTick
           INT   081H
           CALL  _OSIntExit
           POP   ES
           POPA
           IRET

_NewTickISR ENDP

           END
```

multitasking process. Since only one task is created, it will be given control of the CPU by µC/OS.

The *Stat ()* task starts off by installing the tick ISR replacing the BIOS's *INT 08H*. µC/OS's tick ISR is found in *TICK.ASM*.

I added a feature to µC/OS that allows you to determine how much of the CPU is being used by your application. The concept is simple, a 32 bit counter called *OSIdleCtr* is incremented anytime the idle task is running. The higher the value of the counter, the less your application is using the CPU. The following four lines are used to find out how high this counter would be if your application's code was never given control of the CPU:

```
OSTimeDly(1);
OSIdleCtr = 0L;
OSTimeDly(18);
max = (double)OSIdleCtr;
```

The first delay is used to synchronize to the system tick. Next, the idle counter is cleared and then a delay of 18 ticks is executed. Since we only have one task, the idle task will now get the CPU for a whole 18 clock ticks. At the end of the delay, the idle counter contains the highest value it can reach if no other task is executing. From now on (with other tasks executing) all we need to do is to reset the idle counter, delay 18 ticks and compare the value of the idle counter against the maximum obtained. The percentage of the CPU being used is determined by:

```
(1 - OSIdleCtr / max) * 100
```

After determining the maximum value of the idle counter, the ten application tasks are created. Each task uses the reentrant function *Task ()* (described later). Since the *Stat ()* task has the lowest priority, as soon as a task is created, it is given control of the CPU. Since *Task ()* starts with a delay of one tick, control returns to the *Stat ()* task which then completes the creation of the other tasks. Once all tasks are created, the *Stat ()* task begins its infinite loop. The *Stat ()* task now performs two operations. The first operation is to display the following statistics:

1) The number of context switches being performed per second

2) The current CPU usage in percent

3) The current value of the idle counter

4) The maximum value for the idle counter

7

151

I also added a counter that is incremented every time a context switch occurs (see *OSSched()*). For Example #1, the number of context switches is:

```
#Ctx Sw. = Number of interrupts (per 18 ticks) +
           Number of interrupts (per 18 ticks) * 10 tasks
           Number of times Stat() is executed per 18 ticks

#ctx Sw. = 18 + (18 * 10) + 1
         = 199
```

The statistics are displayed at the bottom of the screen.

The second operation performed by the *Stat()* task is to determine if the user desires to quit the program and return to DOS. The program returns to DOS when any key is pressed. Prior to returning to DOS, the PC's BIOS tick ISR is restored, the screen is cleared and the *BP* and *SP* registers are restored to their original state. Note that the code for this example would have to be modified for other memory models.

Task() is a reentrant task which executes every clock tick. The function acquires the random number semaphore, determines a random X and Y coordinate to display its I.D., releases the semaphore and displays its I.D. at this random X and Y coordinate. Note that the function calls *DispChar()*. Since more than one task will be displaying its I.D. on the screen, *DispChar()* ensures that only one task will be able to write to the display at any given time. *DispStr()* is a similar function, except that it displays an ASCII string on the screen.

Example #2

Listing 7.3 presents the code for second example (*EX2.C*). This code creates six tasks:

1) Statistics task

2) Keyboard monitoring task

3) Clock task

4) Task pending on a mailbox

5) Task pending on a queue

6) Task displaying characters at random positions

The code starts execution from *main()*. The screen is first cleared and then the current value of the stack pointer and base pointers are saved to allow for the program to cleanly return to DOS with the same state it had prior to multitasking.

As with Example #1, µC/OS uses the PC's periodic time base (18.20648 Hz or a period of 54.925 mS) as a system tick.

Again, because the PC's BIOS is non-reentrant, a display semaphore is created to provide exclusive access to this resource. The semaphore is initialized to 1 to indicate that only one task may access the display at any given time. A mailbox and a queue are created (described later).

I once again created a task which will create all other tasks. I called this task *TaskStat()* since it will be responsible for displaying run-time statistics. The task is given the lowest priority, i.e. 62. Once the *TaskStat()* task is created, *OSStart()* is called to start the multitasking process. Since only one task is created, it will be given control of the CPU by µC/OS.

TaskStat():

TaskStat() starts off by installing the tick ISR replacing the BIOS's *INT 08H*.µC/OS's tick ISR is found in *TICK.ASM*. As with Example #1, the maximum value taken by the idle counter is determined. *TaskStat()* then creates the other five tasks. Since these tasks have a higher priority than *TaskStat()* µC/OS will preempt *TaskStat()* and give control of the CPU to the highest priority task ready to run. Control will return to *TaskStat()* when all five tasks are unable to execute (are blocked).

The infinite loop in *TaskStat()* performs the same function as in example #1 except that the keyboard is not monitored in this task.

TaskKey():

TaskKey() monitors the keyboard. If the *1* key is pressed, a message is send to *Task1()* through a mailbox. If the *2* key is pressed, a message is sent to *Task2()* through a queue. If the *x* or *X* key is pressed, the application terminates and returns to DOS.

The keyboard task also increments a counter every time it executes. This counter is displayed on the screen to show that the keyboard task is receiving attention from the CPU.

Task1():

Task1() waits for messages from the keyboard task. Messages are received through a mailbox. If a message is not received withing 36 system ticks, a timeout counter is incremented. If a message is received before the timeout, a message counter is incremented. Both counters are displayed.

7

Task2():

Task2() works very much like *Task1()* except that it accepts messages from a queue instead of a mailbox. *Task2()* increments the timeout counter if a message is not received within 72 system ticks.

Task3():

Task3() displays one of 4 characters at random positions on the upper right hand side of the screen. *Task3()* executes every system tick.

TaskClk():

TaskClk() is used to display the current date and time on the screen.

```
                                    Listing 7.3

/*
*******************************************************************************************
*                            uCOS, The Real-Time Kernel
*
*                                    EXAMPLE #2
*******************************************************************************************
*/

#include "INCLUDES.H"

/*
*******************************************************************************************
*                                    CONSTANTS
*******************************************************************************************
*/

#define        TASK_STK_SIZE    1024            /* Size of each task's stacks (# of bytes)   */
#define        KEY_Q_SIZE       10              /* Size of keyboard queue                    */

/*
*******************************************************************************************
*                                    VARIABLES
*******************************************************************************************
*/

UBYTE          TaskStatStk[TASK_STK_SIZE];      /* Statistics task stack                     */
UBYTE          TaskClkStk[TASK_STK_SIZE];       /* Clock       task stack                    */
UBYTE          TaskKeyStk[TASK_STK_SIZE];       /* Keyboard    task stack                    */
UBYTE          Task1Stk[TASK_STK_SIZE];         /* Task #1     task stack                    */
UBYTE          Task2Stk[TASK_STK_SIZE];         /* Task #2     task stack                    */
UBYTE          Task3Stk[TASK_STK_SIZE];         /* Task #3     task stack                    */

OS_EVENT       *DispSemPtr;                      /* Pointer to display   semaphore            */
OS_EVENT       *KeyQPtr;                         /* Pointer to keyboard queue                 */
```

Listing 7.3 *continued*

```
OS_EVENT        *KeyMboxPtr;                        /* Pointer to keyboard mailbox           */

void            *KeyQ[KEY_Q_SIZE];                  /* Keyboard queue                        */

void interrupt (*OldTickISR)(void);
UWORD           OldBP;
UWORD           OldSP;


/*
*******************************************************************************************************
*                                    FUNCTION PROTOTYPES
*******************************************************************************************************
*/

void far        TaskStat(void *data);              /* Function prototypes of tasks          */
void far        TaskKey(void *data);
void far        TaskClk(void *data);
void far        Task1(void *data);
void far        Task2(void *data);
void far        Task3(void *data);

void            DispChar(UBYTE x, UBYTE y, char  c);
void            DispStr(UBYTE x,  UBYTE y, char *s);

void far        NewTickISR(void);


/*$PAGE*/
/*
*******************************************************************************************************
*                                            MAIN
*******************************************************************************************************
*/

void main(void)
{
    UBYTE i;


    clrscr();
    OldBP      = _BP;
    OldSP      = _SP;
    OldTickISR = getvect(0x08);                      /* Get MS-DOS's tick vector             */
    setvect(0x81, OldTickISR);                       /* Store MS-DOS's tick to chain         */
    setvect(uCOS, (void interrupt (*)(void))OSCtxSw); /* uCOS's context switch vector        */
    OSInit();
    DispSemPtr = OSSemCreate(1);                     /* Display  semaphore                   */
    KeyQPtr    = OSQCreate(&KeyQ[0], KEY_Q_SIZE);    /* Keyboard queue                       */
    KeyMboxPtr = OSMboxCreate((void *)0);            /* Keyboard mailbox                     */
    OSTaskCreate(TaskStat, (void *)0, (void *)&TaskStatStk[TASK_STK_SIZE], 62);
    OSStart();                                       /* Start multitasking                   */
}

/*$PAGE*/
```

7

155

Listing 7.3 *continued*

```
/*
********************************************************************************************************
*                                        STATISTICS TASK
********************************************************************************************************
*/

void far TaskStat(void *data)
{
    UBYTE  i;
    char   s[80];
    double max;
    double usage;
    ULONG  idle;
    UWORD  ctxsw;


    data = data;                                              /* Prevent compiler warning              */
    DispStr(0, 0, "uCOS, The Real-Time Kernel");
    OS_ENTER_CRITICAL();                                     /* Install uCOS's clock tick ISR         */
    setvect(0x08, (void interrupt (*)(void))NewTickISR);
    OS_EXIT_CRITICAL();
    DispStr(0, 22, "Determining  CPU's capacity ...");       /* Determine maximum count for OSIdleCtr */
    OSTimeDly(1);                                            /* Synchronize to clock tick             */
    OSIdleCtr = 0L;                                          /* Determine MAX. idle counter value     */
    OSTimeDly(18);
    max        = (double)OSIdleCtr;
    OSTaskCreate(TaskKey, (void *)0, (void *)&TaskKeyStk[TASK_STK_SIZE], 10);
    OSTaskCreate(Task1,   (void *)0, (void *)&Task1Stk[TASK_STK_SIZE],   11);
    OSTaskCreate(Task2,   (void *)0, (void *)&Task2Stk[TASK_STK_SIZE],   12);
    OSTaskCreate(Task3,   (void *)0, (void *)&Task3Stk[TASK_STK_SIZE],   13);
    OSTaskCreate(TaskClk, (void *)0, (void *)&TaskClkStk[TASK_STK_SIZE], 14);
    while (1) {
        OS_ENTER_CRITICAL();

        ctxsw      = OSCtxSwCtr;
        idle       = OSIdleCtr;
        OSCtxSwCtr = 0;                                      /* Reset statistics counters             */
        OSIdleCtr  = 0L;
        OS_EXIT_CRITICAL();
        usage = 100.0 - (100.0 * (double)idle / max);       /* Compute and display statistics        */
        sprintf(s, "Task Switches: %d    CPU Usage: %5.2f %%", ctxsw, usage);
        DispStr(0, 22, s);
        sprintf(s, "Idle Ctr: %7.0f / %7.0f  ", (double)idle, max);
        DispStr(0, 23, s);
        OSTimeDly(18);                                       /* Wait one second                       */
    }
}

/*$PAGE*/
```

Listing 7.3 *continued*

```
/*
*********************************************************************************************
*                                    KEYBOARD TASK
*********************************************************************************************
*/

void far TaskKey(void *data)
{
    UWORD ctr;
    char  s[30];


    data = data;                                        /* Prevent compiler warning        */
    ctr  = 0;
    DispStr(0, 5, "Keyboard Task:");
    DispStr(0, 6, "   Press 1 to send a message to task #1");
    DispStr(0, 7, "   Press 2 to send a message to task #2");
    DispStr(0, 8, "   Press X to quit");
    while (1) {
        OSTimeDly(1);
        sprintf(s, "%05d", ctr);
        DispStr(15, 5, s);
        ctr++;
        if (kbhit()) {
            switch (getch()) {
                case '1': OSMboxPost(KeyMboxPtr, (void *)1);
                          break;

                case '2': OSQPost(KeyQPtr, (void *)1);
                          break;

                case 'x':
                case 'X': OS_ENTER_CRITICAL();
                          setvect(0x08, OldTickISR);
                          OS_EXIT_CRITICAL();
                          clrscr();
                          _BP = OldBP;
                          _SP = OldSP;
                          exit(0);
                          break;
            }
        }
    }
}

/*$PAGE*/
```

7

Listing 7.3 *continued*

```
/*
*******************************************************************************************************
*                                         TASK #1
*******************************************************************************************************
*/

void far Task1(void *data)
{
    UBYTE  err;
    UWORD  toctr;
    UWORD  msgctr;
    char   s[30];


    data  = data;
    msgctr = 0;
    toctr = 0;
    while (1) {
        sprintf(s, "Task #1 Timeout Counter: %05d", toctr);
        DispStr(0, 10, s);
        sprintf(s, "         Message Counter: %05d", msgctr);
        DispStr(0, 11, s);
        OSMboxPend(KeyMboxPtr, 36, &err);
        switch (err) {
            case OS_NO_ERR:
                 msgctr++;
                 break;

            case OS_TIMEOUT:
                 toctr++;
                 break;
        }
    }
}
/*$PAGE*/
/*
*******************************************************************************************************
*                                         TASK #2
*******************************************************************************************************
*/

void far Task2(void *data)
{
    UBYTE  err;
    UWORD  toctr;
    UWORD  msgctr;
    char   s[30];

    data  = data;
    msgctr = 0;
    toctr = 0;
    while (1) {
        sprintf(s, "Task #2 Timeout Counter: %05d", toctr);
```

Listing 7.3 *continued*

```c
        DispStr(0, 15, s);
        sprintf(s, "        Message Counter: %05d", msgctr);
        DispStr(0, 16, s);
        OSQPend(KeyQPtr, 72, &err);
        switch (err) {
            case OS_NO_ERR:
                 msgctr++;
                 break;

            case OS_TIMEOUT:
                 toctr++;
                 break;
        }
    }
}
/*$PAGE*/
/*
*********************************************************************************************************
*                                          TASK #3
*********************************************************************************************************
*/

void far Task3(void *data)
{
    UBYTE   err;
    UBYTE   x;
    UBYTE   y;
    UBYTE   z;


    data = data;
    DispStr(50, 0, "---------- Task #3 ----------");
    while (1) {
        OSTimeDly(1);
        x = random(29);                        /* Find X position where task number will appear    */
        y = random(20);                        /* Find Y position where task number will appear    */
        z = random(4);
        switch (z) {
            case 0: DispChar(x + 50, y + 1, '*');
                    break;

            case 1: DispChar(x + 50, y + 1, '$');
                    break;

            case 2: DispChar(x + 50, y + 1, '#');
                    break;

            case 3: DispChar(x + 50, y + 1, ' ');
                    break;
        }
    }
}

/*$PAGE*/
```

7

Listing 7.3 *continued*

```
/*
*****************************************************************************************************
*                                        CLOCK TASK
*****************************************************************************************************
*/

void far TaskClk(void *data)
{
    struct time now;
    struct date today;
    char        s[40];


    data = data;
    while (1) {
        OSTimeDly(18);
        gettime(&now);
        getdate(&today);
        sprintf(s, "%02d-%02d-%02d   %02d:%02d:%02d",
                    today.da_mon,
                    today.da_day,
                    today.da_year,
                    now.ti_hour,
                    now.ti_min,
                    now.ti_sec);
        DispStr(58, 23, s);
    }
}

/*$PAGE*/
```

Listing 7.3 *continued*

```
/*
***********************************************************************************************
*                                   DISPLAY CHARACTER FUNCTION
***********************************************************************************************
*/

void DispChar(UBYTE x, UBYTE y, char c)
{
    UBYTE err;


    OSSemPend(DispSemPtr, 0, &err);
    gotoxy(x + 1, y + 1);
    putchar(c);
    OSSemPost(DispSemPtr);
}


/*
***********************************************************************************************
*                                   DISPLAY STRING FUNCTION
***********************************************************************************************
*/

void DispStr(UBYTE x, UBYTE y, char *s)
{
    UBYTE err;


    OSSemPend(DispSemPtr, 0, &err);
    gotoxy(x + 1, y + 1);
    puts(s);
    OSSemPost(DispSemPtr);
}
```

7

µC/OS Microprocessor Independent Source Code

```
/*
********************************************************************************************
*                                     uC/OS
*                 Microcomputer Real-Time Multitasking Operating System
*                                SYSTEM DECLARATIONS
*
*                    (c) Copyright 1992, Jean J. Labrosse, Plantation, FL
*                                  All Rights Reserved
*
*
* File : UCOS.H
* By   : Jean J. Labrosse
********************************************************************************************
*/

/*
********************************************************************************************
*                                 uC/OS CONFIGURATION
********************************************************************************************
*/

#define uCOS                    0x80    /* Interrupt vector assigned to uCOS               */

#define OS_MAX_TASKS              20     /* Maximum number of tasks in your application     */
#define OS_MAX_EVENTS             20     /* Maximum number of event control blocks in your application  */
#define OS_MAX_QS                  5     /* Maximum number of queue control blocks in your application  */

#define OS_IDLE_TASK_STK_SIZE   1024     /* Idle task stack size (BYTEs)                    */

/*
********************************************************************************************
*                                 uC/OS ERROR CODES
********************************************************************************************
*/

#define OS_NO_ERR             0          /* ERROR CODES                                    */
#define OS_TIMEOUT           10
#define OS_MBOX_FULL         20
#define OS_Q_FULL            30
#define OS_PRIO_EXIST        40
#define OS_PRIO_ERR          41
#define OS_SEM_ERR           50
#define OS_SEM_OVF           51
#define OS_TASK_DEL_ERR      60
#define OS_TASK_DEL_IDLE     61
#define OS_NO_MORE_TCB       70

/*$PAGE*/
```

A

```
/*
********************************************************************************************
*                                  EVENT CONTROL BLOCK
********************************************************************************************
*/

typedef struct os_event {
    UBYTE  OSEventGrp;                  /* Group corresponding to tasks waiting for event to occur   */
    UBYTE  OSEventTbl[8];               /* List of tasks waiting for event to occur                  */
    WORD   OSEventCnt;                  /* Count of used when event is a semaphore                   */
    void   *OSEventPtr;                 /* Pointer to message or queue structure                     */
} OS_EVENT;


/*
********************************************************************************************
*                                uC/OS TASK CONTROL BLOCK
********************************************************************************************
*/

typedef struct os_tcb {
    void            *OSTCBStkPtr;       /* Pointer to current top of stack                           */
    UBYTE           OSTCBStat;          /* Task status                                               */
    UBYTE           OSTCBPrio;          /* Task priority (0 == highest, 63 == lowest)                */
    UWORD           OSTCBDly;           /* Nbr ticks to delay task or, timeout waiting for event      */
    UBYTE           OSTCBX;             /* Bit position in group  corresponding to task priority (0..7) */
    UBYTE           OSTCBY;             /* Index into ready table corresponding to task priority      */
    UBYTE           OSTCBBitX;          /* Bit mask to access bit position in ready table             */
    UBYTE           OSTCBBitY;          /* Bit mask to access bit position in ready group             */
    OS_EVENT        *OSTCBEventPtr;     /* Pointer to event control block                            */
    struct os_tcb   *OSTCBNext;         /* Pointer to next     TCB in the TCB list                   */
    struct os_tcb   *OSTCBPrev;         /* Pointer to previous TCB in the TCB list                   */
} OS_TCB;


/*
********************************************************************************************
*                                  QUEUE CONTROL BLOCK
********************************************************************************************
*/

typedef struct os_q {
    struct os_q *OSQPtr;                /* Link to next queue control block in list of free blocks   */
    void        **OSQStart;            /* Pointer to start of queue data                            */
    void        **OSQEnd;              /* Pointer to end    of queue data                           */
    void        **OSQIn;               /* Pointer to where next message will be inserted  in   the Q */
    void        **OSQOut;              /* Pointer to where next message will be extracted from the Q */
    UBYTE       OSQSize;               /* Size of queue (maximum number of entries)                 */
    UBYTE       OSQEntries;            /* Current number of entries in the queue                    */
} OS_Q;

/*$PAGE*/
```

```
/*
********************************************************************************************************
*                                    uC/OS GLOBAL VARIABLES
********************************************************************************************************
*/

                                        /* SYSTEM VARIABLES                                        */
extern UWORD      OSCtxSwCtr;           /* Counter of number of context switches                   */
extern ULONG      OSIdleCtr;            /* Idle counter                                            */
extern BOOLEAN    OSRunning;            /* Flag indicating that kernel is running                  */
extern OS_TCB    *OSTCBCur;             /* Pointer to currently running TCB                        */
extern OS_TCB    *OSTCBHighRdy;         /* Pointer to highest priority TCB ready to run            */
extern OS_TCB    *OSTCBPrioTbl[];       /* Table of pointers to all created TCBs                   */

/*
********************************************************************************************************
*                                    uC/OS FUNCTION PROTOTYPES
********************************************************************************************************
*/

void      OSInit(void);
void      OSStart(void);
void      OSStartHighRdy(void);
void      OSSched(void);
void      OSSchedLock(void);
void      OSSchedUnlock(void);
UBYTE     OSTCBInit(UBYTE p, void *stk);

UBYTE     OSTaskCreate(void (far *task)(void *pd), void *pdata, void *pstk, UBYTE prio);
UBYTE     OSTaskDel(UBYTE p);
UBYTE     OSTaskChangePrio(UBYTE oldp, UBYTE newp);

void      OSIntEnter(void);
void      OSIntExit(void);

void      OSIntCtxSw(void);
void far  OSCtxSw(void);

void      OSTimeDly(UWORD ticks);
void      OSTimeTick(void);
void      OSTimeSet(ULONG ticks);
ULONG     OSTimeGet(void);

OS_EVENT *OSSemCreate(WORD value);
UBYTE     OSSemPost(OS_EVENT *pevent);
void      OSSemPend(OS_EVENT *pevent, UWORD timeout, UBYTE *err);

OS_EVENT *OSMboxCreate(void *msg);
UBYTE     OSMboxPost(OS_EVENT *pevent, void *msg);
void     *OSMboxPend(OS_EVENT *pevent, UWORD timeout, UBYTE *err);

OS_EVENT *OSQCreate(void **start, UBYTE size);
UBYTE     OSQPost(OS_EVENT *pevent, void *msg);
void     *OSQPend(OS_EVENT *pevent, UWORD timeout, UBYTE *err);
```

A

165

```
/*
********************************************************************************************
*                                       uC/OS
*                 Microcomputer Real-Time Multitasking Operating System
*                                       KERNEL
*
*                    (c) Copyright 1992, Jean J. Labrosse, Plantation, FL
*                                   All Rights Reserved
*
*
* File : UCOS.C
* By   : Jean J. Labrosse
********************************************************************************************
*/

#include "INCLUDES.H"
#ifdef   TURBOC
#pragma  inline
#endif

/*
********************************************************************************************
*                                     CONSTANTS
********************************************************************************************
*/

#define OS_LO_PRIO          63          /* IDLE task priority                            */

                                        /* TASK STATUS                                   */
#define OS_STAT_RDY          0          /* Ready to run                                  */
#define OS_STAT_SEM          1          /* Pending on semaphore                          */
#define OS_STAT_MBOX         2          /* Pending on mailbox                            */
#define OS_STAT_Q            3          /* Pending on queue                              */

/*$PAGE*/
/*
********************************************************************************************
*                     MAPPING TABLE TO MAP BIT POSITION TO BIT MASK
*
* Note: Index into table is desired bit position, 0..7
*       Indexed value corresponds to bit mask
********************************************************************************************
*/

UBYTE const OSMapTbl[]    = {0x01, 0x02, 0x04, 0x08, 0x10, 0x20, 0x40, 0x80};
```

```
/*
******************************************************************************************************
*                               PRIORITY RESOLUTION TABLE
*
* Note: Index into table is bit pattern to resolve highest priority
*       Indexed value corresponds to highest priority bit position (i.e. 0..7)
******************************************************************************************************
*/

UBYTE const OSUnMapTbl[] = {
    0, 0, 1, 0, 2, 0, 1, 0, 3, 0, 1, 0, 2, 0, 1, 0,
    4, 0, 1, 0, 2, 0, 1, 0, 3, 0, 1, 0, 2, 0, 1, 0,
    5, 0, 1, 0, 2, 0, 1, 0, 3, 0, 1, 0, 2, 0, 1, 0,

    4, 0, 1, 0, 2, 0, 1, 0, 3, 0, 1, 0, 2, 0, 1, 0,
    6, 0, 1, 0, 2, 0, 1, 0, 3, 0, 1, 0, 2, 0, 1, 0,
    4, 0, 1, 0, 2, 0, 1, 0, 3, 0, 1, 0, 2, 0, 1, 0,
    5, 0, 1, 0, 2, 0, 1, 0, 3, 0, 1, 0, 2, 0, 1, 0,
    4, 0, 1, 0, 2, 0, 1, 0, 3, 0, 1, 0, 2, 0, 1, 0,
    7, 0, 1, 0, 2, 0, 1, 0, 3, 0, 1, 0, 2, 0, 1, 0,
    4, 0, 1, 0, 2, 0, 1, 0, 3, 0, 1, 0, 2, 0, 1, 0,
    5, 0, 1, 0, 2, 0, 1, 0, 3, 0, 1, 0, 2, 0, 1, 0,
    4, 0, 1, 0, 2, 0, 1, 0, 3, 0, 1, 0, 2, 0, 1, 0,
    6, 0, 1, 0, 2, 0, 1, 0, 3, 0, 1, 0, 2, 0, 1, 0,
    4, 0, 1, 0, 2, 0, 1, 0, 3, 0, 1, 0, 2, 0, 1, 0,
    5, 0, 1, 0, 2, 0, 1, 0, 3, 0, 1, 0, 2, 0, 1, 0,
    4, 0, 1, 0, 2, 0, 1, 0, 3, 0, 1, 0, 2, 0, 1, 0
};

/*$PAGE*/
/*
******************************************************************************************************
*                                    GLOBAL VARIABLES
******************************************************************************************************
*/

        UWORD       OSCtxSwCtr;         /* Context switch counter                                    */
        ULONG       OSIdleCtr;          /* Counter used in OSTaskIdle()                              */
        BOOLEAN     OSRunning;          /* Flag indicating that uCOS has been started and is running */
        OS_TCB      *OSTCBCur;          /* Pointer to current TCB                                    */
        OS_TCB      *OSTCBHighRdy;      /* Pointer to TCB of highest priority task ready to run      */
        OS_TCB      *OSTCBPrioTbl[64];  /* Table of pointers to created TCBs                         */

/*
******************************************************************************************************
*                                    LOCAL VARIABLES
******************************************************************************************************
*/

static  OS_TCB      *OSTCBList;                          /* Pointer to doubly linked list of TCBs                */
static  UBYTE       OSRdyGrp;                            /* Ready list group                                     */
static  UBYTE       OSRdyTbl[8];                         /* Table of tasks which are ready to run                */
static  UBYTE       OSLockNesting;                       /* Multitasking lock nesting level                      */
static  UBYTE       OSIntNesting;                        /* Interrupt nesting level                              */
static  OS_TCB      *OSTCBFreeList;                      /* Pointer to list of free TCBs                         */
static  OS_EVENT    *OSEventFreeList;                    /* Pointer to list of free EVENT control blocks         */
static  OS_Q        *OSQFreeList;                        /* Pointer to list of free QUEUE control blocks         */
static  ULONG       OSTime;                              /* Current value of system time (in ticks)              */
static  UBYTE       OSIntExitY;                          /* Variable used by 'OSIntExit' to prevent using locals */
static  UBYTE       OSTaskIdleStk[OS_IDLE_TASK_STK_SIZE]; /* Idle task stack                                     */
static  OS_TCB      OSTCBTbl[OS_MAX_TASKS+1];            /* Table of TCBs                                        */
static  OS_EVENT    OSEventTbl[OS_MAX_EVENTS];           /* Table of EVENT control blocks                        */
static  OS_Q        OSQTbl[OS_MAX_QS];                   /* Table of QUEUE control blocks                        */
```

A

```
/*
********************************************************************************************************
*                                    LOCAL FUNCTION PROTOTYPES
********************************************************************************************************
*/

static void        far  OSTaskIdle(void *data);
static void        near OSEventTaskResume(OS_EVENT *pevent);

/*$PAGE*/
/*
********************************************************************************************************
*                                    uC/OS INITIALIZATION
********************************************************************************************************
*/

void OSInit(void)
{
    UBYTE i;


    OSTime         = OL;
    OSTCBHighRdy   = (OS_TCB *)0;
    OSTCBCur       = (OS_TCB *)0;
    OSTCBList      = (OS_TCB *)0;
    OSIntNesting   = 0;
    OSLockNesting  = 0;
    OSRunning      = 0;
    OSRdyGrp       = 0;
    OSIdleCtr      = OL;
    OSCtxSwCtr     = 0;
    for (i = 0; i < 8; i++) {
        OSRdyTbl[i] = 0;
    }
    for (i = 0; i < 64; i++) {
        OSTCBPrioTbl[i] = (OS_TCB *)0;
    }
    for (i = 0; i < OS_MAX_TASKS; i++) {                        /* Init. list of free TCBs             */
        OSTCBTbl[i].OSTCBNext = &OSTCBTbl[i+1];
    }
    OSTCBTbl[OS_MAX_TASKS].OSTCBNext = (OS_TCB *)0;             /* Last OS_TCB is for OSTaskIdle()      */
    OSTCBFreeList                    = &OSTCBTbl[0];
    for (i = 0; i < (OS_MAX_EVENTS - 1); i++) {                 /* Init. list of free EVENT control blocks */
        OSEventTbl[i].OSEventPtr = &OSEventTbl[i+1];
    }
    OSEventTbl[OS_MAX_EVENTS - 1].OSEventPtr = (OS_EVENT *)0;
    OSEventFreeList                          = &OSEventTbl[0];
    for (i = 0; i < (OS_MAX_QS - 1); i++) {                     /* Init. list of free QUEUE control blocks */
        OSQTbl[i].OSQPtr = &OSQTbl[i+1];
    }
    OSQTbl[OS_MAX_QS - 1].OSQPtr = (OS_Q *)0;
    OSQFreeList                  = &OSQTbl[0];
    OSTaskCreate(OSTaskIdle, (void *)0, (void *)&OSTaskIdleStk[OS_IDLE_TASK_STK_SIZE], OS_LO_PRIO);
}
```

```
/*
********************************************************************************************************
*                                          IDLE TASK
********************************************************************************************************
*/

static void far OSTaskIdle(void *data)
{
    data = data;
    while (1) {
        OS_ENTER_CRITICAL();
        OSIdleCtr++;
        OS_EXIT_CRITICAL();
    }
}

/*$PAGE*/
/*
********************************************************************************************************
*                                       START MULTITASKING
********************************************************************************************************
*/

void OSStart(void)
{
    UBYTE y;
    UBYTE x;
    UBYTE p;


    y           = OSUnMapTbl[OSRdyGrp];          /* Find highest priority's task priority number      */
    x           = OSUnMapTbl[OSRdyTbl[y]];
    p           = (y << 3) + x;
    OSTCBHighRdy = OSTCBPrioTbl[p];              /* Point to highest priority task ready to run       */
    OSRunning   = 1;
    OSStartHighRdy();
}


/*
********************************************************************************************************
*                                       uC/OS SCHEDULER
********************************************************************************************************
*/

void OSSched(void)
{
    register UBYTE y;


    OS_ENTER_CRITICAL();
    if ((OSLockNesting | OSIntNesting) == 0) {   /* Task scheduling must be enabled and not ISR level */
        y           = OSUnMapTbl[OSRdyGrp];      /* Get pointer to highest priority task ready to run */
        OSTCBHighRdy = OSTCBPrioTbl[(y << 3) + OSUnMapTbl[OSRdyTbl[y]]];
        if (OSTCBHighRdy != OSTCBCur) {          /* Make sure this is not the current task running    */
            OSCtxSwCtr++;                        /* Increment context switch counter                  */
            OS_TASK_SW();                        /* Perform a context switch                          */
        }
    }
    OS_EXIT_CRITICAL();
}
/*$PAGE*/
```

A

```
/*
*********************************************************************************
*                              PREVENT SCHEDULING
*********************************************************************************
*/

void OSSchedLock(void)
{
    OS_ENTER_CRITICAL();
    OSLockNesting++;                                /* Increment lock nesting level              */
    OS_EXIT_CRITICAL();
}


/*
*********************************************************************************
*                              ENABLE SCHEDULING
*********************************************************************************
*/

void OSSchedUnlock(void)
{
    OS_ENTER_CRITICAL();
    if (OSLockNesting != 0) {
        OSLockNesting--;                                    /* Decrement lock nesting level              */
        if ((OSLockNesting | OSIntNesting) == 0) {   /* See if scheduling re-enabled and not an ISR */
            OS_EXIT_CRITICAL();
            OSSched();                                      /* See if a higher priority task is ready    */
        } else {
            OS_EXIT_CRITICAL();
        }
    } else {
        OS_EXIT_CRITICAL();
    }
}

/*$PAGE*/
/*
*********************************************************************************
*                              INITIALIZE TCB
*********************************************************************************
*/

UBYTE OSTCBInit(UBYTE p, void *stk)
{
    OS_TCB *ptcb;


    OS_ENTER_CRITICAL();
    ptcb = OSTCBFreeList;                            /* Get a free TCB from the free TCB list     */
    if (ptcb != (OS_TCB *)0) {
        OSTCBFreeList        = ptcb->OSTCBNext;      /* Update pointer to free TCB list           */
        OSTCBPrioTbl[p]      = ptcb;
        ptcb->OSTCBStkPtr    = stk;                  /* Load Stack pointer in TCB                 */
        ptcb->OSTCBPrio      = (UBYTE)p;             /* Load task priority into TCB               */
        ptcb->OSTCBStat      = OS_STAT_RDY;          /* Task is ready to run                      */
        ptcb->OSTCBDly       = 0;
        ptcb->OSTCBX         = p & 0x07;
        ptcb->OSTCBBitX      = OSMapTbl[p & 0x07];
        ptcb->OSTCBY         = p >> 3;
        ptcb->OSTCBBitY      = OSMapTbl[p >> 3];
        ptcb->OSTCBEventPtr  = (OS_EVENT *)0;        /* Task is not pending on an event           */
```

```
        ptcb->OSTCBNext        = OSTCBList;                    /* Link into TCB chain                */
        ptcb->OSTCBPrev        = (OS_TCB *)0;
        if (OSTCBList != (OS_TCB *)0) {
            OSTCBList->OSTCBPrev = ptcb;
        }
        OSTCBList              = ptcb;
        OSRdyGrp              |= OSMapTbl[p >> 3];              /* Make task ready to run             */
        OSRdyTbl[p >> 3]     |= OSMapTbl[p & 0x07];

        OS_EXIT_CRITICAL();
        return (OS_NO_ERR);
    } else {
        OS_EXIT_CRITICAL();
        return (OS_NO_MORE_TCB);
    }
}

/*$PAGE*/
/*
*********************************************************************************************************
*                                              ENTER ISR
*********************************************************************************************************
*/

void OSIntEnter(void)
{
    OS_ENTER_CRITICAL();
    OSIntNesting++;                                            /* Increment ISR nesting level        */
    OS_EXIT_CRITICAL();
}


/*
*********************************************************************************************************
*                                              EXIT ISR
*********************************************************************************************************
*/

void OSIntExit(void)
{
    OS_ENTER_CRITICAL();
    if ((--OSIntNesting | OSLockNesting) == 0) { /* Reschedule only if all ISRs completed & not locked */
        OSIntExitY   = OSUnMapTbl[OSRdyGrp];
        OSTCBHighRdy = OSTCBPrioTbl[(OSIntExitY << 3) + OSUnMapTbl[OSRdyTbl[OSIntExitY]]];
        if (OSTCBHighRdy != OSTCBCur) {              /* No context switch if current task is highest ready */
            OSCtxSwCtr++;
            OSIntCtxSw();                                       /* Perform interrupt level context switch */
        }
    }
    OS_EXIT_CRITICAL();
}

/*$PAGE*/
```

A

```
/*
*********************************************************************************************
*                                 CHANGE PRIORITY OF A TASK
*********************************************************************************************
*/

UBYTE OSTaskChangePrio(UBYTE oldp, UBYTE newp)
{
    register OS_TCB   *ptcb;
    register OS_EVENT *pevent;
             BOOLEAN   rdy;

    OS_ENTER_CRITICAL();
    if (OSTCBPrioTbl[newp] != (OS_TCB *)0) {                    /* New priority must not already exist */
        OS_EXIT_CRITICAL();
        return (OS_PRIO_EXIST);
    } else {
        if ((ptcb = OSTCBPrioTbl[oldp]) != (OS_TCB *)0) {       /* Task to change must exist          */
            OSTCBPrioTbl[oldp] = (OS_TCB *)0;                   /* Remove TCB from old priority       */
            pevent             = ptcb->OSTCBEventPtr;           /* Get pointer to event control block */
            if (OSRdyTbl[ptcb->OSTCBY] & ptcb->OSTCBBitX) {     /* If task is ready make it not ready  */
                if ((OSRdyTbl[ptcb->OSTCBY] &= ~ptcb->OSTCBBitX) == 0) {
                    OSRdyGrp &= ~ptcb->OSTCBBitY;
                }
                rdy = TRUE;
            } else {
                rdy = FALSE;
                if (pevent != (OS_EVENT *)0) {                  /* Remove from event wait list        */
                    if ((pevent->OSEventTbl[ptcb->OSTCBY] &= ~ptcb->OSTCBBitX) == 0) {
                        pevent->OSEventGrp &= ~ptcb->OSTCBBitY;
                    }
                }
            }
            if (ptcb->OSTCBPrev == (OS_TCB *)0) {               /* Remove from TCB chain              */
                ptcb->OSTCBNext->OSTCBPrev = (OS_TCB *)0;
                OSTCBList                  = ptcb->OSTCBNext;
            } else {
                ptcb->OSTCBPrev->OSTCBNext = ptcb->OSTCBNext;
                ptcb->OSTCBNext->OSTCBPrev = ptcb->OSTCBPrev;
            }
            OS_EXIT_CRITICAL();
            ptcb->OSTCBPrio = newp;                             /* Setup task control block           */
            ptcb->OSTCBY    = newp >> 3;                        /* ... other fields are unchanged     */
            ptcb->OSTCBBitY = OSMapTbl[newp >> 3];
            ptcb->OSTCBX    = newp & 0x07;
            ptcb->OSTCBBitX = OSMapTbl[newp & 0x07];
            OS_ENTER_CRITICAL();
            if (rdy) {                                          /* If task was ready ...              */
                OSRdyGrp                |= ptcb->OSTCBBitY;     /* ... make new priority ready to run */
                OSRdyTbl[ptcb->OSTCBY]  |= ptcb->OSTCBBitX;
            } else {
                if (pevent != (OS_EVENT *)0) {                  /* Wait for event if was waiting      */
                    pevent->OSEventTbl[ptcb->OSTCBY] |= ptcb->OSTCBBitX;
                    pevent->OSEventGrp               |= ptcb->OSTCBBitY;
                }
            }
            OSTCBPrioTbl[newp]  = ptcb;                         /* Place pointer to TCB @ new priority */
            OSTCBList->OSTCBPrev = ptcb;                        /* Link OS_TCB to OS_TCB chain ...     */
            OSTCBList           = ptcb;                         /* ... we assume idle task is present  */
            OS_EXIT_CRITICAL();
            OSSched();                                          /* Run highest priority task ready    */
            return (OS_NO_ERR);
```

```
        } else {
            OS_EXIT_CRITICAL();
            return (OS_PRIO_ERR);                              /* Task to change didn't exist    */
        }
    }
}

/*$PAGE*/
/*
*********************************************************************************************************
*                                       DELETE A TASK
*********************************************************************************************************
*/

UBYTE OSTaskDel(UBYTE p)
{
    register OS_TCB   *ptcb;
    register OS_EVENT *pevent;


    if (p == OS_LO_PRIO) {                                     /* Not allowed to delete idle task*/
        return (OS_TASK_DEL_IDLE);
    }
    OS_ENTER_CRITICAL();
    if ((ptcb = OSTCBPrioTbl[p]) != (OS_TCB *)0) {             /* Task to delete must exist       */
        OSTCBPrioTbl[p] = (OS_TCB *)0;                         /* Clear old priority entry        */
        if ((OSRdyTbl[ptcb->OSTCBY] &= ~ptcb->OSTCBBitX) == 0) {  /* Make task not ready         */
            OSRdyGrp &= ~ptcb->OSTCBBitY;
        }
        if (ptcb->OSTCBPrev == (OS_TCB *)0) {                  /* Remove from TCB chain           */
            ptcb->OSTCBNext->OSTCBPrev = (OS_TCB *)0;
            OSTCBList                  = ptcb->OSTCBNext;
        } else {
            ptcb->OSTCBPrev->OSTCBNext = ptcb->OSTCBNext;
            ptcb->OSTCBNext->OSTCBPrev = ptcb->OSTCBPrev;
        }
        if ((pevent = ptcb->OSTCBEventPtr) != (OS_EVENT *)0) {     /* If task is waiting on event  */
            if ((pevent->OSEventTbl[ptcb->OSTCBY] &= ~ptcb->OSTCBBitX) == 0) { /* ... remove task from */
                pevent->OSEventGrp &= ~ptcb->OSTCBBitY;                        /* ... event ctrl block */
            }
        }
        ptcb->OSTCBNext = OSTCBFreeList;                       /* Return TCB to free TCB list     */
        OSTCBFreeList   = ptcb;
        OS_EXIT_CRITICAL();
        OSSched();                                             /* Find new highest priority task */
        return (OS_NO_ERR);
    } else {
        OS_EXIT_CRITICAL();
        return (OS_TASK_DEL_ERR);
    }
}
/*$PAGE*/
```

```
/*
********************************************************************************************
*                          DELAY TASK 'n' TICKS    (n from 1 to 65535)
********************************************************************************************
*/

void OSTimeDly(UWORD ticks)
{
    if (ticks > 0) {
        OS_ENTER_CRITICAL();
        if ((OSRdyTbl[OSTCBCur->OSTCBY] &= ~OSTCBCur->OSTCBBitX) == 0) {   /* Delay current task      */
            OSRdyGrp &= ~OSTCBCur->OSTCBBitY;
        }
        OSTCBCur->OSTCBDly = ticks;                                        /* Load ticks in TCB       */
        OS_EXIT_CRITICAL();
        OSSched();
    }
}


/*
********************************************************************************************
*                                    PROCESS SYSTEM TICK
********************************************************************************************
*/

void OSTimeTick(void)
{
    register OS_TCB *ptcb;


    ptcb = OSTCBList;                              /* Point at first TCB in TCB list        */
    while (ptcb->OSTCBPrio != OS_LO_PRIO) {        /* Go through all TCBs in TCB list        */
        OS_ENTER_CRITICAL();
        if (ptcb->OSTCBDly != 0) {                 /* Delayed or waiting for event with TO   */
            if (--ptcb->OSTCBDly == 0) {           /* Decrement nbr of ticks to end of delay */
                OSRdyGrp                |= ptcb->OSTCBBitY; /* Make task ready to run (timer timed out) */
                OSRdyTbl[ptcb->OSTCBY] |= ptcb->OSTCBBitX;
            }
        }
        OS_EXIT_CRITICAL();
        ptcb = ptcb->OSTCBNext;                    /* Point at next TCB in TCB list          */
    }
    OS_ENTER_CRITICAL();
    OSTime++;
    OS_EXIT_CRITICAL();
}

/*$PAGE*/
/*
********************************************************************************************
*                                    SET SYSTEM CLOCK
********************************************************************************************
*/

void OSTimeSet(ULONG ticks)
{
    OS_ENTER_CRITICAL();
    OSTime = ticks;
    OS_EXIT_CRITICAL();
}
```

```
/*
*********************************************************************************************************
*                                    GET CURRENT SYSTEM TIME
*********************************************************************************************************
*/

ULONG OSTimeGet(void)
{
    ULONG ticks;


    OS_ENTER_CRITICAL();
    ticks = OSTime;
    OS_EXIT_CRITICAL();
    return (ticks);
}


/*$PAGE*/
/*
*********************************************************************************************************
*                                      INITIALIZE SEMAPHORE
*********************************************************************************************************
*/

OS_EVENT *OSSemCreate(WORD cnt)
{
    register OS_EVENT *pevent;


    OS_ENTER_CRITICAL();
    pevent = OSEventFreeList;                            /* Get next free event control block          */
    if (OSEventFreeList != (OS_EVENT *)0) {             /* See if pool of free ECB pool was empty      */
        OSEventFreeList = (OS_EVENT *)OSEventFreeList->OSEventPtr;
    }
    OS_EXIT_CRITICAL();
    if (pevent != (OS_EVENT *)0) {                       /* Get an event control block                 */
        if (cnt >= 0) {                                 /* Semaphore cannot start negative            */
            pevent->OSEventCnt    = cnt;                /* Set semaphore value                        */
            pevent->OSEventGrp    = 0x00;              /* Initialize rest of event control block     */
            pevent->OSEventTbl[0] = 0x00;
            pevent->OSEventTbl[1] = 0x00;
            pevent->OSEventTbl[2] = 0x00;
            pevent->OSEventTbl[3] = 0x00;
            pevent->OSEventTbl[4] = 0x00;
            pevent->OSEventTbl[5] = 0x00;
            pevent->OSEventTbl[6] = 0x00;
            pevent->OSEventTbl[7] = 0x00;
            return (pevent);
        } else {
            OS_ENTER_CRITICAL();                        /* Return event control block on error        */
            pevent->OSEventPtr = (void *)OSEventFreeList;
            OSEventFreeList    = pevent;
            OS_EXIT_CRITICAL();
            return ((OS_EVENT *)0);
        }
    } else {
        return ((OS_EVENT *)0);                          /* Ran out of event control blocks            */
    }
}

/*$PAGE*/
```

A

```
/*
********************************************************************************************************
*                                        PEND ON SEMAPHORE
********************************************************************************************************
*/

void OSSemPend(OS_EVENT *pevent, UWORD timeout, UBYTE *err)
{
    OS_ENTER_CRITICAL();
    if (pevent->OSEventCnt-- > 0) {                    /* If semaphore is positive, resource available     */
        OS_EXIT_CRITICAL();
        *err = OS_NO_ERR;
    } else {                                           /* Otherwise, must wait until event occurs           */
        OSTCBCur->OSTCBStat = OS_STAT_SEM;             /* Resource not available, pend on semaphore         */
        OSTCBCur->OSTCBDly  = timeout;                 /* Store pend timeout in TCB                          */
        if ((OSRdyTbl[OSTCBCur->OSTCBY] &= ~OSTCBCur->OSTCBBitX) == 0) {  /* Task no longer ready           */
            OSRdyGrp &= ~OSTCBCur->OSTCBBitY;
        }
        pevent->OSEventTbl[OSTCBCur->OSTCBY] |= OSTCBCur->OSTCBBitX;      /* Put task in waiting list */
        pevent->OSEventGrp                   |= OSTCBCur->OSTCBBitY;
        OS_EXIT_CRITICAL();
        OSSched();                                     /* Find next highest priority task ready to run      */
        OS_ENTER_CRITICAL();
        if (OSTCBCur->OSTCBStat == OS_STAT_SEM) {      /* Must have timed out if still waiting for event*/
            if ((pevent->OSEventTbl[OSTCBCur->OSTCBY] &= ~OSTCBCur->OSTCBBitX) == 0) {
                pevent->OSEventGrp &= ~OSTCBCur->OSTCBBitY;
            }
            OSTCBCur->OSTCBStat     = OS_STAT_RDY;     /* Set status to ready                               */
            OSTCBCur->OSTCBEventPtr = (OS_EVENT *)0;   /* Task is no longer waiting for the event           */
            OS_EXIT_CRITICAL();
            *err = OS_TIMEOUT;                         /* Indicate to caller that didn't get event within TO */
        } else {
            OSTCBCur->OSTCBEventPtr = (OS_EVENT *)0;
            OS_EXIT_CRITICAL();
            *err = OS_NO_ERR;
        }
    }
}

/*$PAGE*/
```

```
/*
********************************************************************************************************
*                                    POST TO A SEMAPHORE
********************************************************************************************************
*/

UBYTE OSSemPost(OS_EVENT *pevent)
{
    OS_ENTER_CRITICAL();
    if (pevent->OSEventCnt < 32766) {              /* Make sure semaphore will not overflow            */
        if (pevent->OSEventCnt++ >= 0) {
            OS_EXIT_CRITICAL();
        } else {                                   /* Negative semaphore value means task(s) pending   */
            if (pevent->OSEventGrp) {              /* See if any task pending on semaphore              */
                OS_EXIT_CRITICAL();
                OSEventTaskResume(pevent);         /* Resume highest priority task pending on semaphore */
                OSSched();                         /* Find highest priority task ready to run           */
            } else {
                OS_EXIT_CRITICAL();
            }
        }
        return (OS_NO_ERR);
    } else {
        OS_EXIT_CRITICAL();
        return (OS_SEM_OVF);
    }
}

/*$PAGE*/
/*
********************************************************************************************************
*                                  INITIALIZE MESSAGE MAILBOX
********************************************************************************************************
*/

OS_EVENT *OSMboxCreate(void *msg)
{
    OS_EVENT *pevent;


    OS_ENTER_CRITICAL();
    pevent = OSEventFreeList;                       /* Get next free event control block               */
    if (OSEventFreeList != (OS_EVENT *)0) {         /* See if pool of free ECB pool was empty          */
        OSEventFreeList = (OS_EVENT *)OSEventFreeList->OSEventPtr;
    }
    OS_EXIT_CRITICAL();
    if (pevent != (OS_EVENT *)0) {
        pevent->OSEventPtr    = msg;               /* Deposit message in event control block          */
        pevent->OSEventGrp    = 0x00;              /* Initialize rest of event control block          */
        pevent->OSEventTbl[0] = 0x00;
        pevent->OSEventTbl[1] = 0x00;
        pevent->OSEventTbl[2] = 0x00;
        pevent->OSEventTbl[3] = 0x00;
        pevent->OSEventTbl[4] = 0x00;
        pevent->OSEventTbl[5] = 0x00;
        pevent->OSEventTbl[6] = 0x00;
        pevent->OSEventTbl[7] = 0x00;
    }
    return (pevent);                               /* Return pointer to event control block           */
}

/*$PAGE*/
```

A

```
/*
*********************************************************************************************
*                             PEND ON MAILBOX FOR A MESSAGE
*********************************************************************************************
*/

void *OSMboxPend(OS_EVENT *pevent, UWORD timeout, UBYTE *err)
{

    void   *msg;

    OS_ENTER_CRITICAL();
    if ((msg = pevent->OSEventPtr) != (void *)0) {       /* See if there is already a message      */
        pevent->OSEventPtr = (void *)0;                  /* Clear the mailbox                      */
        OS_EXIT_CRITICAL();
        *err = OS_NO_ERR;
    } else {
        OSTCBCur->OSTCBStat = OS_STAT_MBOX;              /* Message not available, task will pend  */
        OSTCBCur->OSTCBDly  = timeout;                   /* Load timeout in TCB                    */
        if ((OSRdyTbl[OSTCBCur->OSTCBY] &= ~OSTCBCur->OSTCBBitX) == 0) {  /* Task no longer ready  */
            OSRdyGrp &= ~OSTCBCur->OSTCBBitY;
        }

        pevent->OSEventTbl[OSTCBCur->OSTCBY] |= OSTCBCur->OSTCBBitX;      /* Put task in waiting list */
        pevent->OSEventGrp                   |= OSTCBCur->OSTCBBitY;
        OS_EXIT_CRITICAL();
        OSSched();                                       /* Find next highest priority task ready to run */
        OS_ENTER_CRITICAL();
        if (OSTCBCur->OSTCBStat == OS_STAT_MBOX) {       /* If status is not OS_STAT_RDY, timeout occured */
            if ((pevent->OSEventTbl[OSTCBCur->OSTCBY] &= ~OSTCBCur->OSTCBBitX) == 0) {
                pevent->OSEventGrp &= ~OSTCBCur->OSTCBBitY;
            }
            OSTCBCur->OSTCBStat     = OS_STAT_RDY;        /* Set status to ready                    */
            OSTCBCur->OSTCBEventPtr = (OS_EVENT *)0;
            msg                     = (void *)0;          /* Set message contents to NULL           */
            OS_EXIT_CRITICAL();
            *err                    = OS_TIMEOUT;         /* Indicate that a timeout occured        */
        } else {
            msg                     = pevent->OSEventPtr; /* Message received                       */
            pevent->OSEventPtr      = (void *)0;          /* Clear the mailbox                      */
            OS_EXIT_CRITICAL();
            *err                    = OS_NO_ERR;
        }
    }
    return (msg);                                        /* Return the message received (or NULL)  */
}

/*$PAGE*/
```

```
/*
********************************************************************************************************
*                                    POST MESSAGE TO A MAILBOX
********************************************************************************************************
*/

UBYTE OSMboxPost(OS_EVENT *pevent, void *msg)
{
    OS_ENTER_CRITICAL();
    if (pevent->OSEventPtr != (void *)0) {          /* Make sure mailbox doesn't already contain a msg    */
        OS_EXIT_CRITICAL();
        return (OS_MBOX_FULL);
    } else {
        pevent->OSEventPtr = msg;                    /* Place message in mailbox                           */
        if (pevent->OSEventGrp) {                    /* See if any task pending on mailbox                 */
            OS_EXIT_CRITICAL();
            OSEventTaskResume(pevent);               /* Resume highest priority task pending on mailbox    */
            OSSched();                               /* Find highest priority task ready to run            */
        } else {
            OS_EXIT_CRITICAL();
        }
        return (OS_NO_ERR);
    }
}

/*$PAGE*/
```

```
/*
*********************************************************************************************
*                              INITIALIZE MESSAGE QUEUE
*********************************************************************************************
*/

OS_EVENT *OSQCreate(void **start, UBYTE size)
{
    OS_EVENT *pevent;
    OS_Q      *pq;


    OS_ENTER_CRITICAL();
    pevent = OSEventFreeList;                    /* Get next free event control block          */
    if (OSEventFreeList != (OS_EVENT *)0) {      /* See if pool of free ECB pool was empty      */
        OSEventFreeList = (OS_EVENT *)OSEventFreeList->OSEventPtr;
    }
    OS_EXIT_CRITICAL();
    if (pevent != (OS_EVENT *)0) {               /* See if we have an event control block       */
        OS_ENTER_CRITICAL();                     /* Get a free queue control block              */
        pq = OSQFreeList;
        if (OSQFreeList != (OS_Q *)0) {
            OSQFreeList = OSQFreeList->OSQPtr;
        }
        OS_EXIT_CRITICAL();
        if (pq != (OS_Q *)0) {                   /* See if we were able to get a queue control block */
            pq->OSQStart      = start;           /* Yes, initialize the queue                   */
            pq->OSQEnd        = &start[size];
            pq->OSQIn         = start;
            pq->OSQOut        = start;
            pq->OSQSize       = size;
            pq->OSQEntries    = 0;
            pevent->OSEventPtr    = pq;
            pevent->OSEventGrp    = 0x00;        /* Initialize rest of event control block      */
            pevent->OSEventTbl[0] = 0x00;
            pevent->OSEventTbl[1] = 0x00;
            pevent->OSEventTbl[2] = 0x00;
            pevent->OSEventTbl[3] = 0x00;
            pevent->OSEventTbl[4] = 0x00;
            pevent->OSEventTbl[5] = 0x00;
            pevent->OSEventTbl[6] = 0x00;
            pevent->OSEventTbl[7] = 0x00;
        } else {                                 /* No, since we couldn't get a queue control block */
            OS_ENTER_CRITICAL();                              /* Return event control block on error */
            pevent->OSEventPtr = (void *)OSEventFreeList;
            OSEventFreeList    = pevent;
            OS_EXIT_CRITICAL();
            pevent = (OS_EVENT *)0;
        }
    }
    return (pevent);
}
/*$PAGE*/
```

```
/*
*********************************************************************************************
*                                PEND ON A QUEUE FOR A MESSAGE
*********************************************************************************************
*/

void *OSQPend(OS_EVENT *pevent, UWORD timeout, UBYTE *err)
{
    void   *msg;
    OS_Q   *pq;

    OS_ENTER_CRITICAL();
    pq = pevent->OSEventPtr;                          /* Point at queue control block                */
    if (pq->OSQEntries != 0) {                        /* See if any messages in the queue            */
        msg = *pq->OSQOut++;                          /* Yes, extract oldest message from the queue   */
        pq->OSQEntries--;                             /* Update the number of entries in the queue    */
        if (pq->OSQOut == pq->OSQEnd) {               /* Wrap OUT pointer if we are at the end of the queue */
            pq->OSQOut = pq->OSQStart;
        }
        OS_EXIT_CRITICAL();
        *err = OS_NO_ERR;
    } else {
        OSTCBCur->OSTCBStat = OS_STAT_Q;              /* Task will have to pend for a message to be posted */
        OSTCBCur->OSTCBDly  = timeout;               /* Load timeout into TCB                        */
        if ((OSRdyTbl[OSTCBCur->OSTCBY] &= ~OSTCBCur->OSTCBBitX) == 0) {  /* Task no longer ready    */
            OSRdyGrp &= ~OSTCBCur->OSTCBBitY;
        }
        pevent->OSEventTbl[OSTCBCur->OSTCBY] |= OSTCBCur->OSTCBBitX;       /* Put task in waiting list */
        pevent->OSEventGrp                   |= OSTCBCur->OSTCBBitY;
        OS_EXIT_CRITICAL();
        OSSched();                                    /* Find next highest priority task ready to run */
        OS_ENTER_CRITICAL();
        if (OSTCBCur->OSTCBStat == OS_STAT_Q) {   /* Timeout occured if status indicates pending on Q */
            if ((pevent->OSEventTbl[OSTCBCur->OSTCBY] &= ~OSTCBCur->OSTCBBitX) == 0) {
                pevent->OSEventGrp &= ~OSTCBCur->OSTCBBitY;
            }
            OSTCBCur->OSTCBStat     = OS_STAT_RDY;    /* Set status to ready                          */
            OSTCBCur->OSTCBEventPtr = (OS_EVENT *)0;  /* No longer waiting for event                  */
            msg                     = (void *)0;      /* No message received                          */
            OS_EXIT_CRITICAL();
            *err                    = OS_TIMEOUT;     /* Indicate a timeout occured                   */
        } else {
            msg = *pq->OSQOut++;                       /* Message received, extract from queue         */
            pq->OSQEntries--;                         /* Update the number of entries in the queue    */
            if (pq->OSQOut == pq->OSQEnd) {           /* Wrap OUT pointer if we are at the end of the queue */
                pq->OSQOut = pq->OSQStart;
            }
            OS_EXIT_CRITICAL();
            *err = OS_NO_ERR;
        }
    }                                                 /* Return message received (or NULL)           */
    return (msg);
}
/*$PAGE*/
```

```
/*
*********************************************************************************************************
*                                   POST MESSAGE TO A QUEUE
*********************************************************************************************************
*/

UBYTE OSQPost(OS_EVENT *pevent, void *msg)
{
    OS_Q  *pq;

    OS_ENTER_CRITICAL();
    pq = pevent->OSEventPtr;                     /* Point to queue control block                       */
    if (pq->OSQEntries >= pq->OSQSize) {         /* Make sure queue is not full                        */
        OS_EXIT_CRITICAL();
        return (OS_Q_FULL);
    } else {
        *pq->OSQIn++ = msg;                      /* Insert message into queue                          */
        pq->OSQEntries++;                        /* Update the number of entries in the queue          */
        if (pq->OSQIn == pq->OSQEnd) {           /* Wrap IN pointer if we are at the end of the queue  */
            pq->OSQIn = pq->OSQStart;
        }
        if (pevent->OSEventGrp) {                /* See if any task pending on queue                   */
            OS_EXIT_CRITICAL();
            OSEventTaskResume(pevent);           /* Yes, resume highest priority task pending on queue */
            OSSched();                           /* Find highest priority task ready to run            */
        } else {
            OS_EXIT_CRITICAL();
        }
        return (OS_NO_ERR);
    }
}

/*$PAGE*/
```

```
/*
*********************************************************************************************************
*                                MAKE TASK WAITING FOR EVENT READY TO RUN
*********************************************************************************************************
*/

static void near OSEventTaskResume(OS_EVENT *pevent)
{
    OS_TCB *ptcb;
    UBYTE   x;
    UBYTE   y;
    UBYTE   bitx;
    UBYTE   bity;
    UBYTE   p;


    OS_ENTER_CRITICAL();
    y    = OSUnMapTbl[pevent->OSEventGrp];             /* Find highest priority task pending on event  */
    bity = OSMapTbl[y];
    x    = OSUnMapTbl[pevent->OSEventTbl[y]];
    bitx = OSMapTbl[x];
    p    = (y << 3) + x;
    if ((pevent->OSEventTbl[y] &= ~bitx) == 0) {       /* Remove this task from the waiting list        */
        pevent->OSEventGrp &= ~bity;
    }
    ptcb                = OSTCBPrioTbl[p];              /* Point to this task's OS_TCB                   */
    ptcb->OSTCBDly      = 0;                            /* Prevent OSTimeTick() from readying this task  */
    ptcb->OSTCBStat     = OS_STAT_RDY;                  /* Task is ready to run                          */
    ptcb->OSTCBEventPtr = (OS_EVENT *)0;               /* Unlink event control block from this task    */
    OSRdyGrp           |= bity;                         /* Put task in the ready to run list             */
    OSRdyTbl[y]        |= bitx;
    OS_EXIT_CRITICAL();
}
```

A

80186/80188 Microprocessor Specific Source Code

```
/*
********************************************************************************************
*                                      uC/OS
*                Microcomputer Real-Time Multitasking Operating System
*
*                  (c) Copyright 1992, Jean J. Labrosse, Plantation, FL
*                                  All Rights Reserved
*
*                              80186/80188 Specific code
*                                 SMALL MEMORY MODEL
*
* File : 80186S.H
* By   : Jean J. Labrosse
********************************************************************************************
*/

/*
********************************************************************************************
*                                    CONSTANTS
********************************************************************************************
*/

#define  FALSE     0
#define  TRUE      1

/*
********************************************************************************************
*                                     MACROS
********************************************************************************************
*/

#define  OS_ENTER_CRITICAL()   asm CLI
#define  OS_EXIT_CRITICAL()    asm STI
#define  OS_TASK_SW()          asm INT   uCOS

/*
********************************************************************************************
*                                   DATA TYPES
********************************************************************************************
*/

typedef unsigned char BOOLEAN;
typedef unsigned char UBYTE;                /* Unsigned  8 bit quantity                 */
typedef signed   char BYTE;                 /* Signed    8 bit quantity                 */
typedef unsigned int  UWORD;                /* Unsigned 16 bit quantity                 */
typedef signed   int  WORD;                 /* Signed   16 bit quantity                 */
typedef unsigned long ULONG;                /* Unsigned 32 bit quantity                 */
typedef signed   long LONG;                 /* Signed   32 bit quantity                 */
```

```
/*
********************************************************************************************************
*                                            uC/OS
*                        Microcomputer Real-Time Multitasking Operating System
*
*                        (c) Copyright 1992, Jean J. Labrosse, Plantation, FL
*                                        All Rights Reserved
*
*                                    80186/80188 Specific code
*                                        SMALL MEMORY MODEL
*
* File : 80186S_C.C
* By   : Jean J. Labrosse
********************************************************************************************************
*/

#include "INCLUDES.H"

/*
********************************************************************************************************
*                                          CREATE A TASK
********************************************************************************************************
*/
UBYTE OSTaskCreate(void (far *task)(void *pd), void *pdata, void *pstk, UBYTE p)
{
    UWORD *stk;
    UBYTE  err;


    OS_ENTER_CRITICAL();
    if (OSTCBPrioTbl[p] == (OS_TCB *)0) {   /* Make sure task doesn't already exist at this priority   */
        OS_EXIT_CRITICAL();
        stk    = (UWORD *)pstk;             /* Load stack pointer                                      */
        *--stk = (UWORD)FP_OFF(pdata);      /* Simulate call to function with argument                 */
        *--stk = (UWORD)FP_SEG(task);
        *--stk = (UWORD)FP_OFF(task);
        *--stk = (UWORD)0x0200;             /* PSW = Interrupts enabled                                */
        *--stk = (UWORD)FP_SEG(task);       /* Put pointer to task    on top of stack                  */
        *--stk = (UWORD)FP_OFF(task);
        *--stk = (UWORD)0x0000;             /* AX = 0                                                  */
        *--stk = (UWORD)0x0000;             /* CX = 0                                                  */
        *--stk = (UWORD)0x0000;             /* DX = 0                                                  */
        *--stk = (UWORD)0x0000;             /* BX = 0                                                  */
        *--stk = (UWORD)0x0000;             /* SP = 0                                                  */
        *--stk = (UWORD)0x0000;             /* BP = 0                                                  */
        *--stk = (UWORD)0x0000;             /* SI = 0                                                  */
        *--stk = (UWORD)0x0000;             /* DI = 0                                                  */
        *--stk = (UWORD)0x0000;             /* ES = 0                                                  */
        err = OSTCBInit(p, (void *)stk);    /* Get and initialize a TCB                                */
        if (err == OS_NO_ERR) {
            if (OSRunning) {                /* Find highest priority task if multitasking has started  */
                OSSched();
            }
        }
        return (err);
    } else {
        OS_EXIT_CRITICAL();
        return (OS_PRIO_EXIST);
    }
}
```

B

```
;************************************************************************************************
;                                      uC/OS
;                Microcomputer Real-Time Multitasking Operating System
;
;                    (c) Copyright 1992, Jean J. Labrosse, Plantation, FL
;                                  All Rights Reserved
;
;
;
;                                  80186/80188 Specific code
;                                   SMALL MEMORY MODEL
;
; File : 80186S_A.ASM
; By   : Jean J. Labrosse
;************************************************************************************************

           PUBLIC  _OSStartHighRdy
           PUBLIC  _OSCtxSw
           PUBLIC  _OSIntCtxSw

           EXTRN   _OSIntEnter:NEAR
           EXTRN   _OSIntExit:NEAR
           EXTRN   _OSTimeTick:NEAR
           EXTRN   _OSTCBCur:WORD
           EXTRN   _OSTCBHighRdy:WORD

.MODEL     SMALL
.CODE
.186


;************************************************************************************************
;                                   START MULTITASKING
;                                void OSStartHighRdy(void)
;
; Total execution time : 123 bus cycles
;************************************************************************************************

_OSStartHighRdy    PROC NEAR

           MOV     BX,[_OSTCBHighRdy]        ; 9~, Point to TCB of highest priority task ready to run
           MOV     [_OSTCBCur],BX           ; 12~
           MOV     AX,[BX]                  ; 9~, Point to task's top of stack
           MOV     SP,AX                    ; 2~
           MOV     AX,DS                    ; 2~, Stacks are in DATA segment thus set SS to DS
           MOV     SS,AX                    ; 2~
           POP     ES                       ; 8~
           POPA                             ; 51~
           IRET                             ; 28~, Run task

_OSStartHighRdy    ENDP

           PAGE                             ; /*$PAGE*/
```

```
;************************************************************************************************
;                          PERFORM A CONTEXT SWITCH (From task level)
;                                  void OSCtxSw(void)
;
; Total execution time : 182 bus cycles
;************************************************************************************************

_OSCtxSw       PROC    FAR

               PUSHA                            ; 36~, Save current task's context
               PUSH    ES                       ;  8~
               MOV     BX,[_OSTCBCur]           ;  9~, Save stack pointer in preempted task's TCB
               MOV     [BX],SP                  ; 12~
               MOV     BX,[_OSTCBHighRdy]       ;  9~, Point to TCB of highest priority task
               MOV     [_OSTCBCur],BX           ; 12~, This is now current TCB
               MOV     SP,[BX]                  ;  9~, Get new task's stack pointer
               POP     ES                       ;  8~
               POPA                             ; 51~
               IRET                             ; 28~, Return to new task

_OSCtxSw       ENDP

               PAGE                             ; /*$PAGE*/
;************************************************************************************************
;                          PERFORM A CONTEXT SWITCH (From an ISR)
;                                  void OSIntCtxSw(void)
;
; Total execution time : 142 bus cycles
;************************************************************************************************

_OSIntCtxSw PROC    NEAR

               ADD     SP,6                     ;  4~, Ignore calls to OSIntExit and OSIntCtxSw
               MOV     BX,[_OSTCBCur]           ;  9~, Save stack pointer in old TCB
               MOV     [BX],SP                  ; 12~
               MOV     BX,[_OSTCBHighRdy]       ;  9~, Point to TCB of highest prio. task ready to run
               MOV     [_OSTCBCur],BX           ; 12~, This is now current the TCB
               MOV     SP,[BX]                  ;  9~, Get new task's stack pointer
               POP     ES                       ;  8~
               POPA                             ; 51~
               IRET                             ; 28~, Return to new task

_OSIntCtxSw ENDP

               END
```

Software Development Conventions

Conventions must be established early in a project. These conventions are necessary to maintain consistency throughout the project. Adopting conventions increases productivity and simplifies project maintenance. In this section I will describe the conventions I have used to develop μC/OS and other products.

Directory Structure

Adopting a consistent directory structure avoids confusion when either more than one programmer is involved in a project, or you are involved in many projects. This section shows the directory structure that I use on a daily basis. All software development projects are placed in a \SOFTWARE sub-directory from the root directory. I prefer to create the \SOFTWARE sub-directory since it avoids having a large number of directories in the root directory. All files related to μC/OS are located in the following sub-directories:

    \SOFTWARE\UCOS\SOURCE

This sub-directory contains the files *UCOS.C* and *UCOS.H*. These files are target microprocessor independent.

    \SOFTWARE\UCOS\80186S\SOURCE

This directory contains the μC/OS target specific files for the Intel 80186/80188 microprocessor assuming the SMALL memory model (thus the *S* in the sub-directory name). *80186S_C.C*, *80186S_C.H* and *80186S_A.ASM* are the source files for this target microprocessor. *_C* and *_A* in the file names are used to indicate that the source files are in C or assembly language, respectively.

Since μC/OS can be ported to other microprocessors, the following are suggested directory names for the source code for these targets. Note that μC/OS is not limited to these microprocessors.

    \SOFTWARE\UCOS\80186L\SOURCE
    \SOFTWARE\UCOS\68HC11\SOURCE
    \SOFTWARE\UCOS\6809\SOURCE
    \SOFTWARE\UCOS\68000\SOURCE
    \SOFTWARE\UCOS\Z80\SOURCE

Each project which will use µC/OS should be placed in a sub-directory by itself under the *SOFTWARE* directory. Instead of having all files in a project located in a single sub-directory I like to split project related files in these sub-directories. (There is nothing like looking at a project sub-directory containing dozens of files!).

```
\SOFTWARE\project\SOURCE
\SOFTWARE\project\DOC
\SOFTWARE\project\OBJ
\SOFTWARE\project\TEST
```

The *SOURCE* sub-directory contains *pure* project specific source code (i.e. your application's C and assembly language source files). By *pure* I mean source code which is not used to debug or test your application (see the *TEST* sub-directory).

The *DOC* sub-directory contains documentation specific to you application.

The *OBJ* sub-directory will hold the object files created by the compiler and the assembler.

I don't like to mix product build files with project source code. I place all product build files in a *TEST* sub-directory. The *TEST* sub-directory contains product build files (Borland *.PRJ* files, make files, batch files etc.) for creating a test version of the product. A test version will build your product assuming the source code located in the *SOURCE* sub-directory and any *TEST* specific source code you may want to include to verify your application. Note that test source code should be placed in the *TEST* directory and not the *SOURCE* directory. The target executable file (either *EPROM HEX* file or *DOS EXE* file) will also be placed in this directory.

To remove the frustration of navigating through these sub- directories, I wrote a utility program that allows you to *jump* to a directory without having to use the DOS change directory command. This utility is called *TO.EXE* and is described in Appendix E.

C Programming Style

Overview

There are many ways to code a program in C (or any other language). The style you use is just as good as any other as long as you strive to attain the following goals:

- Portability
- Consistency
- Neatness
- Easy maintenance
- Easy understanding
- Simplicity

C

Whichever style you use, I would emphasize that it should be adopted consistently throughout all your projects. I would further insist that a single style be adopted by all team members in a large project. To this end, I would recommend that a C programming style document be formalized for your organization. Adopting a common coding style reduces code maintenance headaches and costs. Adopting a common style will avoid code rewrites. This section describes the C programming style I use. The main emphasis on the programming style presented here is to make the source code easy to follow and maintain.

I don't like to limit the width of my C source code to 80 characters just because today's monitors only allow you to display 80 characters wide. My limitation is actually how many characters can be printed on an 8.5" by 11" page using compressed mode (17 characters per inch). Using compressed mode, you can accommodate up to 132 characters and have enough room on the left of the page for holes for insertion in a three ring binder. Allowing 132 characters per line prevents having to interleave source code with comments.

Header

The header of a C source file looks as shown below. Your company name and address can be on the first few lines followed by a title describing the contents of the file. A copyright notice is included to give warning of the proprietary nature of the software.

```
/*
********************************************************************
*                          Company Name
*                            Address
*
*             (c) Copyright 19xx, Company Name, City, State
*                        All Rights Reserved
*
*
* Filename    :
* Programmer(s):
* Description :
********************************************************************
*/
/*$PAGE*/
```

The name of the file is supplied followed by the name of the programmer(s). The name of the programmer who created the file is given first.The last item in the header is a description of the contents of the file.

I like to dictate when page breaks will occur. This is done by inserting the special comment /*$PAGE*/ whenever a page break is desired. The file is printed using a utility that I wrote called *LISTC* (see Appendix D). When *LISTC* encounters this comment, it sends a form feed character to the printer.

Revision History

Because of the dynamic nature of software, I always include a section in the source file to describe changes made to the file. You may either maintain version control manually or automate the process by using a version control software package. I prefer to use version control software because it takes care of a number of chores automatically. The version control section contains the different revision levels, date and time and a short description of each of the different revision levels. Revision history should start on a page boundary.

Include Files

The required header files immediately follow the revision history section. You may either list only the header files required for the module or combine header files in a single header file. I like to use the latter (shown below) since it prevents you from having to remember which header file goes with which source, file especially when new modules are added. The only inconvenience is that it takes longer to compile each file.

```
/*
*******************************************************************
*                          INCLUDE FILES
*******************************************************************
*/

#include "INCLUDES.H"
```

Naming Identifiers

C compilers which conform to the ANSI X3J11 standard allow up to 32 characters for identifier names. Identifiers are variables, structure/union members, functions, macros, #defines, etc.. Descriptive identifiers can be formulated using this 32 character feature and the use of acronyms, abbreviations and mnemonics (see Acronyms, Abbreviations and Mnemonics). Identifier names should reflect what the identifier is used for. I like to use a hierarchical method when creating an identifier. For instance, the function *OSSemPend()* indicates that it is part of the operating system, it is a semaphore and the operation being performed is to wait (*pend*) for the semaphore. This method allows me to group all functions related to semaphores together.

Variable names should be declared on separate lines rather than combining them on a single line. Separate lines make it easy to provide a descriptive comment for each variable.

I use the file name as a prefix for variables that are either local (static) or global to the file. This makes it clear that the variables are being used locally and globally. For example, local and global variables of a file named KEY.C are declared as follows:

```
static UWORD KeyCharCnt;         /* Number of keys pressed      */
static char  KeyInBuf[100];      /* Storage buffer to hold chars */
       char  KeyInChar;          /* Character typed             */
```

Upper case characters are used to separate words in an identifier. I prefer to use this technique versus making use of the underscore character, ("_") because underscores do not add any meaning to names and also use up character spaces.

Global variables (external to the file) can use any name as long as they contain a mixture of upper case and lower case characters and are prefixed with the module/file name (i.e. all global keyboard related variable names would be prefixed with the word *Key*).

Formal arguments to a function and local variables within a function are declared in lower case. The lower case makes it obvious that such variables are local to a function; global variables will contain a mixture of upper and lower case characters.

Within functions, certain variable names can be reserved to always have the same meaning. Some examples are given below but others can be used as long as consistency is maintained.

```
i, j  and k     for loop counters.
p1, p2 ... pn   for pointers.
c, c1  ... cn   for characters.
s, s1  ... sn   for strings.
ix, iy and iz   for intermediate integer variables
fx, fy and fz   for intermediate floating point variables
etc.
```

To summarize:

formal parameters in a function declaration should only contain lower case characters.

auto variable names should only contain lower case characters.

static variables or functions should use the file/module name (or a portion of it) as a prefix and should make use of upper/lower case characters.

extern variables or functions should use the file/module name (or a portion of it) as a prefix and should make use of upper/lower case characters.

Acronyms, Abbreviations & Mnemonics

When creating names for variables and functions (identifiers), it is often the practice to use acronyms (e.g. *OS*, *ISR*, *TCB*, etc.), abbreviations (buf, doc etc.) and mnemonics (clr, cmp, etc.). The use of acronyms, abbreviations and mnemonics allows an identifier to be descriptive while requiring fewer characters. Unfortunately, if acronyms, abbreviations and mnemonics are not used consistently, they may add confusion. To ensure consistency, I have opted to create a list of acronyms, abbreviations and mnemonics that I use in all my projects. The same acronym, abbreviation or mnemonic is used throughout, once it is assigned. I call this list the Acronym, Abbreviation and Mnemonic Dictionary. As I need more acronyms, abbreviations or mnemonics, I simply add them to the list.

There might be instances where one list for all products doesn't make sense. For instance, if you are an engineering firm working on a project for different clients and the products that you develop are totally unrelated, then a different list for each project would be more appropriate; the vocabulary for the farming industry is not the same as the vocabulary for the defense industry. I use the rule that if all products are similar, they use the same dictionary.

A common dictionary to a project team will also increase the team's productivity. It is important that consistency be maintained throughout a project, irrespective of the individual programmer(s). Once *buf* has been agreed to mean *buffer* it should be used by all project members instead of having some individuals use *buffer* and others use *bfr*. To further this concept, you should always use *buf* even if your identifier can accommodate the full name; stick to *buf* even if you can fully write the word *buffer*.

Table C.1 shows an example of an acronyms, abbreviations and mnemonics dictionary. Note that some of the words are the same in both columns. This is done to indicate that there is no acronym, abbreviation or mnemonic which would better describe the word on the left. When variations of a word can map to the same acronym, abbreviation or mnemonic, the variations are listed on the same line.

Table C.1

Acronyms, Abbreviations & Mnemonics Dictionary

Description	Acronym, abbreviation or mnemonic
Bit	Bit
Buffer	Buf
Change	Change
Clear	Clr
Command	Cmd
Compare	Cmp
Context	Ctx
Count	Cnt
Current	Cur
Delete	Del
Delay	Dly
Empty	Empty
Entries	Entries
Error(s)	Err
Event(s)	Event
Free	Free
Full	Full
Get	Get
Group(s)	Grp
High	High
High Priority Task	HPT
Idle	Idle
Input(s)	In
Initialize, Initialization	Init
Interrupt	Int
Interrupt Service Routine	ISR
List	List
Low, Lower, Lowest	Low
Low Priority Task	LPT
Lock	Lock
Maximum	Max

C

Table C.1 *continued*

Mailbox	Mbox
Minimum	Min
Message	Msg
Number of	N
Nesting	Nesting
New	New
Next	Next
Old	Old
Operating System	OS
Output	Out
Overflow	Ovf
Previous	Prev
Printer	Prt
Priority	Prio
Pointer	Ptr
Put	Put
Queue	Q
Ready	Rdy
Real Time	RT
Resume	Resume
Running	Running
Schedule, Scheduler	Sched
Semaphore	Sem
Start	Start
Status, Statistic	Stat
Stack	Stk
Stop	Stop
Suspend	Suspend
Switch	Sw
Task	Task
Table	Tbl
Tick	Tick
Time	Time
Unlock	Unlock

Comments

I find it very difficult to mentally separate code from comments when code and comments are interleaved. Because of this, I never interleave code with comments. Comments are written to the right of the actual C code. When large comments are necessary, they are written in the function description header.

Comments are lined up as shown in the following example. The comment terminators (*/) do not need to be lined up, but for neatness I prefer to do so. It is not necessary to have one comment per line since a comment could apply to a few lines.

```c
/*
*******************************************************************************************************************
*                                              atoi()
*
* Description : Function to convert string 's' to an integer.
* Arguments   : ASCII string to convert to integer.
*                (All characters in the string must be decimal digits (0..9))
* Returns     : String converted to an 'int'
*******************************************************************************************************************
*/

int atoi(char *s)
{
    int n;                                  /* Partial result of conversion                          */

    n = 0;                                  /* Initialize result                                     */
    while (*s >= '0' && *s <= '9' && *s) {  /* For all valid characters and not end of string        */
        n = 10 * n + *s - '0';              /* Convert current char to int and add to partial result */
        s++;                                /* Position on next character to convert                 */
    }
    return (n);                             /* Return the result of the converted string             */
}
```

#DEFINES

Header files (.H) and C source files (.C) might require that constants and macros be defined. Constants and macros are always written in upper case with the underscore character used to separate words. Note that hexadecimal numbers are always written with a lower case *x* and all upper case letters for hexadecimal *A* through *F*.

```
/*
*********************************************************************
*                        CONSTANTS & MACROS
*********************************************************************
*/

#define KEY_FF          0x0F
#define KEY_CR          0x0D

#define KEY_BUF_FULL()  (KeyNRd > 0)
```

Data Types

C allows you to create new data types using the *typedef* keyword. I declare all data types using upper case characters, and thus follow the same rule used for constants and macros. There is never a problem confusing constants, macros, and data types; because of the context in which they are used. Since different microprocessors have different word length, I like to declare the following data types (assuming Borland C++ V3.x):

```
typedef unsigned char BOOLEAN;      /* Boolean        */
typedef unsigned char UBYTE;        /*  8 bit unsigned */
typedef char          BYTE;         /*  8 bit signed  */
typedef unsigned int  UWORD;        /* 16 bit unsigned */
typedef int           WORD;         /* 16 bit signed  */
typedef unsigned long ULONG;        /* 32 bit unsigned */
typedef long          LONG;         /* 32 bit signed  */
typedef float         FP;           /* Floating Point */

Using these data types, you will always know the size of each.
```

Local Variables

Some source modules will require that local variables be available. These variables are only needed for the source file (file scope) and should thus be hidden from the other modules. Hiding these variables is accomplished in C by using the *static* keyword. Variables can either be listed in alphabetical order, or in functional order.

```
/*
*******************************************************************
*                       LOCAL VARIABLES
*******************************************************************
*/

static char KeyBuf[100];
static WORD KeyNRd;
```

Function Prototypes

This section contains the prototypes (or calling conventions) used by the functions declared in the file. The order in which functions are prototyped should be the order in which the functions are declared in the file. This order allows you to quickly locate the position of a function when the file is printed.

```
/*
*******************************************************************
*                     FUNCTION PROTOTYPES
*******************************************************************
*/

       void      KeyClrBuf(void);
static BOOLEAN KeyChkStat(void);
static WORD    KeyGetCnt(int ch);
```

Also note that the *static* keyword, the returned data type, and the function names are all aligned.

Function Declarations

As much as possible, there should only be one function per page when code listings are printed on a line printer. A comment block should precede each function. All comment blocks should look as shown below. A description of the function should be given and should include as much information as necessary. If the combination of the comment block and the source code extends past a printed page, a page break should be forced (preferably between the end of the comment block and the start of the function). This allows the function to be on a page by itself and prevents having a page break in the middle of the function. If the function itself is longer than a printed page then it should be broken by a page break comment (/*$PAGE*/) in a logical location (i.e. at the end of an *if*, *for* etc. statement instead of in the middle of one).

More than one small function can be declared on a single page. They should all, however, contain the comment block describing the function. The beginning of a function should start at least two lines after the end of the previous function.

```
/*
*********************************************************************
*                        CLEAR KEYBOARD BUFFER
*
* Description : Flush keyboard buffer
* Arguments   : none
* Returns     : none
* Notes       : none
*********************************************************************
*/

void KeyClrBuf(void)
{
}
/*$PAGE*/
```

Functions that are only used within the file should be declared *static* to hide them from other functions in different files.

Function names should make use of the file name as a prefix. This prefix makes it easy to locate function declarations in medium to large projects. It also makes it very easy to know where these functions are declared. For example, all functions in a file named *KEY.C* and functions in a file named *VIDEO.C* could be declared as follows:

```
KEY.C

    KeyGetChar()
    KeyGetLine()
    KeyGetFnctKey()
```

```
VIDEO.C

    VideoGetAttr()
    VideoPutChar()
    VideoPutStr()
    VideoSetAttr()
```

C

It's not necessary to use the whole file/module name as a prefix. For example, a file called *KEYBOARD.C* could have functions starting with *Key* instead of *Keyboard*.

It is also preferable to use upper case characters to separate words in a function name instead of using underscores. Again, underscores don't add any meaning to names and they use up character spaces. As mentioned previously, formal parameters and local variables should be in lower case. This makes it clear that such variables have a scope limited to the function.

Each local variable name **MUST** be declared on its own line. This allows the programmer to comment each one as needed. Local variables are indented four spaces. The statements for the function are separated from the local variables by three spaces. Declarations of local variables should be physically separated from the statements because they are different.

Indentation

Indentation is important to show the flow of the function. The question is, how many spaces are needed for indentation? One space is obviously not enough while 8 spaces is too much. The compromise I use is four spaces. I also never use TABs, because various printers will interpret TABs differently; and your code may not look as you want. Avoiding TABs does not mean that you can't use the TAB key on your keyboard. A good editor will give you the option to replace TABs with spaces (in this case, 4 spaces).

A space follows the keywords *if, for, while* and *do'*. *The keyword else* has the privilege of having one before and one after it if curly braces are used. I write *if (condition)* on its own line and the statement(s) to execute on the next following line(s) as follows:

```
if (x < 0)
        z = 25;

if (y > 2) {
        z = 10;
        x = 100;
        p++;
}
```

instead of the following method.

```
if (x < 0) z = 25;
if (y > 2) {z = 10; x = 100; p++;}
```

There are two reasons for this method. The first is that I like to keep the decision portion apart from the execution statement(s). The second reason is consistency with the method I use for *while, for* and *do* statements.

switch statements are treated as any other conditional statement. Note that the case statements are lined up with the case label. The important point here is that *switch* statements must be easy to follow. *cases* should also be separated from one another.

```
if (x > 0) {
    y = 10;
    z =  5;
}


if (z < LIM) {
    x = y + z;
    z = 10;
} else {
    x = y - z;
    z = -25;
}


for (i = 0; i < MAX_ITER; i++) {
    *p2++ = *p1++;
    xx[i] = 0;
}


while (*p1) {
    *p2++ = *p1++;
    cnt++;
}
```

C

```
do {
    cnt--;
    *p2++ = *p1++;
} while (cnt > 0);



switch (key) {
    case KEY_BS :
        if (cnt > 0) {
            p--;
            cnt--;
        }
        break;

    case KEY_CR :
        *p = NUL;
        break;

    case KEY_LINE_FEED :
        p++;
        break;

    default:
        *p++ = key;
        cnt++;
        break;
}
```

Statements & Expressions

All statements and expressions should be made to fit on a single source line. I never use more than one assignment per line such as:

```
x = y = z = 1;
```

Even though this is correct in C, when the variable names get more complicated, the intent might not be as obvious.

The following operators are written with no space around them:

```
->      Structure pointer operator     p->m
.       Structure member  operator     s.m
[]      Array subscripting             a[i]
```

Parentheses after function names have no space(s) before them. A space should be introduced after each comma to separate each actual argument in a function. Expressions within parentheses are written with no space after the opening parenthesis and no space before the closing parenthesis. Commas and semicolons should have one space after them.

```
strncat(t, s, n);
for (i = 0; i < n; i++)
```

The unary operators are written with no space between them and their operands:

```
!p    ~b    ++i    --j    (long)m    *p    &x    sizeof(k)
```

The binary operators is preceded and followed by one or more spaces, as is the ternary operator:

```
c1 = c2      x + y      i += 2      n > 0 ? n : -n;
```

The keywords *if*, *while*, *for*, *switch* and *return* is followed by one space.

For assignments, numbers are lined up in columns as if you were to add them. The equal signs are also lined up.

```
x        = 100.567;
temp     =  12.700;
var5     =   0.768;
variable =  12;
storage  = &array[0];
```

Structures and Unions

Structures are *typedef* since this allows a single name to represent the structure. The structure *type* is declared using all upper case characters with underscore characters used to separate words.

```
typedef struct line {      /* Structure that defines a LINE      */
    int   LineStartX;      /* 'X' & 'Y' starting coordinate      */
    int   LineStartY;
    int   LineEndX;        /* 'X' & 'Y' ending   coordinate      */
    int   LineEndY;
    int   LineColor;       /* Color of line to draw              */
} LINE;
```

```
typedef struct point {          /* Structure that defines a POINT      */
    int  PointPosX;             /* 'X' & 'Y' coordinate of point       */
    int  PointPosY;
    int  PointColor;            /* Color of point                      */
} POINT;
```

Structure members start with the same prefix (as shown in the examples above).
Member names should start with the name of the structure type (or a portion of it).
This makes it clear when pointers are used to reference members of a structure such
as:

```
    p->LineColor;               /* We know that 'p' is a pointer to LINE */
```

Reserved Keywords

The following keywords should never be used for identifiers. These keywords are
reserved in the C++ language as defined by Bjarne Stroustrup and are thus reserved
for future compatibility.

```
asm
class
delete
overload
private
protected
public
friend
handle
new
operator
template
this
virtual
```

Appendix D

LISTC & HPLISTC

LISTC and *HPLISTC* are utilities to print C source files. *LISTC* is used to print C source code on a dot matrix printer, while *HPLISTC* is used to print C source code on an HP Laserjet printer.

Both *LISTC* and *HPLISTC* will print your source code in compressed mode; 17 characters per inch (CPI). An 8.5" by 11" page (portrait) will accommodate up to 132 characters. An 11" by 8.5" page (landscape) will accommodate up to 175 characters. Once the source code is printed, *LISTC* and *HPLISTC* return the printer to its normal print mode.

LISTC and *HPLISTC* print the current date and time, the filename, its extension and the page number at the top of each page. An optional title can also be printed at the top of each page. As *LISTC HPLISTC* prints the source code, it looks for two special comments: /*$TITLE=*/ or /*$title=*/ and /*$PAGE*/ or /*$page*/.

The /*$TITLE=*/ comment is used to specify the title to be printed on the second line of each page. You can define a new title for each page by using the /*$TITLE=*/ comment. The new title will be printed at the top of the next page. For example:

    /*$TITLE=uC/OS Task Creation Function*/

will set the title for the next page to *uC/OS Task Creation Function*, and this title will be printed on each subsequent page of your source code until the title is changed again.

The /*$PAGE*/ comment is used to force a page break in you source code listing. *LISTC* and *HPLISTC* will not eject the page unless you specifically specify the /*$PAGE*/ comment. If you do not force a page break using the /*$PAGE*/ comment, a short function may be printed on two separate pages if a page break is forced by the printer upon reaching its maximum number of lines per page. The page number on the top of each page actually indicates the number of occurrences of the /*$PAGE*/ comment encountered by *LISTC* or *HPLISTC*.

Before each line is printed, *LISTC* and *HPLISTC* print a line count that can be used for reference purposes.

Both programs work identically, except that *HPLISTC* also allows you to print source code in landscape mode, but *LISTC* only prints in portrait mode.

The programs are invoked as follows:

```
LISTC filename.ext [destination]

HPLISTC filename.ext [L | l] [destination]
```

where:

filename.ext is the name of the file to print and

destination is the destination of the printout.

L or l means to print the file in landscape mode.

Since *LISTC* and *HPLISTC* send the output to *stdout*, the printout can be redirected to a file, a printer (*PRN, LPT1, LPT2* etc.) or a *COM* port (*COM1, COM2* etc.) by using >.By default, *LISTC* and *HPLISTC* output to the monitor.

HPLISTC allows you to print the source file in landscape mode. This allows you to print about 175 columns wide!

The source code for both *LISTC* and *HPLISTC* is shown on the following pages.

```
/*$TITLE=Program to list C source files*/
/*
********************************************************************************
*                                    LISTC
*
*                          Program to list C source files.
*
*
*
* Filename     : LISTC.C
* Programmer(s): Jean J. Labrosse
********************************************************************************
*
*
* Program use :
*
*        LISTC filename.ext [>destination]
*
*        where :
*
*            filename.ext        Is the name of the file to list (with extension)
*            [>destination]      Is the destination of the listed file, it can be:
*                                >PRN       for the printer
*                                >file.ext  for redirecting it to a file
*
* Note: This program is compiled using the Borland International C++ compiler Version 3.0
********************************************************************************
*/

/*
********************************************************************************
*                                  INCLUDES
********************************************************************************
*/

#include <STDIO.H>
#include <STRING.H>
#include <DOS.H>

/*$PAGE*/
/*
********************************************************************************
*                               LOCAL CONSTANTS
********************************************************************************
*/
#define  PRINTER_FORM_FEED        0x0C
#define  PRINTER_COMPRESSED_MODE  "\017"      /* String to set    printer in compressed mode (SI)  */
#define  PRINTER_NORMAL_MODE      "\022"      /* String to return printer to normal    mode (DC2) */
#define  NUL                      0x00
#define  NULLPTR                  (char *)0

#define  TRUE                     1
#define  FALSE                    0
```

209

```
/*
********************************************************************************************
*                                    TYPE DECLARATIONS
********************************************************************************************
*/

typedef  unsigned char BOOLEAN;


typedef struct cmd {                            /* Special comment COMMANDS structure          */
    char  *CmdName;                             /* Name of COMMAND                             */
    void (*CmdFnct)(char *s);                   /* Function to execute when COMMAND is found   */
} CMD;


/*
********************************************************************************************
*                                    FUNCTION PROTOTYPES
********************************************************************************************
*/

        void    main(int argc, char *argv[]);
static  void    ListcInit(void);
static  BOOLEAN ListcChkCmd(char *s);
static  void    ListcNewPage(char *s);
static  void    ListcChangeTitle(char *s);
static  void    ListcHdr(void);
static  void    ListcGetDate(char *s);
static  void    ListcGetTime(char *s);

/*$PAGE*/
/*
********************************************************************************************
*                                    GLOBAL VARIABLES
********************************************************************************************
*/

static  char    ListcInStr[256];               /* Input  String                               */
static  char    ListcDate[30];                  /* Current Date                                */
static  char    ListcTime[30];                  /* Current Time                                */
static  char    ListcFileName[100];            /* File Name                                   */
static  int     ListcLineN;                     /* Line counter                                */
static  int     ListcPageN;                     /* Page counter                                */
static  char    ListcTitle[150];               /* Page TITLE                                  */
static  FILE    *ListcSrcFile;                  /* File pointer (Input file)                   */

/*
********************************************************************************************
*                                    TABLES
********************************************************************************************
*/

static  char    *ListcMonths[] = {              /* Table of MONTHs                             */
    "",
    "January",
    "February",
    "March",
    "April",
    "May",
```

```
        "June",
        "July",
        "August",
        "September",
        "October",

        "November",
        "December"
};


static  CMD  ListcCmdTable[] = {                        /* Table of comment COMMANDS            */
    {"page",    ListcNewPage},                          /* PAGE break command                  */
    {"PAGE",    ListcNewPage},
    {"title",   ListcChangeTitle},                      /* TITLE command                       */
    {"TITLE",   ListcChangeTitle},
    {"",        (void (*)())0}
};

/*$PAGE*/
/*
**********************************************************************************************************
*                                    LISTC ENTRY POINT
**********************************************************************************************************
*/

void main(int argc, char *argv[])
{
    if (argc < 2 || argc > 3) {                         /* Valid number of arguments ?         */
        fprintf(stdout, "\n\n");
        fprintf(stdout, "Name of file to print missing, use:\n\n"); /* Display program invocation */
        fprintf(stdout, "     LISTC filename.ext [>destination]\n");
        return;
    }
    ListcInit();                                        /* Perform initializations             */
    strcpy(ListcFileName, argv[1]);                     /* Get file name                       */
    ListcSrcFile = fopen(ListcFileName, "r");           /* Open file to list                   */
    if (ListcSrcFile == NULL) {                         /* Make sure that file got opened      */
        fprintf(stdout, "Cannot open %s.\n", ListcFileName); /* Display error message          */
        return;
    }
    ListcHdr();                                         /* Print page header                   */
    while (fgets(ListcInStr, 250, ListcSrcFile) != NULL) { /* Print code                       */
        if (ListcChkCmd(ListcInStr) == FALSE) {         /* See if input line is a command      */
            fprintf(stdout, "%04d  %s", ListcLineN, ListcInStr);
        }
        ListcLineN++;
    }
    fclose(ListcSrcFile);                               /* Close input file                    */
    fprintf(stdout, "%c", PRINTER_FORM_FEED);
    fprintf(stdout, "%s", PRINTER_NORMAL_MODE);         /* Set printer to normal mode          */
}
```

```
/*
*********************************************************************************************
*                                   INITIALIZE LISTC
*********************************************************************************************
*/

static void ListcInit(void)
{
    ListcLineN = 1;
    ListcPageN = 1;
    strcpy(ListcTitle, "");                          /* No TITLE when we start                 */
    ListcGetDate(ListcDate);                         /* Get the current date 'Month day, year' */

    ListcGetTime(ListcTime);                         /* Get the current time 'HH:MM:SS'        */
    fprintf(stdout, "%s", PRINTER_COMPRESSED_MODE);  /* Force printer into compressed mode     */
}

/*$PAGE*/
/*
*********************************************************************************************
*                                CHECK FOR LISTC COMMAND
*********************************************************************************************
*/

static BOOLEAN ListcChkCmd(char *s)
{
    char  *p1;                                       /* Pointer to command name                */
    char  *p2;                                       /* Pointer to command buffer              */
    CMD   *ptr;                                      /* Pointer to table of available cmds     */
    char  cmd[80];                                   /* Buffer to hold the command name        */


    cmd[0] = NUL;
    p1     = strchr(s, '$');                         /* Look for '$' in string                 */
    if (p1 != NULLPTR) {                             /* See if we found a '$'                  */
        p1++;                                        /* We did, position on next character     */
        p2 = &cmd[0];                                /* Set up to copy command to buffer       */
        while (*p1 != NUL && strchr(" =*", *p1) == NULLPTR) {  /* Copy cmd until '=', '*', ' ' or NUL */
            *p2++ = *p1++;
        }
        *p2 = NUL;                                   /* Append NUL at end of command           */
        ptr = &ListcCmdTable[0];                     /* Search for command in command table    */
        while (ptr->CmdName[0] != NUL) {             /* Go through the whole command table     */
            if (strcmp(ptr->CmdName, cmd) == 0) {    /* See if we found the cmd to execute     */
                ptr->CmdFnct(p1);                    /* We found the command name,             */
                return (TRUE);                       /* ... execute the function               */
            } else {
                ptr++;                               /* Look for next entry in cmd table       */
            }
        }
    }
    return (FALSE);
}

/*$PAGE*/
```

D

```c
/*
********************************************************************************************
*                              LISTC 'PAGE' COMMAND HANDLER
********************************************************************************************
*/

static void ListcNewPage(char *s)
{
    s[0] = s[0];                                        /* Prevent compiler warning              */
    ListcPageN++;                                       /* Increment the page counter            */
    fprintf(stdout, "%c", PRINTER_FORM_FEED);           /* Issue a form feed                     */
    ListcHdr();                                         /* Make the page header                  */
}


/*
********************************************************************************************
*                              LISTC 'TITLE' COMMAND HANDLER
********************************************************************************************
*/

static void ListcChangeTitle(char *s)
{
    char *p1;


    ListcTitle[0] = NUL;                                /* Initialize the TITLE to empty         */
    p1            = &ListcTitle[0];                     /* Position at beginning of destination  */
    s++;                                                /* Ignore the '='                        */
    while (*s != NUL && strchr("*", *s) == NULLPTR) {   /* Copy command until '*' or NUL         */
        *p1++ = *s++;
    }
    *p1 = NUL;                                          /* Append NUL terminator at end of command */
}

/*$PAGE*/
/*
********************************************************************************************
*                                   PRINT PAGE HEADER
********************************************************************************************
*/

static void ListcHdr(void)
{
    fprintf(stdout, "                   ");
    fprintf(stdout, "%-15s          ", ListcDate);
    fprintf(stdout, "%-15s          ", ListcTime);
    fprintf(stdout, "%-20s          ", ListcFileName);
    fprintf(stdout, "  Page: %03d\n", ListcPageN);
    if (ListcTitle[0] != NUL) {
        fprintf(stdout, "                        %s\n", ListcTitle);      /* Output TITLE if we have a title    */
    }
    fprintf(stdout, "\n\n");
}
```

```
/*
******************************************************************************************
*                                 GET CURRENT DATE
******************************************************************************************
*/

static void ListcGetDate(char *str)
{
    struct date today;                          /* Structure to hold current date        */

    getdate(&today);                            /* Function to get the current DATE       */
    sprintf(str, "%s %2d, %4d", ListcMonths[today.da_mon], today.da_day, today.da_year);
}


/*
******************************************************************************************
*                                 GET CURRENT TIME
******************************************************************************************
*/

static void ListcGetTime(char *str)
{
    struct time now;                            /* Structure to hold current time        */

    gettime(&now);                              /* Function to get the current TIME       */
    sprintf(str, "%02d:%02d:%02d", now.ti_hour, now.ti_min, now.ti_sec);
}
```

```
/*$TITLE=Program to list C source files on an HP Laserjet printer*/
/*
*******************************************************************************************************
*                                          HPLISTC
*
*                     Program to list C source files on an HP Laserjet Printer
*
*
*
* Filename     : HPLISTC.C
* Programmer(s): Jean J. Labrosse
*******************************************************************************************************
*
*
* Program use :
*
*         HPLISTC filename.ext [L | P] [>destination]
*
*         where :
*
*              filename.ext        Is the name of the file to list (with extension)
*              [L]                 Indicates that the printer will print in LANDSCAPE mode
*              [P]                 Indicates that the printer will print in PORTRAIT  mode (default)
*              [>destination]      Is the destination of the listed file, it can be:
*                                       >PRN       for the printer
*                                       >file.ext  for redirecting it to a file
*
* Note: This program is compiled using the Borland International C++ compiler Version 3.0
*******************************************************************************************************
*/




/*
*******************************************************************************************************
*                                          INCLUDES
*******************************************************************************************************
*/

#include <STDIO.H>
#include <STRING.H>
#include <DOS.H>

/*$PAGE*/
```

```
/*
********************************************************************************
*                              LOCAL CONSTANTS
********************************************************************************
*/
#define  PRINTER_FORM_FEED        0x0C
#define  PRINTER_COMPRESSED_MODE  "\x01B(11U\x01B(s0P\x01B(s16.6H\x01B(s8.5V"  /* String to set    Laser-
Jet in compressed mode.*/
#define  PRINTER_LANDSCAPE        "\x01B&l1O"                                 /* String to set    Laser-
Jet in LANDSCAPE  mode.*/
#define  PRINTER_NORMAL_MODE      "\x01B&l0O\033E"                            /* String to return Laser-
Jet to normal    mode.*/
#define  PRINTER_PAGE_LENGTH      "\x01B&l2E\x01B&l7.6C\x01B&l66F"            /* String to set    Laser-
Jet to 66 lines/page.   */
#define  NUL                      0x00
#define  NULLPTR                  (char *)0

#define  PORTRAIT                 0
#define  LANDSCAPE                1

#define  TRUE                     1

#define  FALSE                    0



/*
********************************************************************************
*                              TYPE DECLARATIONS
********************************************************************************
*/

typedef  unsigned char BOOLEAN;


typedef struct cmd {                          /* Special comment COMMANDS structure          */
    char   *CmdName;                          /* Name of COMMAND                             */
    void (*CmdFnct)(char *s);                 /* Function to execute when COMMAND is found   */
} CMD;




/*
********************************************************************************
*                              FUNCTION PROTOTYPES
********************************************************************************
*/


        void      main(int argc, char *argv[]);
static  void      ListcInit(void);
static  BOOLEAN   ListcChkCmd(char *s);
static  void      ListcNewPage(char *s);
static  void      ListcChangeTitle(char *s);
static  void      ListcHdr(void);
static  void      ListcGetDate(char *s);
static  void      ListcGetTime(char *s);

/*$PAGE*/
```

216

```
/*
******************************************************************************************************
*                                     GLOBAL VARIABLES
******************************************************************************************************
*/

static  char        ListcInStr[256];              /* Input  String                          */
static  char        ListcDate[30];                /* Current Date                           */
static  char        ListcTime[30];                /* Current Time                           */
static  char        ListcFileName[100];           /* File Name                              */
static  int         ListcLineN;                   /* Line counter                           */
static  int         ListcPageN;                   /* Page counter                           */
static  char        ListcTitle[150];              /* Page TITLE                             */
static  FILE        *ListcSrcFile;                /* File pointer (Input file)              */
static  int         ListcMode;


/*
******************************************************************************************************
*                                          TABLES
******************************************************************************************************
*/

static  char        *ListcMonths[] = {            /* Table of MONTHs                        */
    "",
    "January",
    "February",

    "March",
    "April",
    "May",
    "June",
    "July",
    "August",
    "September",
    "October",
    "November",
    "December"
};




static  CMD  ListcCmdTable[] = {                  /* Table of comment COMMANDS              */
    {"page",    ListcNewPage},                    /* PAGE break command                     */
    {"PAGE",    ListcNewPage},
    {"title",   ListcChangeTitle},                /* TITLE command                          */
    {"TITLE",   ListcChangeTitle},
    {"",        (void (*)())0}
};


/*$PAGE*/
```

D

```
/*
*********************************************************************************************
*                                   LISTC ENTRY POINT
*********************************************************************************************
*/

void main(int argc, char *argv[])
{
    if (argc < 2 || argc > 3) {                              /* Valid number of arguments ?   */
        fprintf(stdout, "\n\n");
        fprintf(stdout, "Name of file to print missing, use:\n\n");
        fprintf(stdout, "     HPLISTC filename.ext [L | l | P | p] [>destination]\n\n\n");
        fprintf(stdout, "     where:\n");
        fprintf(stdout, "          filename.ext is the name of the file to print\n");
        fprintf(stdout, "          L | l       indicates to put the printer in LANDSCAPE mode\n");
        fprintf(stdout, "          P | p       indicates to put the printer in PORTRAIT  mode (Dflt)\n");
        fprintf(stdout, "          destination is the redirected destination of the file\n");
        fprintf(stdout, "                          >PRN      to redirect the file to the printer\n");
        fprintf(stdout, "                          >file.ext to redirect to a file\n");
        return;
    }
    ListcMode = PORTRAIT;                                    /* Default to PORTRAIT mode      */
    if (argc > 2) {                                          /* See if mode is specified      */
        if ((strcmp(argv[2], "L") == 0) || (strcmp(argv[2], "l") == 0))
            ListcMode = LANDSCAPE;                           /* Force to LANDSCAPE mode       */
    }
    ListcInit();                                             /* Perform initializations       */
    strcpy(ListcFileName, argv[1]);                          /* Get file name                 */
    ListcSrcFile = fopen(ListcFileName, "r");               /* Open file to list             */
    if (ListcSrcFile == NULL) {                              /* Make sure that file got opened */
        fprintf(stdout, "Cannot open %s.\n", ListcFileName); /* Display error message         */
        return;
    }
    ListcHdr();                                              /* Print page header             */
    while (fgets(ListcInStr, 250, ListcSrcFile) != NULL) {   /* Print code                    */
        if (ListcChkCmd(ListcInStr) == FALSE) {             /* See if input line is a command */
            fprintf(stdout, "%04d  %s", ListcLineN, ListcInStr);
        }
        ListcLineN++;
    }
    fclose(ListcSrcFile);                                    /* Close input file              */
    fprintf(stdout, "%c", PRINTER_FORM_FEED);
    fprintf(stdout, "%s", PRINTER_NORMAL_MODE);             /* Set printer to normal mode    */
}

/*$PAGE*/
/*
*********************************************************************************************
*                                   INITIALIZE LISTC
*********************************************************************************************
*/

static void ListcInit(void)
{
    ListcLineN = 1;
    ListcPageN = 1;
    strcpy(ListcTitle, "");                                  /* No TITLE when we start        */
    ListcGetDate(ListcDate);                                 /* Get the current date 'Month day, year' */
    ListcGetTime(ListcTime);                                 /* Get the current time 'HH:MM:SS' */
```

218

```
    fprintf(stdout, "%s", PRINTER_PAGE_LENGTH);            /* Set page length to 66 lines per page.  */
    fprintf(stdout, "%s", PRINTER_COMPRESSED_MODE);        /* Force printer into compressed mode      */
    if (ListcMode == LANDSCAPE) {
        fprintf(stdout, "%s", PRINTER_LANDSCAPE);          /* Force printer into LANDSCAPE  mode      */
    }
}


/*
********************************************************************************************
*                                CHECK FOR LISTC COMMAND
********************************************************************************************
*/

static BOOLEAN ListcChkCmd(char *s)
{
    char  *p1;                                             /* Pointer to command name                */
    char  *p2;                                             /* Pointer to command buffer              */
    CMD   *ptr;                                            /* Pointer to table of available cmds     */
    char  cmd[80];                                         /* Buffer to hold the command name        */


    cmd[0] = NUL;
    p1     = strchr(s, '$');                               /* Look for '$' in string                 */
    if (p1 != NULLPTR) {                                   /* See if we found a '$'                   */
        p1++;                                              /* We did, position on next character     */
        p2 = &cmd[0];                                      /* Set up to copy command to buffer       */
        while (*p1 != NUL && strchr(" =*", *p1) == NULLPTR) {  /* Copy cmd until '=', '*', ' ' or NUL */
            *p2++ = *p1++;
        }
        *p2 = NUL;                                         /* Append NUL at end of command           */
        ptr = &ListcCmdTable[0];                           /* Search for command in command table    */
        while (ptr->CmdName[0] != NUL) {                   /* Go through the whole command table     */
            if (strcmp(ptr->CmdName, cmd) == 0) {          /* See if we found the cmd to execute     */
                ptr->CmdFnct(p1);                          /* We found the command name,             */
                return (TRUE);                             /* ... execute the function               */
            } else {
                ptr++;                                     /* Look for next entry in cmd table       */
            }
        }
    }
    return (FALSE);
}


/*$PAGE*/
/*
********************************************************************************************
*                             LISTC 'PAGE' COMMAND HANDLER
********************************************************************************************
*/

static void ListcNewPage(char *s)
{
    s[0] = s[0];                                           /* Prevent compiler warning               */
    ListcPageN++;                                          /* Increment the page counter             */
    fprintf(stdout, "%c", PRINTER_FORM_FEED);              /* Issue a form feed                      */
    ListcHdr();                                            /* Make the page header                   */
}
```

```
/*
*******************************************************************************************************
*                                   LISTC 'TITLE' COMMAND HANDLER
*******************************************************************************************************
*/

static void ListcChangeTitle(char *s)
{
    char *p1;


    ListcTitle[0] = NUL;                                /* Initialize the TITLE to empty            */
    p1          = &ListcTitle[0];                       /* Position at beginning of destination     */
    s++;                                                /* Ignore the '='                           */
    while (*s != NUL && strchr("*", *s) == NULLPTR) {   /* Copy command until '*' or NUL            */
        *p1++ = *s++;
    }
    *p1 = NUL;                                          /* Append NUL terminator at end of command  */
}

/*$PAGE*/
/*
*******************************************************************************************************
*                                       PRINT PAGE HEADER
*******************************************************************************************************
*/

static void ListcHdr(void)
{
    fprintf(stdout, "               ");
    fprintf(stdout, "%-15s      ", ListcDate);
    fprintf(stdout, "%-15s      ", ListcTime);
    fprintf(stdout, "%-20s      ", ListcFileName);
    fprintf(stdout, " Page: %03d\n", ListcPageN);
    if (ListcTitle[0] != NUL) {
        fprintf(stdout, "               %s\n", ListcTitle);   /* Output TITLE if we have a title    */
    }
    fprintf(stdout, "\n\n");
}
```

```
/*
****************************************************************************************************
*                                   GET CURRENT DATE
****************************************************************************************************
*/


static void ListcGetDate(char *str)
{
    struct date today;                              /* Structure to hold current date        */


    getdate(&today);                                /* Function to get the current DATE       */
    sprintf(str, "%s %2d, %4d", ListcMonths[today.da_mon], today.da_day, today.da_year);
}




/*
****************************************************************************************************
*                                   GET CURRENT TIME
****************************************************************************************************
*/

static void ListcGetTime(char *str)
{
    struct time now;                                /* Structure to hold current time        */


    gettime(&now);                                  /* Function to get the current TIME       */
    sprintf(str, "%02d:%02d:%02d", now.ti_hour, now.ti_min, now.ti_sec);
}
```

D

TO

TO is an MS-DOS utility that allows you to go to a directory without having to type:

```
CD path
```
or
```
CD ..\path
```

TO is probably the utility I use the most, since it allows me to move between directories very quickly. At the DOS prompt, you simply type *TO* followed by the *name* you associated with a directory and then press *Enter* as follows:

```
TO name
```

where *name* is a name you associated with a path. The names and paths are placed in an ASCII file called *TO.TBL* which resides in the root directory of the current drive. TO scans *TO.TBL* for the name you specified on the command line; if the name exists in *TO.TBL*, the directory is changed to the path specified with the name. If *name* is not found in *TO.TBL*, the message *Invalid NAME.* is displayed.

The format of *TO.TBL* is shown below and an example of *TO.TBL* is shown in Figure E.1:

```
name, path
name, path
   .      .
   .      .
name, path
```

You may optionally add an entry by typing the *path* associated with a *name* on the command line prompt as follows:

```
TO name path
```

In this case, TO will append this new entry at the end of *TO.TBL*. This avoids having to use a text editor to add a new entry to *TO.TBL*.

E

```
                        Figure E.1

    A,              ..\SOURCE
    C,              ..\SOURCE
    D,              ..\DOC
    L,              ..\LST
    O,              ..\OBJ
    P,              ..\PROD
    W,              ..\WORK
    LOG,            ..\LOG
    UCOS,           \SOFTWARE\UCOS\SOURCE
    186S,           \SOFTWARE\UCOS\80186S\SOURCE
    186L,           \SOFTWARE\UCOS\80186L\SOURCE
    11,             \SOFTWARE\UCOS\68HC11\SOURCE
    80,             \SOFTWARE\UCOS\Z80\SOURCE
    09,             \SOFTWARE\UCOS\6809\SOURCE
    TO,             \SOFTWARE\TO\SOURCE
    LISTC,          \SOFTWARE\LISTC\SOURCE
```

Referring again to Figure E.1, by simply typing *TO UCOS*, TO will change directory to *\SOFTWARE\UCOS\SOURCE*. Similarly, by typing *TO 11*, TO will change directory to *\SOFTWARE\UCOS\68HC11\SOURCE*. *TO.TBL* can be as long as needed, but each name must be unique. Note that two names can be associated with the same directory as shown in Figure E.1. If you add entries in *TO.TBL* using a text editor, all entries **MUST** be entered in upper case. When you invoke TO at the DOS prompt, the name you specify is converted to upper case prior to searching through the table. *TO.TBL* is searched linearly from the first entry to the last. For faster response, you may want to place your most frequently used directories at the beginning of the file.

The source code for TO is shown on the following pages.

```
/*$TITLE=Command to jump 'TO' a specified project*/
/*
********************************************************************************************
*                                          TO
*
*                             Command to jump TO a specified project
*
*
*
* Filename      : TO.C
* Programmer(s) : Jean J. Labrosse
********************************************************************************************
*
* This program allows the user to change directory by simply specifying a name which is associated with
* the directory's path.
*
*
* Program use:
*
*        TO name [path]
*
*        where :
*
*            name              Is the name associated with a path
*            [path]            Is an optional path used to specify the path associated with the project
*
*        Notes : TO assumes the presence of the file TO.TBL on the root directory of the current drive
*                TO.TBL is an ASCII file which has the following format:
*
*                    name, path
*                    name, path
*                       .    .
*                       .    .
*                    name, path
*
*                where, 'name' is the name associated with 'path'
********************************************************************************************
*/
/*$PAGE*/
/*
********************************************************************************************
*                                      INCLUDE FILES
********************************************************************************************
*/

#include <DIR.H>
#include <STDIO.H>
#include <STRING.H>
#include <CTYPE.H>
#include <CONIO.H>
```

E

```
/*
******************************************************************************************
*                                    CONSTANTS
******************************************************************************************
*/

#define  NUL          0x00
#define  TO_NOT_EOF      0
#define  TO_EOF         -1

#define  TRUE           1
#define  FALSE          0

/*
******************************************************************************************
*                                FUNCTION PROTOTYPES
******************************************************************************************
*/

        void   main(int argc, char *argv[]);
static  void   ToDispUsage(void);
static  void   ToErrNoFile(void);
static  void   ToFindPath(char *project);
static  int    ToAddPath(char *project, char *path);
static  int    ToRdLine(void);

/*
******************************************************************************************
*                                 GLOBAL VARIABLES
******************************************************************************************
*/

static  char   ToName[100];
static  char   ToPath[200];
static  char   ToLine[300];
static  char   ToLineRd[300];
static  FILE  *ToFilePtr;
static  FILE  *ToTempFilePtr;

/*$PAGE*/
```

```
/*
****************************************************************************************************
*                                      TO ENTRY POINT
****************************************************************************************************
*/

void main(int argc, char *argv[])
{
    int stat;


    switch (argc) {
        case 1:  ToDispUsage();                                        /* TO                        */
                 break;

        case 2:  ToFilePtr = fopen("\\TO.TBL", "r");                   /* TO <name>                 */
                 if (ToFilePtr != NULL) {
                     ToFindPath(argv[1]);                              /* Find path assoicated with name */
                     fclose(ToFilePtr);



                 } else {
                     ToErrNoFile();                                    /* \TO.TBL does not exist    */
                 }
                 break;

        case 3:  ToFilePtr     = fopen("\\TO.TBL", "r");               /* TO <name> <path>          */
                 ToTempFilePtr = fopen("ZZZZZZZZ.ZZZ", "w");           /* Create temporary file     */
                 if (ToFilePtr != NULL && ToTempFilePtr != NULL) {
                     stat = ToAddPath(argv[1], argv[2]);               /* Add new entry in \TO.TBL  */
                     fclose(ToFilePtr);
                     fclose(ToTempFilePtr);
                     if (stat == 1) {                                  /* See if unique name ...    */
                         ToFilePtr     = fopen("\\TO.TBL", "w");       /* ... ZZZZZZZZ.ZZZ -> \TO.TBL */
                         ToTempFilePtr = fopen("ZZZZZZZZ.ZZZ", "r");
                         while (fgets(ToLine, 100, ToTempFilePtr) != NULL) {
                             fputs(ToLine, ToFilePtr);
                         }
                         fclose(ToFilePtr);
                         fclose(ToTempFilePtr);
                     }
                     remove("ZZZZZZZZ.ZZZ");                           /* Delete temporary file     */
                 } else {
                     ToErrNoFile();
                 }
                 break;

        default: ToDispUsage();                                        /* default                   */
                 break;

    }
}
/*$PAGE*/
```

E

```
/*
*********************************************************************************************************
*                                DISPLAY THE USAGE OF THIS PROGRAM
*********************************************************************************************************
*/

static void ToDispUsage(void)
{
    printf("TO.EXE\n\n");
    printf("Program to change directory:\n");
    printf("    This program reads a file in the ROOT directory called \"\\TO.TBL\".\n");
    printf("    This file is an ASCII file.\n");
    printf("    This file contains a table of names and their path.\n");
    printf("    This name is separated from the directory by a comma.\n\n");
    printf("Usage:  TO <name> [path]\n\n");
    printf("    To add a new name:\n");
    printf("        Type TO followed by the name and finally, its path\n");
}


/*
*********************************************************************************************************
*                            DISPLAY ERROR MESSAGE SINCE \TO.TBL NOT FOUND
*********************************************************************************************************
*/

static void ToErrNoFile(void)

{
    printf("Error:\n");
    printf("    \"\\TO.TBL\" does not exist.\n");
    printf("    \"\\TO.TBL\" is an ASCII file that contains a name and a path.\n");
    printf("    The file is organized as follows:\n");
    printf("        <name>, <path>\n");
}
/*$PAGE*/
```

```
/*
********************************************************************************************************
*                                    FIND PATH ASSOCIATED WITH NAME
********************************************************************************************************
*/

static void ToFindPath(char *name)

{
    int  stat;
    char *ptr;


    ptr = name;                             /* Convert name to upper case                  */
    while (*ptr) {
        *ptr = toupper(*ptr);
        ptr++;
    }
    do {
        stat = ToRdLine();                  /* Read line from \TO.TBL and extract name & path */
        if (strcmp(name, ToName) == 0) {    /* See if found desired name                    */
            clrscr();                       /* Clear the screen                            */
            chdir(ToPath);                  /* Change directory to path associated with name */
            return;
        }
    } while (stat != TO_EOF);               /* Read all lines from \TO.TBL                  */
    printf("Invalid NAME.\n");              /* Name not found in \TO.TBL                    */
}


/*$PAGE*/
```

E

```
/*
*******************************************************************************************************
*                          ADD PATH ASSOCIATED WITH NAME TO \TO.TBL
*******************************************************************************************************
*/

static int ToAddPath(char *name, char *path)
{
    char *ptr;
    char  buf[20];


    ptr = name;                                        /* Convert name name to upper case          */
    while (*ptr) {
        *ptr = toupper(*ptr);
        ptr++;
    }
    while (ToRdLine() != TO_EOF) {                      /* Read line from \TO.TBL                    */
        if (strcmp(name, ToName) == 0) {               /* See if name already in \TO.TBL            */
            clrscr();                                  /* Clear the screen                          */
            printf("Name <%s> already exist.\n", name); /* Indicate that already exist              */
            return (0);
        }
        fprintf(ToTempFilePtr, "%s", ToLineRd);
    }
    strcpy(buf, "           ");                         /* Place name name within 11 characters      */
    ptr = &buf[0];
    while (*name)
        *ptr++ = *name++;
    *ptr++ = ',';
    ptr    = path;                                     /* Convert path to upper case characters      */
    while (*ptr) {
        *ptr = toupper(*ptr);
        ptr++;
    }
    fprintf(ToTempFilePtr, "%s%s\n", buf, path);       /* Add new name & path at the end of TO.TBL   */
    return (1);
}

/*$PAGE*/
```

```
/*
********************************************************************************************************
*                          READ A LINE FROM \TO.TBL AND SEPARATE TOKENS
********************************************************************************************************
*/

static int ToRdLine(void)
{
    char *ptr;
    char *source;
    char *desti;


    if (fgets(ToLine, 100, ToFilePtr) != NULL) {
        strcpy(ToLineRd, ToLine);
        ptr = strchr(ToLine, '\n');                    /* Remove the newline character        */
        if (ptr != NULL) {
            *ptr = NUL;
        }
        ptr    = strtok(ToLine, ",");                  /* Get name                            */
        source = ptr;                                  /* Remove any spaces                   */
        desti  = &ToName[0];
        while (*source) {
            if (*source != ' ') {
                *desti++ = toupper(*source);
                source++;
            } else {
                source++;
            }
        }
        *desti = NUL;
        ptr    = strtok(NULL, ",");                    /* Get path                            */
        source = ptr;                                  /* Remove any spaces                   */
        desti  = &ToPath[0];
        while (*source) {
            if (*source != ' ') {
                *desti++ = *source++;
            } else {
                source++;
            }
        }
        *desti = NUL;
        return (TO_NOT_EOF);
    } else {
        return (TO_EOF);
    }
}
```

E

Real-Time Kernel Manufacturers

Two recent surveys, one in *Embedded Systems Programming* magazine (January 1992) and the other in *Computer Design* (June 1992), identified about 40 real-time kernel manufacturers. Products are available for 8, 16 and 32 bit microprocessors. Some of these packages are complete operating systems and include a real-time kernel, input/output executive, file management executive, network manager, language interface libraries, debugger and cross-platform compilers. The decision whether you should design your own kernel or purchase one depends on many factors.

BUYING A KERNEL

If you can afford to buy a kernel for your application, do it. Generally, what is important is to get your application quickly to market. Designing your own kernel may delay getting your product out. Buying an off the shelf kernel may give you some piece of mind. Most of these products have been around for some time and are mature (bug free), but this is not always the case. A few years ago, I purchased a kernel from a reputable kernel manufacturer and encountered a serious bug. Unfortunately, it took over one year to get the manufacturer to fix the bug. Excluding this bad experience, kernel manufacturers are generally responsive to getting bugs fixed (or at least they should be). Most kernel manufacturers will also support multiple target microprocessors. This is a benefit since you can port your applications to different environments if needed. As time goes on, kernel manufacturers will also add features to their products.

There are also some drawbacks when purchasing a kernel. The most obvious one is the cost. Pricing varies from one kernel manufacturer to the next. You can buy a real-time kernel for as little as $100 and as much as $10,000. The manufacturer may or may not require royalties on a per system basis. Royalties on the software are treated as if you purchased a chip which gets included with each unit. The manufacturers call this silicon software. Royalties vary between $5.00 to about $250.00 per copy. As with most software products, you also have to consider software maintenance costs that may vary between $100 and $2000 per year. The final cost item is the time it will take you to evaluate the kernels and make a decision. Deciding which kernel to chose is not cut and dry.

The kernel manufacturer may or may not provide you with performance data on its product. I have a hard time with this situation. How can a manufacturer of a real-time kernel not provide you with this information? If performance data is

F

provided, make sure you understand how it was obtained, since performance data can be misleading. Here are some questions to ask:

- How long are interrupts being disabled

- What is and how do you define interrupt latency

- Are kernel services deterministic

- Is performance affected by the number of tasks

- How soon will a higher priority task execute following an event

Also, some kernels are designed around a microprocessor family such as the Intel 80x86. Are there special versions of the kernel for the 8086, 80186, 80286, 80386 etc.? Are there special versions for the SMALL, MEDIUM, LARGE etc. memory models? When evaluating performance data, the target microprocessor used, as well as the memory model must be considered.

Another consideration is whether you can purchase the source code. This is an important factor, since the manufacturer may not be around a few years from now, and you will need to support the kernel yourself. Having the source code does not mean that it's going to be easy to support the kernel. If source code is available, ask to get a sample to see what it looks like.

Writing Your Own Kernel

Writing your own kernel is not a small endeavor, and the time required is often underestimated. When designing your own kernel, you have to account for the time to document, debug, and maintain the kernel.

There are a number of advantages to writing your own. Since you wrote the kernel, you can easily make changes, add features, port it to different target microprocessors, use only the features needed for the application, etc. You also don't have to pay royalties and maintenance fees.

Real-time Kernel Survey

The following tables shows the survey of real-time kernel manufacturers conducted by *Embedded Systems Programming* magazine in the January, 1992 issue. Table F.1 lists the vendors, contacts, systems and chips supported. Table F.2 lists the chips found in the survey. Table F.3 displays the vendors correlated with the systems supported.

Table F.1

Vendor:
   Accelerated Technology Inc.
   P.O. Box 850245
   Mobile, Alabama 36685

Contact:
   Neil Henderson
   (205) 450-0700

Product Name:
   Nucleus RTX

Microprocessor(s) Supported:
   68HC11
   8088/86
   80188/186
   80286
   290xx
   32x32
   680x0
   683xx
   80386/486
   80960
   MIPS
   SPARC

Vendor:
   A.T. Barrett & Assoc.
   11501 Chimney Rock, Ste. R
   Houston, Texas 77035

Contact:
   Ron Hodge
   (800) 525-4302

Product Name:
   RTXC, RTXC/MP

Microprocessor(s) Supported:
   64180/Z80
   68HC11
   8051
   68HC16
   8088/86
   80188/86
   80286
   8096/80196
   V-Series
   680x0
   683xx
   80386/486
   Transputer

F

Table F.1 *continued*

Vendor:
Byte-BOS Integrated Systems
451 Zuni Dr.
Del Mar, California 92014

Contact:
Nick Andrews
(619) 755-8836

Product Name:
Byte-BOS

Microprocessor(s) Supported:
64180/Z80
6800/01/02/03
68HC11
8051
H8/300
68HC16
8088/86
80188/86
80286
8096/80196
V-Series
7700
H8/500
680x0
683xx
80386/486

Vendor:
CMX Company
19 Indian Head Heights
Framingham, Mass. 01701

Contact:
Charles Behrmann
(508) 872-7675

Product Name:
Real-Time Multi-Tasking OS

Microprocessor(s) Supported:
64180/Z80
6800/01/02/03
68HC11
8051
H8/300
Z8
68HC16
8096/80196

Vendor:
Diab Data
323 Vintage Park Dr.
Foster City, CA 94404

Contact:
Richard Kopatschek
(415) 571-1700

Product Name:
D-NIX

Microprocessor(s) Supported:
680x0
88000

Table F.1 *continued*

Vendor:
Digital Equipment Corp.
29 Parker St., Mailstop PK03-2/3K
Maynard, MA 01754-2198

Contact:
Dick Day
(508) 493-6717

Product Name:
VAX ELM, DEC ELX, DEC OSF/1

Microprocessor(s) Supported:
VAX   (ELM)
680x0 (ELX)
MIPS (ELX, OSF/1)

Vendor:
Emerge Systems
114 Sixth Ave.
Indialantic, FL 32903

Contact:
Frank Aaron
(407) 723-0444

Product Name:
RTUX, RTUX-EX, RTUX-SA

Microprocessor(s): Supported
680x0
683xx
88000

Vendor:
Digital Research Inc.
Box DRI
Monterey, CA 93942

Contact:
Bill Fitler
(800) 649-3896

Ptoduct Name:
FlexOS

Microprocessor(s) Supported:
80188/186
80286
80386/486

Vendor:
Encore
6901 W. Sunrise Blvd.
Ft. Lauderdale, FL 33340

Contact:
Richard G. Stone
(305) 797-5403

Product Name:
90 Family

Microprocessor(s) Supported:
88000

F

Table F.1 *continued*

Vendor:
   Enea Data AB
   Box 232, Nytorpsvagen 5B
   S-183 23 Taby, Sweden

Contact:
   Lars Sjoberg
   (46) 87922500

Product Name:
   OSE

Microprocessor(s) Supported:
   64180/Z80
   6800/01/02/03
   68HC11
   8051
   8088/86
   80188/186
   80286
   680x0
   683xx

Vendor:
   Eurostart
   2433 Frances Dr.
   Loveland, Colo. 80537-0722

Contact:
   Sirio Sconzo
   (303) 669-5068

Product Name:
   RTXDOS

Microprocessor(s) Supported:
   80286
   80386/486

Vendor:
   Eyring
   1455 West 820 North
   Provo, Utah 84601

Contact:
   PDOS Sales Dept.
   (800) 375-2434

Product Name:
   PDOS, VMEPROM

Microprocessor(s) Supported:
   680x0

Vendor:
   FORTH Inc.
   111 N. Sepulveda Blvd.
   Manhattan Beach, CA 90266-6861

Contact:
   Randy Leberknight
   (800) 553-6784

Product Name:
   polyFORTH/pFX, chipFORTH/pFX

Microprocessor(s)	Name:
6800/01/02/03	(chipFORTH/pFX)
68HC11	(chipFORTH/pFX)
8051	(chipFORTH/pFX)
8088/86	(polyFORTH/pFX)
80286	(polyFORTH/pFX)
RTX-2000	(polyFORTH/pFX)
680x0	(chipFORTH/pFX & polyFORTH/pFX)
683xx	(chipFORTH/pFX)
80386/486	(polyFORTH/pFX)
i860	(polyFORTH/pFX)
VAX	(polyFORTH/pFX)

Table F.1 *continued*

Vendor:
Genelogic
87 Cherry Ridge Rd.
Hewitt, NJ 07421

Contact:
Gene V. Hartsell
(201) 853-1333

Product Name:
GX/Kernel

Microprocessor(s) Supported:
68HC11

Vendor:
Hewlett Packard Co.
19091 Pruneridge Ave.
Cupertino, CA 95014

Contact:
David Fastenau
(408) 447-5381

Product Name:
HP 1000 RTE-A

Microprocessor(s) Supported:
Proprietary

Vendor:
General Software
P.O. Box 2571
Redmond, WA 98073

Contact:
Stephen Jones
(206) 391-4285

Product Name:
Embedded DOS

Microprocessor(s) Supported:
8088/86
80188/186
80286
V-Series
80386/486

Vendor:
Industrial Programming Inc.
100 Jericho Quadrangle
Jericho, NY 11753

Contact:
Carole Sigda
(516) 938-6600

Product Name:
MTOS-UX

Microprocessor(s) Supported:
6800/01/02/03
8088/86
80188/186
80286
V-Series
680x0
80386/486
88000
i860

F

Table F.1 *continued*

Vendor:
Innovative Integration
4086 Little Hollow Place
Moorepark, CA 93021

Contact:
Jim Henderson
(805) 529-7570

Product Name:
II FORTH, II Monitor

Microprocessor(s) Supported:
RTX-2000

Vendor:
Intel Corp.
5200 N.E. Elam Young Pkwy.
Hillsboro, OR 97124

Contact:
Intel Literature Dept.
(800) 548-4725

Product Name:
iRMX

Microprocessor(s) Supported:
8088/86
80188/86
80286
80386/486

Vendor:
JMI Software Consultants Inc.
P.O. Box 481
Spring House, PA 19477

Contact:
Ed Rathje
(215) 628-0840

Product Name:
C EXECUTIVE

Microprocessor(s) Supported:
64180/Z80
6809
8080/85
8088/86
80188/186
80286
LSI-11
34010/20
290xx
32x32
680x0
683xx
80386/486
80960
i860
MIPS
SPARC
Transputer

Table F.1 *continued*

Vendor:
Kadak Products Ltd.
1847 W. Broadway Ave., Ste. 206
Vencouver, B.C., Canada V6J 1Y5

Contact:
Bill Renwick
(604) 734-2796

Product Name:
AMX

Microprocessor(s) Supported:
64180/Z80
6809
8080/85
8088/86
80188/186
80286
V-Series
680x0
683xx
80386/486

Vendor:
Lynx Real-Time Systems Inc.
16780 Lark Ave.
Los Gatos, CA 95030

Contact:
George Kohli
(408) 354-7770

Product Name:
LynxOS

Microprocessor(s) Supported:
680x0
80386/486
88000
i860
MIPS
SPARC

Vendor:
Micro Digital Inc.
6402 Tulagi St.
Cypress, CA 90630

Contact:
Ralph Moore
(800) 366-2491

Product Name:
SMX

Microprocessor(s) Supported:
8088/86
80188/86
80286
80386/486

F

Table F.1 *continued*

Vendor:
Microware Systems Corp
1900 N.W. 114th St
Des Moines, Iowa 50322

Contact:
Andy Ball
(515) 224-1929

Product Name:
OS-9, OS-9000

Microprocessor(s) Supported:
680x0   (OS-9 & OS-9000)
683xx   (OS-9)
80386/486   (OS-9000)

Vendor: Motorola Microcomputer
Division
2900 South Diablo Wy.
Tempe, AZ 85282

Contact:
Dick Vanderlin
(602) 438-3244

Product Name:
VME exec Microprocessor(s) Supported:
680x0
88000

Vendor:
Modcomp
1650 W. McNab Rd.
Ft. Lauderdale, FL 33309-1088

Contact:
Alan Scharf
(305) 977-1320

Product Name:
REAL/IX

Microprocessor(s) Supported:
680x0
80386/486
88000

Vendor:
Objective:Systems
5430 Bernieres
Saint-Leonard, Quebec
Canada H1R 1N1

Contact:
Louis Lamarche
(514) 325-7139

Product Name:
Interactors C++

Microprocessor(s) Supported:
8088/86
80188/186
80286
80386/486

Table F.1 *continued*

Vendor:
> OnTime Marketing
> Karolinenstrasse 32
> D-2000 Hamburg 36
> Germany

Contact:
> 49-40-43 74 72

Product Name:
> RTKernel

Microprocessor(s) Supported:
> 80286
> 80386/486

Vendor:
> Precise Software Technologies
> P.O. Box 6934, Station J
> Ottawa, Ontario
> Canada K2A 3Z5

Contact:
> Craig Honegger
> (613) 596-2251

Product Name:
> Precise/MPE

Microprocessor(s) Supported:
> 8088/86
> 80188/186
> 80286
> 680x0
> 683xx
> 80386/486
> 88000
> SPARC

Vendor:
> Quantum Software Systems Ltd.
> 175 Terrence Matthews Crescent
> Kanata, Ontario
> Canada K2M 1W8

Contact:
> Tom Anzai
> (800) 363-9001

Product Name:
> QNX

Microprocessor(s) Supported:
> 8088/86
> 80188/186
> 80286
> 80386/486

Vendor:
> Ready Systems
> 470 Potrero Ave.
> Sunnyvale, CA 94086

Contact:
> Jeanie Maceri
> (408) 522-7140

Product Name:
> VRTX

Microprocessor(s) Supported:
> 8088/86
> 80188/186
> 80286
> 80386/486
> 680x0
> 683xx
> 80386/486
> SPARC

F

Table F.1 *continued*

Vendor:
    Real-Time Intelligent Systems Corp.
    16 Summerhill Ave.
    Worcester, MA 01606

Contact:
    James Morrison
    (508) 852-4822

Product Name:
    Activation Framework

Microprocessor(s) Supported:
    80286
    80386/486
    MIPS
    SPARC

Vendor:
    RTMX-Uniflex
    800 Eastowne Dr., Ste. 111
    Chapel Hill, NC 27514

Contact:
    Randy Lewis
    (919) 493-1451

Product Name:
    UniFLEX

Microprocessor(s) Supported:
    680x0
    80386/486
    88000
    i860
    MIPS
    SPARC

Vendor:
    Schneider Software Systems
    3430 List Place #1006
    Minneapolis, MN 55416

Contact:
    AL Schneider
    (612) 926-7979

Product Name:
    IXOS

Microprocessor(s) Supported:
    8088/86
    80286
    80386/486

Vendor:
    Software Components Group
    3260 Jay St.
    Santa Clara, CA 95054

Contact:
    Guy Occhipinti
    (408) 980-1500

Product Name:
    pSOS, pSOS+

Microprocessor(s)	Name:
8088/86	(pSOS)
680x0	(pSOS+)
683xx	(pSOS+)
80386/486	(pSOS+)
80960	(pSOS+)
88000	(pSOS+)

Table F.1 *continued*

Vendor:
Spectron Microsystems Inc.
5266 Hollister Ave.
Santa Barbara, CA 93111

Contact:
Mike Stein
(805) 967-0503

Product Name:
SPOX

Microprocessor(s) Supported:
680x0
683xx
SPARC
MIPS
i960

Vendor:
Talton/Louley Engineering
9550 Ridgehaven Ct.
San Diego, CA 92123

Contact:
Frank Bunton
(619) 565-6656

Product Name:
T/L Executive

Microprocessor(s) Supported:
8088/86
80188/186
80286
V-Series
80386/486

Vendor:
TeleSoft
5959 Cornerstone Ct. W
San Diego, CA 92121

Contact:
TeleSoft Sales
(619) 457-2700

Product Name:
TeleGen2

Microprocessor(s) Supported:
1750A
680x0
80386/486
80960
SPARC
MIPS

F

Table F.1 *continued*

Vendor:
U.S. Software Corp.
14215 N.W. Science Park Dr.
Portland, OR 97229

Contact:
Rich Burns
(503) 641-8446

Product Name:
MultiTask! C Executive

Microprocessor(s) Supported:
64180/Z80
68HC11
8051
68HC16
8088/86
80188/186
80286
8096/80196
V-Series
680x0
683xx
80386/486
80960

Vendor:
VenturCom Inc.
215 First St.
Cambridge, MA 02142

Contact:
Betty Pool
(617) 661-1230

Product Name:
VENIX, E-VENIX

Microprocessor(s) Supported:
80286
80386/486

Vendor:
Willies' Computer Software Co.
2470 S. Dairy Ashford, Suite 188
Houston, TX 77077

Contact:
(713) 498-4832

Product Name:
MTASK

Microprocessor(s) Supported:
80188/186
80286
80386/486

Table F.1 *continued*

Vendor:
Wind River Systems Inc.
1351 Ocean Ave.
Emeryville, CA 94608

Contact:
Mary Stewart
(510) 814-2041

Product Name:
VxWorks

Microprocessor(s) Supported:
680x0
683xx
80960
SPARC
MIPS

Table F.2

MICROPROCESSOR LIST

6800/01/02/03
6809
68HC11
68HC16
680x0
683xx
88000
8051
8080/85
8086/88
80186/188
80286
80386/486
8096/196
80960
i860
V-series
Z80/64180
Z8
H8/300
290xx
32x32
MIPS
SPARC
Transputer
VAX
LSI-11
1750A
34010/020
7700
H8/500
RTX-2000

F

Table F.3

Company	Proprietary	RTX-2000	7700	34010/020	1750A	LSI-11	VAX	Transputer	SPARC	MIPS	32x32	290xx	H8/500	H8/300	Z8	Z80/64180	V-Series	i860	80960	8096/196	80386/486	80286	80186/188	8086/88	8080/85	8051	88000	683xx	680x0	68HC16	68HC11	6809	6800/01/02/03
Accelerated Technology Inc.									●	●	●	●							●		●	●	●	●				●	●	●	●		
A.T. Barret & Assoc.			●					●												●	●	●	●	●		●		●	●	●	●		●
Byte-BOS Integrated Systems														●		●	●			●	●	●	●	●		●		●	●	●	●		●
CMX Company													●	●	●	●				●						●			●	●	●		
Diab Data																													●				
Digital Equipment Corp.							●			●																							
Digital Research Corp.																					●	●	●										
Emerge Systems																											●						
Encore																																	
Enea Data AB																●					●			●		●		●	●		●		●
Eurostart																																	
Eyring																					●	●						●	●			●	
FORTH Inc.		●					●									●					●	●	●	●		●		●	●		●	●	●
Genelogic																	●																
General Software																					●	●	●	●	●	●		●	●				
Hewlett Packard	●																																
Industrial Programming Inc.																●		●	●		●	●	●	●									
Innovative Integration		●																		●	●	●	●	●									
Intel Corp.				●		●		●	●	●	●	●							●		●	●	●	●	●								
JMI Software Consultants Inc.																					●	●	●	●				●	●			●	●
Kadak Products Ltd.																					●	●	●	●				●	●			●	●
Lynx Real-Time Systems Inc.									●	●							●				●	●	●	●					●				
Micro Digital Inc.																					●					●		●					
Microware Systems Corp.																		●			●			●			●	●	●				
Modcomp																											●						
Motorola Microcomputer Div.																											●			●			
Objective:Systems																					●	●	●	●					●				
OnTime Marketing																					●	●	●	●									
Precise Software Technologies																					●	●	●	●					●				
Quantum Software Systems Ltd																					●	●	●	●									
Ready Systems										●											●	●	●	●					●				
Real-Time Intelligent Systems Corp.																					●												

Table F.3 *continued*

Manufacturer	6800/01/02/03	6809	68HC11	68HC16	680x0	683xx	88000	8051	8080/85	8086/88	80186/188	80286	80386/486	80960/196	80960	1860	V-Series	Z80/64180	Z8	H8/300	H8/500	290xx	32x32	MIPS	SPARC	Transputer	VAX	LSI-11	1750A	34010/020	7700	RTX-2000	Proprietary
RTMX-Uniflex					●		●						●			●								●	●								
Schneider Software Systems							●					●	●																				
Software Components Group					●	●				●			●		●									●	●								
Spectron Microsystems Inc.					●	●				●					●		●																
Talton/Louley Engineering										●	●	●	●																				
TeleSoft													●											●	●				●				
U.S. Software Corp.			●	●	●	●		●		●	●	●	●	●	●		●	●															
VenturCom Inc.												●	●																				
Willies' Computer Software Co.					●	●					●	●	●																				
Wind River Systems Inc.															●									●	●								

Bibliography

Allworth, Steve T.
Introduction To Real-Time Software Design
New York, New York
Springer-Verlag, 1981

Bal Sathe, Dhananjay
"Fast Algorithm Determines Priority"
EDN, (India), Sept. 1988, p.237

Comer, Douglas
Operating System Design, The XINU Approach
Englewood Cliffs, New Jersey
Prentice-Hall, Inc., 1984

Deitel, Harvey M. and Kogan, Michael S.
The Design Of OS/2
Reading, Massachusetts
Addison-Wesley Publishing Company, 1992

Hunter & Ready
VRTX Technical Tips
Palo Alto, California
Hunter & Ready, Inc., 1986

Hunter & Ready
Dijkstra Semaphores, Application Note
Palo Alto, California
Hunter & Ready, Inc., 1983

G

Hunter & Ready
VRTX and Event Flags
Palo Alto, California
Hunter & Ready, Inc., 1986

Intel Corp.
"Algorithms Star In Multipurpose Systems"
Electronics, March, 1983

Intel Corp.
iAPX186/188 User's Manual and Programmer's Reference
Santa Clara, California
Intel Corp., 1983

Labrosse, Jean J.
"A Portable Real-Time Kernel in C"
Embedded Systems Programming, May 1992 p40-53

Labrosse, Jean J.
Implementing a Real-Time Kernel
Embedded Systems Programming, June 1992 p44-49

Madnick, E. Stuart and Donovan, John J.
Operating Systems
New York, New York
McGraw-Hill Book Company, 1974

Plum, Thomas
C Programming Guidelines
Cardiff, New Jersey
Plum Hall, Inc., 1984

Ready Systems
VRTX32/86 User's Guide
Sunnyvale, California
Ready Systems, Inc., 1989

Ready Systems
VRTX32 C User's Guide
Sunnyvale, California
Ready Systems, Inc., 1987

Ripps, David L.
An Implementation Guide To Real-Time Programming
Englewood Cliffs, New Jersey
Yourdon Press, 1989

Savitzky, Stephen R.
Real-Time Microprocessor Systems
New York, New York
Van Nostrand Reinhold Company, 1985

Ward, Robert
MS-DOS System Programming
Lawrence, Kansas
R & D Publications, Inc., 1990

G

Appendix H

Companion Disk

Don't waste your time entering the code from this book.

R & D Publications has created a Companion Disk to μC/OS, *The Real-Time Kernel*, available on either 5 1/4 inch or 3 1/2 inch MS-DOS format. The disk contains all of the source files from this book. It is an essential resource for anyone who wants to forgo the drudgery of typing code (and the time required to find and correct those inevitable typing errors).

The Companion Disk to μC/OS, The Real-Time Kernel is available only through R & D Publications. To order, use the special reply card provided at the end of the book. If the card has already been used, send $24.95, plus $3.50 for domestic postage and handling, $15.00 for foreign orders to:

R & D Publications
1601 W. 23rd St. Ste 200
Lawrence, KS 66046

or call 913-841-1631 / FAX 913-841-2624.

Please specify 5 1/4 inch or 3 1/2 inch format. Payment must be in U.S. funds. You may pay by check or money order (payable to R & D Publications) or by VISA, or Master-Card; please include both your credit card number and the expiration date. All orders are shipped within 48 hours upon receipt of order to R & D.

Licensing

The code in this book is protected by copyright. You may either transcribe the code to machine readable form or purchase the companion disk for your own personal use. You do not need a license to use this code in your application , if your application is distributed in object format. You should, however, indicate in your product literature that you are using μC/OS, The Real-Time Kernel. If you distribute μC/OS in source code , you must obtain a license.

For licensing information, contact:

Jean J. Labrosse
9540 N. W. 9th Court
Plantation, FL 33324

or call 305 472-5094

H

Hardware/Software Requirements

Hardware:	IBM-PC AT (or compatible system)
Fixed Disk Capacity:	2 Megabytes free
System Memory:	640K bytes of RAM
Operating System:	IBM PC-DOS or MS-DOS (version 3.3 or newer)
Software:	µC/OS, The Real-Time Kernel companion disk

Installation

Before installation, make backup copies of the companion disk to µC/OS, The Real-Time Kernel.

To install the companion disk to µC/OS, The Real-Time Kernel, follow these steps:

1) Load DOS and specify the C: drive as the default drive

2) Insert the companion disk to µC/OS, The Real-Time Kernel in drive A:

3) Enter *A:INSTALL [drive]*

where *[drive]* is an optional drive letter indicating the destination disk on which µC/OS, The Real-Time Kernel will be installed. If you do not specify a drive, µC/OS, The Real-Time Kernel will be installed on the current drive.

INSTALL will create the following directory on the specified destination drive:

\SOFTWARE

INSTALL will then change the directory to *\SOFTWARE* and copy the file *UCOS.EXE* from the *A:* drive to this directory. *INSTALL* will then execute *UCOS.EXE* which will then create all other directories under *\SOFTWARE* and transfer all source files presented in this book (see **Directory Structure**). Upon completion, *INSTALL* will delete *UCOS.EXE* and change the directory to *\SOFTWARE\UCOS\SOURCE* where you will find the source code for the kernel portion.

Read the *READ.ME* file for last minute changes and notes.

Directory Structure

Once *INSTALL* has completed, you destination drive will contain the following sub-directories:

    \SOFTWARE

The main directory from the root where all software related files are placed.

    \SOFTWARE\UCOS

The μC/OS project directory.

    \SOFTWARE\UCOS\SOURCE

Contains the source files UCOS.C and UCOS.H. These files are target independent.

    \SOFTWARE\UCOS\80186S

This directory contains the μC/OS target specific files for the Intel 80186/80188 microprocessor (assuming the SMALL memory model), comprising the following files: *80186S_C.C, 80186S_C.H* and *80186S_A.ASM*.

    \SOFTWARE\UCOS\EX1\SOURCE

This directory contains the source files for the Example #1 and should contain the following files: *EX1.C, EX1.DSK, EX1.PRJ, INCLUDES.H*, and *TICK.ASM*.

    \SOFTWARE\UCOS\EX1\OBJ

This directory contains the object files and the executable file for Example #1 and should contain the following files: *UCOS.OBJ, 80186S_C.OBJ, 80186S_A.OBJ, TICK.OBJ, EX1.OBJ, EX1.EXE* and *EX1.MAP*.

    \SOFTWARE\UCOS\EX2\SOURCE

This directory contains the source files for Example #2 and should contain the following files: *EX2.C, EX2.DSK, EX2.PRJ, INCLUDES.H*, and *TICK.ASM*.

    \SOFTWARE\UCOS\EX2\OBJ

This directory contains the object files and the executable file for Example #2 and should contain the following files: *UCOS.OBJ, 80186S_C.OBJ, 80186S_A.OBJ, TICK.OBJ, EX2.OBJ, EX2.EXE* and *EX2.MAP*.

    \SOFTWARE\LISTC

This is the *LISTC* and *HPLISTC* project directory.

H

\SOFTWARE\LISTC\SOURCE

This directory contains the source files for *LISTC* and *HPLISTC* and should contain the following files: *LISTC.C, HPLISTC.C.*

\SOFTWARE\LISTC\OBJ

This directory contains the object and executable files for *LISTC* and *HPLISTC* and should contain the following files: *LISTC.OBJ, LISTC.EXE, HPLISTC.OBJ* and *HPLISTC.C.*

\SOFTWARE\TO

This is the *TO* project directory.

\SOFTWARE\TO\SOURCE

This directory contains the source files for *TO* and should contain the following files: *TO.C.*

\SOFTWARE\TO\OBJ

This directory contains the object and executable files for *TO* and should contain the following files: *TO.OBJ, TO.EXE.*

Index

I

E

F

H

I

I

I

T

U

V

I

W

||||

BUSINESS REPLY MAIL

FIRST CLASS PERMIT NO. 682 LAWRENCE, KS

Postage will be paid by addressee

publications, inc.
1601 W. 23rd St., Suite 200
Lawrence, KS 66046-9950